Sertorius and the Struggle for Spain

Sertorius and the Struggle for Spain

Philip Matyszak

Pen & Sword
MILITARY

First published in Great Britain in 2013
and republished in this format in 2021 by
Pen & Sword Military
an imprint of
Pen & Sword Books Ltd
Yorkshire – Philadelphia

ISBN 978-1-39901-313-0

Typeset in Ehrhardt by Mac Style
Printed in the UK by CPI Group (UK) Ltd, Croydon, CR0 4YY

Pen & Sword Books Limited incorporates the imprints of Atlas,
Archaeology, Aviation, Discovery, Family History, Fiction, History,
Maritime, Military, Military Classics, Politics, Select, Transport, True
Crime, Air World, Frontline Publishing, Leo Cooper, Remember When,
Seaforth Publishing, The Praetorian Press, Wharncliffe Local History,
Wharncliffe Transport, Wharncliffe True Crime and White Owl.

For a complete list of Pen & Sword titles please contact

PEN & SWORD BOOKS LIMITED
47 Church Street, Barnsley, South Yorkshire, S70 2AS, England
E-mail: enquiries@pen-and-sword.co.uk
Website: www.pen-and-sword.co.uk

Or
PEN AND SWORD BOOKS
1950 Lawrence Rd, Havertown, PA 19083, USA
E-mail: Uspen-and-sword@casematepublishers.com
Website: www.penandswordbooks.com

Contents

To the memory of Krystyna Dzuirdzik 1938–2012

Acknowledgements

This book required detailed information from people familiar with areas of Spain and Portugal where I have not been myself. So thanks to those who have been my eyes on the ground – particularly Felix Paulinski, Fernando Quesada Sanz, Director. Dpto. de Arqueología, Universidad Autónoma de Madrid, Beatriz Ezquerra Lebrón, Conservadora del Museo de Teruel, and Alberto Pérez of Desperto Ferro magazine. Thanks also go to Jean-Luc Féraud, the re-enactor who posed for the pictures of a legionary of the 1st century BC and Jasper Oorthuys of *Ancient Warfare* magazine, who stepped in to help at the last minute. The nature of the work required discussing 'what if?' scenarios with a number of ancient historians, all of whom participated enthusiastically in the discussion and considerably influenced the final text. Finally, I'd like to thank those people who, having bought previous books, have taken the time to write and tell me what they particularly enjoyed about them. Hearing from readers always makes my day.

List of Illustrations

1. Bust believed to be of Caius Marius, now in the Munich Glyptothek. (*Picture: Geoffry Faldene. Used with kind permission*)
2. Bust of Gnaeus Pompey, now in the Munich Glyptothek. (*Picture: Adrian Goldsworthy, used with his kind permission*)
3. The Roman theatre at Zaragoza, Spain. (*Picture: Philip Matyszak*)
4. Bolskan silver denarius. (*Copyright: Museo de Teruel, Spain; used with kind permission*)
5. Aerial view of excavations at La Caridad. (*Copyright: Museo de Teruel, Spain. Used with kind permission*)
6. Excavations at Clunia. (*Picture: Felix Paulinski, used with kind permission*)
7. Spear points from La Caridad. (*Copyright: Museo de Teruel, Spain. Pictures: Jorge Escudero; used with kind permission*)
8. Remains of a *scorpio* from La Caridad (*Copyright: Museo de Teruel, Spain. Pictures: Jorge Escudero; used with kind permission*)
9. Lead slingshot ammunition from La Caridad. (*Copyright: Museo de Teruel, Spain. Pictures: Jorge Escudero; used with kind permission*)
10. Iron shield boss from La Caridad. (*Copyright: Museo de Teruel, Spain. Pictures: Jorge Escudero; used with kind permission*)
11. Falcata sword. (*Copyright: Museo de Teruel, Spain. Picture: Jorge Escudero; picture used with kind permission*)
12. Spanish sword. (*Copyright: Museo de Teruel, Spain. Picture: Jorge Escudero; used with kind permission*)
13. Bas relief of Iberian *caetratus* from Osuna, southern Spain. (*Picture courtesy of Fernando Quesada Sanz, Universidad Autónoma de Madrid*)
14. Bas relief of Iberian heavy infantryman from Osuna, southern Spain. (*Picture courtesy of Fernando Quesada Sanz, Universidad Autónoma de Madrid*)
15. Montefortino helmet now in the British Museum (*Picture: P. Matyszak*)
16. Iron light pilum shank (*Copyright: Museo de Teruel, Spain*)

Maps

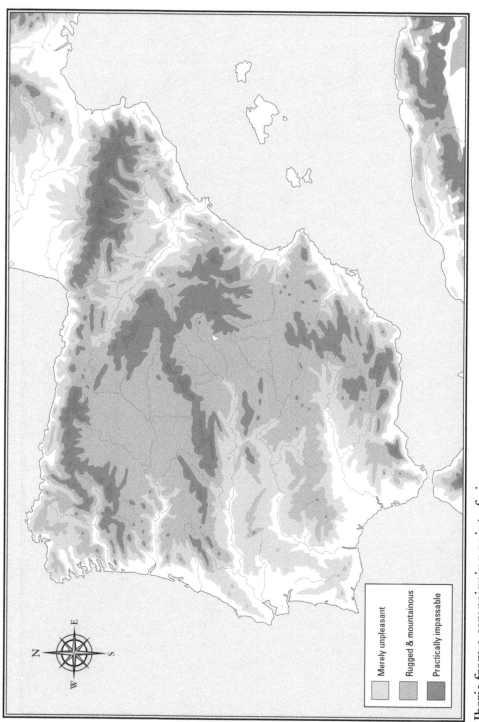

Iberia from a campaigning point of view.

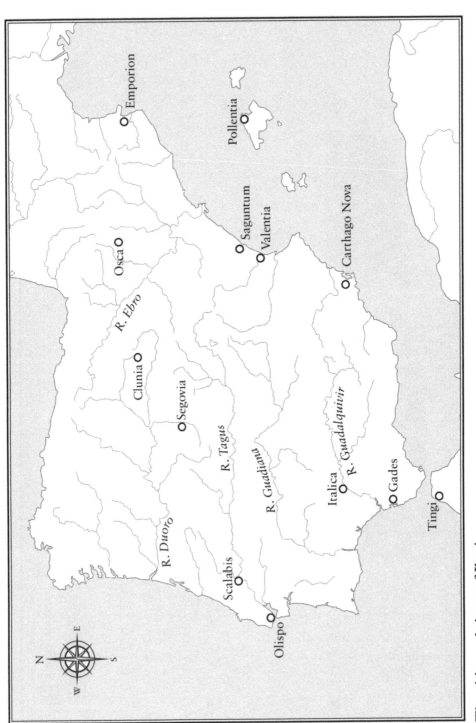

The cities and rivers of Iberia.

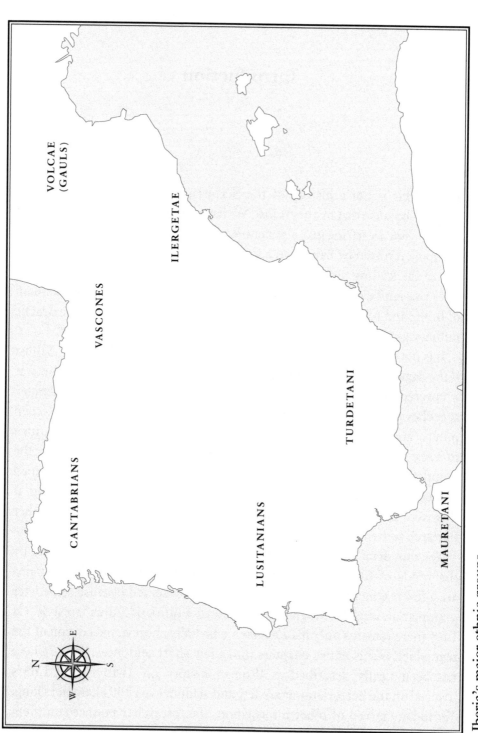

Iberia's major ethnic groups.

Introduction

This is not a history of the Sertorian war in Iberia of 82–71 BC, because that history is lost. We have a good record of the Jugurthan war in Africa just a generation before, and a generation later we are spoiled rotten by having an account of the Gallic war written for us by one of the leading protagonists – Julius Caesar himself. Yet between these wars two entire provinces fell from the control of the central government of Rome and remained for almost a decade under the rule of a charismatic military genius – and precisely what happened is largely a mystery.

It is not that the war was considered unimportant. The historian Sallust – the same man who brought us detailed reporting of the Jugurthan war – covered the war in Iberia in considerable depth. Individual actions, speeches and an organized chronology explained the war to the Roman public, and if anyone wanted a second opinion, they had only to turn to Livy's magisterial *Ab urbe condita*. The 'history of Rome from the foundation' covered the war in Hispania at the same time as it described contemporary events and wars all around the Mediterranean. And if this were not enough, the character of Sertorius inspired the biographer Plutarch to write the story of his life.

Yet this detailed mass of information is largely gone, blown apart by the winds of time. Of the war as described by Sallust all that remains are a few fragmentary pieces of text, usually preserved because some later grammarian used the fragment to illustrate a quirk of Sallustian style. Of Livy there remains only his *Epitome* – a brutally abbreviated edition of the text which crams entire chapters into a few short sentences. The *Epitome* has been neatly described as 'Roman history on Twitter' and Livy's 'tweets' on the Sertorian war are few and seldom even 140 characters long. Yet today, starved of other information, the researcher pounces on them gratefully.

This leaves us with Plutarch, and without Plutarch one would have to abandon the entire project. Plutarch's *Life of Sertorius* survived, and survived almost entirely intact. But the biography of a general is not the history of a war, especially if our biographer is the un-military Plutarch. Plutarch tells us of the mood of his hero (and for Plutarch, Sertorius is definitely a hero) at times when we would rather like to know things like army numbers and deployments. And because Plutarch keeps the spotlight unwaveringly on his protagonist we are left to discover elsewhere that (for example) a lot of the war was fought by a highly competent second-in-command whom Plutarch does not even mention.

Fortunately for later historians the Sertorian war was a very big deal at the time, and it reverberated through Roman history to an extent where we can pick up the echoes. Valerius Maximus wrote on the *Doings and Sayings of Famous Men*, and some of those who fought in the Sertorian war were famous indeed. So from Valerius Maximus we get anecdotes and snippets of a personal nature. The Sertorian war was also a masterclass exercise in generalship on both sides – as the high attrition rate of lesser generals demonstrates. Therefore when a later commander called Frontinus collected a book of anecdotes illuminating the art of generalship, a good many of his exemplars were taken from the Sertorian war.

Even at the end (chronologically speaking) of the Roman empire, with almost a thousand years of history to relate, writers such as Florus and Orosius dedicated several pages to Sertorius; another historian, Appian, gave the war a cursory and occasionally inaccurate treatment as a lead-in to his main topic: the struggle between Caesar and Pompey.

Despite the existence of such brief and fragmentary accounts, it is fair to say that unless further documentation comes to light, the full story of Sertorius and his war is lost beyond retelling. So this book is not a history. It is a reconstruction. Using Plutarch's account as a scaffold, the other fragments and anecdotes can be carefully fitted around his narrative. The result is a sort of sudoku played with scraps of evidence. The trick is to place each fragment within a timeline to create a narrative. Each fragment must be both internally consistent with other fragments and with what is known of wider contemporary Roman history. So, for example, when Cicero gives an offhand mention that a character was in Rome in a particular year, we can place the first fragment describing that character's activity in Iberia soon after that date, and so tentatively date a fragment which says only 'it was late in the season'.

The problem with such a reconstruction is that we can end up with a 'Ptolemaic universe'. The Ptolemaic universe was an ancient description of the universe which accounted for all known astronomical phenomena in a manner which was totally internally consistent and completely wrong. Thus while this reconstruction of the Sertorian war has put all the known evidence together in a manner which effectively re-creates the history of the war, it remains just that – a recreation. Given what we do know, this is the story of how things might have happened. Nothing in the account which follows disagrees with the ancient evidence, even when at times the ancient evidence seems to disagree with itself.

This book is a straightforward narrative of what happened in the Sertorian war. It makes sense, has a consistent chronology and is told as much as possible in the words of the original narrators. It is not and cannot be a history of that war. But it may be as close as we are going to get.

Given the problems with assembling such a narrative, one might ask why it was worth doing at all. Indeed, this book is probably the first attempt since Livy to tell the full story of the Sertorian war, precisely for that reason. Yet the story is worth reconstructing, and now is a good time to do so.

One reason is that academia has recently turned its attention to the Sertorius war, and from several interesting papers and discussions a framework of consensus has emerged. The work of Spann must be mentioned here, and above all the contribution of C.F. Conrad, whose book *Plutarch's Sertorius: A Historical Commentary* is a towering masterpiece of research, and an obligatory text for anyone approaching the topic. It is largely thanks to such dedicated work by academics at the coalface of historical analysis that it has now become possible for a historian such as myself to assemble these detailed studies into a history for the general reader. So one reason why the story of the Sertorian war is told in the following pages is because it is now possible for this to be done.

Where my conclusions differ from the eminent scholars above (mainly in chronology, often in emphasis, occasionally in geography) I have hastened to buttress my points with both data and argument. Where the state of the evidence allows only a balance of probability, I have not, unlike the academics above, carefully discussed the options in detail, but opted for that which I considered best, and informed the reader of my choice with either a brief mention in the text (the word 'probably' occurs a lot) or in a footnote. As mentioned above, neither conclusion is 'wrong' insofar as the evidence often allows for multiple conclusions. Opinions may legitimately differ as to which interpretation comes closest to describing the elusive ideal of 'what really happened'.

The second reason for describing this war is that 'what really happened' can be seen on many different levels. At one level, this was a brutal, futile war fought to an inevitable finish to the accompaniment of wasted lives and needless destruction. Sertorius fought not for an ideal, but for survival once his side had come second in an Italian civil war which was even more brutal, wasteful and pointless. And his was a war which, given the mismatch of resources, only the other side could win.

On another level, this war is the story of Sertorius – a military genius who spent his adult life fighting on the losing side in three different wars. From hopeless situation to utter disaster, Sertorius constantly battled the headwinds of misfortune, retrieving what he could, occasionally turning disaster to triumph, and however discouraged he might become, always indomitably soldiering on. If life is all about postponing the inevitable, Sertorius certainly lived life to the full. In the end he lost, but his stubborn defiance made his enemies work long and hard for their victory, and pay for it dearly. For many of those for whom there is no light at the end of the tunnel, the story of Sertorius should be an example and an inspiration.

Again, there is a larger story. The war of 82–71 BC was not, as heretofore, the Iberian peoples against Rome. Even though those fighting did not realize it at the time, the Sertorian war marked a crucial turning point in the history of the Iberian people. Before Sertorius the peninsula was occupied by various tribes which often had little in common besides geographical proximity and a dislike of Romans. During the war, both sides identified with Rome, albeit with different ideas of who should rule there. Afterwards, this decade of war was the catalyst for the creation of Hispania as a unified entity, a part of a greater empire, but proudly rooted in its own culture and tradition.

The Romano-Iberian fusion proved a happy blend which led to centuries of peace in the peninsula, and the creation of a national identity. Given the fissiparous forces tearing at Spain today, it is well worth another look at the events which brought the country together in the first place.

Finally, and most importantly, this is a story worth telling for its own sake. Like so many of the half-forgotten events of two thousand years ago, it is a thundering good yarn. It has a gallant, and occasionally brooding protagonist, a fine set of complex villains, heroic battles, ingenious ruses and epic sieges. We even have pirates and giants. Had history not unaccountably omitted a damsel in distress we would have had *Sertorius: the opera* long before now.

It is time to re-introduce the world to Sertorius.

Rossland, British Columbia
September 2012

Chapter 1

A Portrait of the Rebel as a Young Man

In the year 81 BC the life of Quintus Sertorius appeared to have little direction or purpose. At the time he and his followers had just captured the city of Tinga (Tangier), in North Africa. This was not because Sertorius had anything against this city, or any urgent reason for capturing it. However, the operation provided an outlet for his considerable energy and military talent.

Certainly, Sertorius seems barely to have cared one way or the other for Ascalis, the would-be-king whose ambitions he had thwarted by this endeavour. One reason for engaging on the enterprise seems to have been annoyance with the Cilician pirates with whom he had recently parted company. The pirates had supported Ascalis, so Sertorius chose the opposite side. However, the main reason for the enterprise was that if Sertorius did not do something – anything – with the men who followed him, the small force at his command would eventually lose interest and disband.

Then Sertorius, once considered the rising star of his generation, would be alone – a refugee and the last rebel in a lost cause. At this point Sertorius must have wondered what he was fighting for and whether he was doomed to spend the rest of his life in such pointless adventures. His enemies were both too strong to resist and too implacable to make peace. What was he to do?

Only a few weeks before, Sertorius had seriously considered getting away from it all, and basically becoming a beach bum in the Canary Isles.

He fell into the company of some sailors. These were recently returned from the Atlantic Islands... They call these The Isles of the Blessed. The rain is moderate, and does not fall that often, but the soft winds precipitate heavy dews. As a result, the rich soil is excellent for crops and orchards, but in any case, enough nutritious and plentiful fruit grows wild to feed – without work or even undue effort – those who can't be bothered to do more.

On these islands the wind is soft and healthy, and the seasons moderate. Out there the blasts of the north and east winds have lost their power... The southern and western winds are for the most part cool breezes which moisten and enrich the soil. Even the barbarians believe this is the home of the blessed, the Elysian Fields of which Homer sang.

(Plutarch, *Life of Sertorius*, 8)

After listening to the sailors, Sertorius decided that this was the life for him: 'a quiet life, free from tyranny and unending wars.'

Though not yet thirty years old, Sertorius had already experienced enough action, excitement and adventure to fill three normal lifetimes. Nor had his experience of his fellow human beings been particularly inspiring. Between bouts of warfare, massacre and betrayal Sertorius had found himself in the political cesspit of contemporary Roman politics. Political life at the centre of Rome's growing empire had routinely involved bribery, nepotism and riots, enlivened by the occasional murder and lynching. But recently the process had tipped over into a full-scale civil war resulting in tens of thousands of deaths up and down the Italian peninsula – and Sertorius had personally added more than his share to that total.

It was not the life his parents had planned for him. He was born in Sabine country, in Nursia, a town that had already been ancient centuries before Romulus came to found Rome. (The area appears to have been inhabited since Neolithic times, and remains so today as Norcia, a pleasant and scenic city conveniently located between the Sibillini Hills and a fertile plain.) Rome had taken control of the city during the Sabine wars, and by 268 BC considered its citizens sufficiently Romanized to make them full citizens of the Republic.

The Sertorius family were minor aristocrats – almost certainly *Equites Romani*, the class of Romans directly below senators in rank. The parents appear to have doted on their intelligent and athletic child. It was an affection which young Sertorius heartily reciprocated. When his father died, his widow focused all her energies on raising her precocious son. Of this mother, we know little other than that her name was apparently Rhea, and that she ensured that her son had the best education possible for a young man of his status. In return, sniffs his biographer Plutarch, Sertorius became 'excessively fond' of his mother.

It was unbecoming for a contemporary Roman man to show sentiment for the opposite sex. Sertorius' contemporary and later opponent, Gnaeus Pompey, was teased for his 'effeminacy' for no other reason than that while he was married to them, his different wives had all loved him. Another contemporary, the orator Cicero, was at pains to stress that he had not married his ward Publilia because he loved her, but because he needed her money. Certainly, and like many an Italian lad since, Sertorius found no other woman the equal of his mother. In his case it appears that he not only never married, but did not even have a serious relationship with anyone of the female gender once he had left home.

Leaving home, filial affection notwithstanding, was something Sertorius did while in his mid-to-late teens. His education, like that of his contemporaries, had given him a working knowledge of the law and the classics. That is, he learned the epics of Homer and histories of Latin worthies such as the elder Cato, but his education would have concentrated on rhetoric – the art of oratory. A Roman student orator learned not just what to say, but how to time his delivery and the appropriate style of dress and gesture that should accompany the words. Speeches were the principal means by which the upper classes communicated with the voters, soldiers in the army and even large groups of their peers. Good rhetoric was essential for a public career, and listeners had a keen appreciation of cadence, gesture and stance. (Which is why statues of Romans which may seem somewhat contrived today were, for contemporary viewers, rich in symbolic meaning.) Sertorius would also have learned how to ride a horse, wrestle, and become skilled in the use of sword and javelin.

His mind filled with tales of heroic deeds, and his body trained in practical techniques for emulating them, Sertorius was too ambitious to settle into the bucolic ranks of the *domi nobiles*, those country men who were important in their own towns but unknown elsewhere. Sertorius was determined to make it big in Rome.

A young man arriving in Rome would bring with him letters of introduction to those of as high a social status as his parents or local connections were able to contact. The hope was that the new arrival would obtain the patronage of a political insider who would smooth the way to a successful career. The young Tullius Cicero would follow the same path several years later, seeking the patronage of the great jurist Mucius Scaevola (who thereafter steered Cicero away from his first love of poetry into a career as a forensic orator). Just as Cicero switched from poetry to oratory on his arrival in the big city, Sertorius switched from oratory to a more direct form of persuasion. He joined the army.

It appears, despite his mother's illusions, that the rhetoric of her son was not as polished and sophisticated as she may have fondly believed. Certainly, Sertorius made enough of an impression on the young Cicero to merit special mention in a later treatise on oratory –

> Of all the totally illiterate and crude orators, well, actually ranters, I ever knew – and I might as well add 'completely coarse and rustic' – the roughest and readiest were Q. Sertorius ...
>
> (Cicero, *Brutus*, 180)

In his defence – assuming he possessed the oratical skill to offer one – Sertorius could have pointed out that he was only entering his late teens. In fact, his biographer Plutarch offers exactly that argument, remarking that Sertorius won some influence by his youthful eloquence.[1] This influence gained Sertorius a position in the Roman army of Caepio, for youth was no impediment to an aristocratic Roman set on a military career. A law passed in the previous generation by Gaius Gracchus forbade the conscription of those under the age of seventeen, but the upper classes could volunteer earlier. Gracchus himself was probably around sixteen years old when he entered military service.[2]

At this time the army was beginning a state of transition which later historians have given the portmanteau description of 'the Marian reforms' though is debatable how many of these reforms were actually instituted by Marius and how many were the *de facto* recognition of existing changes. One such change was to the position of military tribune. The *tribunus militum* was originally of senatorial rank, and was one of a group of six who commanded a Roman legion under the overall command of the magistrate – usually a consul or proconsul – who commanded the entire army.

At the turn of the second century, the position mutated to become one where only a single senatorial military tribune remained – as understudy to the legate who now commanded the legion. The remaining tribunes were junior officers of the equestrian class, there to learn the art of soldiering and to acquire the political favour of their commanders.

Whether or not his position was formally described as such, Sertorius was probably of the latter class of military tribune. This rank placed him among the *cohors amicorum,* the 'body of friends' who accompanied the commander; in this case the Roman proconsul Servilius Caepio. Serving with a senior general gave the young Sertorius a first-hand set of enduring lessons on how not to command an army. As bunglers go, Caepio was particularly lethal. After he had alienated his fellow general and broken up potential peace negotiations, Caepio took his hapless legions through a series of strategic misjudgements followed by tactical blunders that resulted in his army being wiped out almost to the last man.

The wiping out was done in Transalpine Gaul at the Battle of Arausio (also sometimes called the Battle of the Rhone) in 104 BC. The wipers who did the deed were a massive confederation of Germanic tribes usually referred to as the Cimbri, though there were Teutones, Ambrones and various other migrants and warriors of opportunity in the mix. In fairness to Caepio, his was but the most disastrous of the series of defeats and débâcles which up to 103 made up the Roman contribution to the Cimbric wars.

The Cimbri had started somewhere around modern Denmark, and had moved in a slow tribal migration along the Vistula and Danube. They first met and almost annihilated the Romans in 113 BC in battle at Noreia, north-east of the Alps in modern Austria. Unfortunately for Gaul, the Cimbri did not follow up this success by marching on Rome but instead embarked on the leisurely looting of Gaul for much of the next decade. When the Cimbri next arrived on the frontiers of Roman territory it was 104 BC and the point of contact was in the Roman province of Gallia Transalpina near the small town of Arausio on the Rhone. Here Caepio marched to meet them.

It is a habit of Roman historians to give blow-by-blow descriptions of battles in which they were victorious, often with the inclusion of elegantly composed pre-battle speeches. Yet when it comes to defeats, these same historians generally reveal only the basic details in a few tight-lipped sentences. It also does not help that our sources for this period are fragmentary in any case. So for one of the most dramatic battles of the late second century, and certainly the first and largest battle in the entire extensive military career of Sertorius, our best account is this brief summary of Book 67 of Livy's history of Rome.

> The consul Gnaeus Manlius and proconsul Quintus Servilius Caepio were defeated, and both their camps were plundered. So Valerius Antias [an earlier historian] relates. Casualties [of the battle] near Arausio amounted to 80,000 soldiers and 40,000 servants and camp followers killed. Caepio, caused the defeat by his rashness. He was condemned for this and his [proconsular] powers were stripped from him. His possessions were confiscated – the first time this punishment had been inflicted since the time of king Tarquin.

Both consul and proconsul survived the battle which obliterated their armies. An account of the battle was written by the church historian Orosius in late antiquity. If this is to be credited, the two generals were among just ten survivors from the slaughter.[3] Seven of the remainder remain unknown, but the eighth was Sertorius. Plutarch takes up the tale.

> After the Romans had been defeated and put to flight [which suggests that more than ten fled, at least initially], he made his way across the Rhone. He swam against a strongly adverse current, wearing shield, breastplate and all, though he had lost his horse and had taken a body wound – so tough was his body and so trained was he to bear hardship.
>
> (Plutarch, *Life of Sertorius*, 2)

At this point the history of Rome itself might have come to an abrupt close, for the only Roman armies capable of stopping the Cimbric hordes had been massacred beside the river. It is quite possible that all that saved the city was that the autumn was now setting in (the battle was fought in the first week of October), and the Cimbri were reluctant to cross the Alps in these conditions.[4] Instead the migrating horde turned its attention to Spain, giving the Romans precious time to regroup.

We now get a rare hint as to the physical appearance of our hero. Sertorius transferred his allegiance to Rome's new commander, Caius Marius, but chose to serve with the enemy. That is, he became a spy. It was absolutely essential that Rome should know exactly how much time was available to rebuild the city's shattered armies, and the only way to do this was to keep a close eye on the Cimbri. Sertorius volunteered to join the Cimbric army in the guise of a Gallic recruit.

> He dressed himself as a Celt, and acquired some of the basics of the language for use as necessary. Then he mingled with the barbarians to see and hear anything of importance.
>
> (Plutarch, *Life of Sertorius*, 3)

Three items stand out in these singular sentences. The first is that even if we allow little credence to the cliché that all Celts were tall and fair and all Romans were shorter and swarthier, it is clear that Sertorius expected to pass as a Celt once he was dressed as one. An inarticulate, well-built, blue-eyed blond might pass muster.[5] On the other hand, a spy who combined 'stereotypical Roman' looks with basic Celtic would probably have a reduced life expectancy. On balance therefore, we can postulate Sertorius looked at least as Celtic as he did Roman.

The second point is that Sertorius had apparently only the basics of the Celtic tongue. This must have hugely increased the risk of discovery, even given the multinational and consequently multilingual nature of the Cimbric horde. But it must have also greatly reduced Sertorius' ability to hear anything of value unless he remained with the horde for a matter of years and increased his linguistic prowess as he went along.

The third point to consider is that this early experience of life among 'barbarian' warriors would have greatly increased the sensitivity of Sertorius as to what was and was not distinctively Roman. Awareness of such distinctions is not intuitive among those brought up in a single culture, and such people often fail to check whether an outside party in a negotiation shares their understanding of events. The later life of Sertorius involved extensive dealings with non-Romans. The fact that Sertorius actually went on to have a later life shows that he made a keen study of specifically Roman attitudes and conduct, and was able to separate these from more general behaviour. This empathy with non-Romans would have made Sertorius a more sympathetic and competent negotiator at a time when his contemporaries were becoming notorious for not seeing anyone's point of view but their own.

We have no idea how long Sertorius spent as a barbarian warrior, or where he was in the years before the Cimbri returned again to the Roman frontier. As suggested above, if Plutarch is serious that Sertorius overheard valuable information, he must have been with the invaders long enough to have acquired some proficiency at least in listening to the language. In fact, there is no reason why he could not have remained in the role of spy until 103 BC. During this period, the invading army split up, and if Sertorius stayed with the Cimbri he would have gone with them to Iberia, while the Teutones and Ambrones remained to trouble south-western Gaul.

The Cimbri did not fare well in Iberia. The Celtiberian people of the central interior gave them the same welcome that they had given to generations of Roman invaders (see next chapter). The Cimbri proved even less capable of dealing with the heat, sudden ambushes and hostile terrain than the Romans had been, and quickly retreated to the relatively friendly climes of southern Gaul. There they re-joined the rest of the horde. Their arrival quickly finished off the already fast-diminishing food supplies in the area, and in 102 the migrants resolved to make a serious attempt to enter Italy. It may be that it was only at this late date that Sertorius 'came back to Marius, and was rewarded for his valour'.[6]

The 'Marius' in question was the current Roman consul. The relationship between the two men changed the life of Sertorius forever, and indirectly resulted in Sertorius becoming the rebel ruler of Hispania. Therefore it is worth taking some time to examine the character and career of Marius up to the point where he joins the narrative. Like Sertorius and Cicero, Marius was a lad from the country who had come to Rome to make good. In fact, Marius was from Arpinum, Cicero's home town. (It is indicative of the close relations between Italian aristocrats of the time that marriage ties linked not only the families of Cicero and Marius but also Marius and the Julii Caesares, the family of the later general and dictator Gaius Julius Caesar.)

Like Sertorius, Marius first distinguished himself as a soldier. In Marius' case this was the Numantia campaign which Scipio Aemilianus fought against the Celtiberians in 133 BC. On returning to Rome Marius obtained the patronage of the aristocratic Caecilii Metelli and launched his political career. Like Sertorius, Marius too was rough-spoken and unpolished, but he overcame these handicaps by bull-headed determination and a certain amount of guile. He quickly decided to make it plain that he was no Caecilian poodle, and once elected as tribune of the plebs he showed in no uncertain terms that he was his own man. This he did by taking a firmly populist line in matters such as voting reform which endeared him to the masses, but put the aristocratic noses of the Metelli out of joint.

Marius had the habit of attempting to get his own way, and if he failed he would attempt an insincere compromise which only alienated those who had supported him thus far. So it was characteristic that later in his tribuneship he tried to appease the aristocracy but instead simply turned the common people against him while the aristocracy despised him no less.

This rather stalled his political career, and Marius failed to be elected aedile. However, he persevered with the obstinacy which distinguished his character, and wore down the electorate until they made him praetor, albeit last among the successful candidates, and only after a prosecution for bribing his way into the office.

As did Sertorius in later years, Marius served in Hispania as a propraetor (though Sertorius' appointment was considerably less official). As a provincial governor Marius did much to establish the silver mines and suppress brigandage. Overall, he was both more honest and considerably more competent than most of his predecessors. This helped greatly in preparing a favourable reception in Iberia for those who later fought in his name – as did Sertorius even after Marius was dead.

Any hopes of reconciliation between Marius and his former patrons came to an end when Marius rejoined the army and served as legate under the overall command of the consul, another of the Caecilii Metelli. At the time Rome was fighting an African war against the renegade king Jugurtha of Numidia.[7] Marius nursed ambitions of taking his career much further, and as ever, had little compunction in how he set about doing so.

He had earned the trust of the common soldiers by his undoubted bravery and his willingness to share their hardships and diet. Metellus may eventually have become aware that the purpose of this gallant behaviour was to turn the army against him. So he eventually decided to be rid of his subversive subordinate by allowing him back to Rome to stand for the consulship. Originally Metellus had insultingly suggested that Marius should campaign to become consul together with his son, a lad who eventually achieved that office about twenty-five years later. (That son, Metellus Pius, was later to become one of the most intractable opponents of Sertorius in Spain, as will be seen.)

Though he gave Marius permission to go to Rome to campaign for the consulship, Metellus had done his best to ensure that Marius would not actually win it. For that reason he allowed Marius to leave camp only twelve days before the actual election. In that time his insolent subordinate would have to cross the Mediterranean, travel up Italy, and then launch and complete an election campaign.

Metellus had underestimated the man, and underestimated the man's good fortune. A fortuitous following wind allowed Marius to cross the Mediterranean in just three days. When he arrived in Rome, Marius proceeded to give his personal confirmation of all the slanders against Metellus that his agents had been busily spreading for weeks beforehand. Marius made the promise – which appeared rash enough at the time – that within a year he would bring to an end the Numidian war which had been dragging on through fits and starts since 112 BC.

Once again, an apparently impetuous move by Marius was in fact based on sound strategy and calculation. In this case he was well aware of the fact that Metellus had prepared a sound strategy for bringing the war against Jugurtha to a conclusion, and all that Marius had to do was implement those parts which Metellus had not already completed. The war was well on the way to being successfully wrapped up when Marius returned to Africa to claim the glory.

> Metellus was furious, since he had practically finished the war and all that now remained was the actual capture of Jugurtha. Now – after coming to power by stabbing his commander in the back – along came Marius to enjoy the crown and the triumph. In his jealousy Metellus would not even agree to meet Marius. Instead he left the country as a private citizen and let the army be handed over by Rutilius [Rufus, who had become Metellus' legate after the departure of Marius for Rome].
>
> But Nemesis got Marius in the end, for just as Marius robbed Metellus of his glory, so Sulla robbed Marius.
>
> (Plutarch, *Life of Marius*, 10)

The Sulla in question was Cornelius Sulla, a rising aristocrat from a family which had until then withered almost into insignificance. While serving with the African army, Sulla led a daring undercover operation which took him to the court of the king of Mauritania, where Jugurtha was hoping for sanctuary from the victorious Romans. Once at the court, Sulla persuaded the king to hand Jugurtha over to his custody. Sulla's capture of Jugurtha left those in the ever-growing ranks of Marius' enemies to claim that Metellus had masterminded the conclusion of the war and Sulla had actually finished it. This left Marius an insignificant cipher in the middle.

Marius was now highly popular with the common people – for he had indeed kept his election promise to bring the troops home after a successful war. However, there was enough truth in his enemies' claim that Marius' popularity was undeserved to rankle him. Ever insecure, and – given the number and quality of his enemies – quite justifiably paranoid, Marius became suspicious and jealous of Sulla.

So popular was Marius that an irresistible wave of public opinion swept him into office for an unconstitutional second consulship.[8] Taking advantage of the Cimbric detour into Iberia over the next few years, Marius – whom the Roman people trustingly re-elected each year – had thrown himself into re-organizing and training the army. (In fact, he adopted and implemented many of the ideas of Metellus' second-in-command, Rutilius Rufus, but naturally kept the credit to himself.)

While Marius had been rising to supreme command, Sertorius had been missing, presumably off adventuring somewhere with the barbarian host. At some time before the Cimbri renewed their assault on Italy Sertorius left their army, shaved off his beard, and re-joined the legions. Some hard fighting lay ahead.

As with his politics, Marius was a careful soldier who liked to ensure that he fought his battles on ground he had carefully prepared beforehand. His favourite tactic was to prepare a well-fortified and well-provisioned camp, and let the enemy become exhausted and frustrated by attacking it. (In a later war, an exasperated enemy demanded 'If you are such a great general, why won't you come out and fight?' To which Marius replied 'If you think you are any good, why can't you make me?') Then, when the enemy eventually moved on Marius would cautiously follow, always at a distance which allowed time for his highly-practised legions to throw up another well-fortified camp at the drop of a javelin.

When the enemy finally made a mistake, Marius would pounce. Usually by then his own army were just as furious and frustrated as the enemy, and fought like demons to avoid being cooped up in camp and enduring the jeers of the enemy yet again. It helped that, by the time Marius actually offered battle, the enemy were eager to come to grips at almost any price, which meant that Marius got to choose his own ground.

At Aquae Sextae in 102 BC Marius demonstrated that for all his annoying qualities he knew how to general an army. He first caught the enemy off guard at river crossing, and used their misjudgement to give them a handy impromptu beating. A more formal battle followed shortly afterwards. The Teutones and Ambrones charged up a hill which Marius had carefully selected for steepness and poor footing. The legions were waiting on more level ground near the crest, with orders not to counter-charge, but simply to push the enemy back. Because of the slope and the enemy's difficulty with the ground underfoot, this was easily accomplished.

Then, while the main body of the enemy army consisted of tight-packed, stationary and confused warriors, Marius unleashed the four thousand men he had concealed in ambush behind the lines. These hit the back of an already somewhat demoralized barbarian horde, and precipitated the immediate collapse of their battle line.

Thus, payment was exacted for the Roman defeat at Arausio with over 100,000 of the invaders killed or captured by the victorious legions. The local peasantry, who had been comprehensively plundered by the Cimbri over the preceding months, now gained a certain measure of recompense. They not only fenced their fields and vineyards with the bones of the enemy but also enjoyed years of bumper harvests from those fields fertilized by the decomposing dead.

This was probably Sertorius' second battle. It is, however, not completely certain that he was present. All his biographer tells us is that on Sertorius' return from his espionage mission 'he performed many feats requiring both calculation and courage'. Presumably participation in the battle was one of these feats. It was certainly an educational experience. Sertorius would have learned that battles were not won by heroism alone, but by a general who understood the psychology of both his own men and the enemy, and used this understanding to bring about battle on terms most advantageous to himself. It was not always advisable to offer battle at the first opportunity (or in the case of Marius, not at the second, third or tenth opportunity either). After all, the enemy were not going to go away, and if they did, one could always follow them until a suitable chance for victory presented itself.

This was not heroic, but it worked. With the Teutones and Ambrones disposed of by Marius, Rome's other consul, Lutatius Catulus demonstrated the failings of the heroic approach when he tried to take on the Cimbri at the first chance he got. At this point the Cimbri had split from the Teutones and Ambrones. Because each tribal grouping considerably outnumbered the Roman forces combined, it made sense for the invaders to try to defeat the Romans in detail while simultaneously easing the supply problem of feeding their own huge combined force.

Marius had accustomed his soldiers to gazing down at their enemies from the security of their camp ramparts. In fighting off the impatient attempts of the barbarians to take their camp by storm, the legionaries had learned that the invaders could be beaten. In short, among the legionaries of Marius familiarity had bred a certain degree of contempt. The soldiers of Catulus had no such experience. Their first sight of the Cimbri was of a massive horde drawn up in impressive battle array on the plains near the river Po.

Catulus observed the panicky state of his army and belatedly opted for the better part of valour by withdrawing his men to safety across the river. With the victory of Marius in Gaul, he had no need to hurry events. Once the Roman army was combined, he could hope it would be the enemy who would be defeated in detail, with the Cimbri going down in defeat as the Teutons and Ambrones had done already.

And so it proved. The Cimbric threat to Rome was forever crushed in 101 BC at Vercellae, in what is sometimes called the Battle of the Raudine Plain. There were some 52,000 Romans in the battle, facing what the Romans estimated to be 180,000 of the enemy. (Modern historians are always somewhat sceptical of the overwhelming odds against which the legions invariably are reported to have battled, but there remains no way to dispute the figure today.)

Contrary to usual Marian practice, the battle was fought at a mutually agreed time and place. It was the Cimbri who were more eager for battle, as thanks to capable work by one of Catulus' subordinates, the local alpine tribes had kept the Romans generously stocked with provisions. For the battle it appears that the two sides chose highly compatible strategies. Marius chose to deploy his legions on the left and right wings, with Catulus' men in the centre. The idea was that the wings would advance while the centre mainly 'folded in' on itself. Plutarch rather unfairly claims that the intention was to give Marius maximum glory while downplaying Catulus' role, but it must be remembered that the morale of the Marian legionaries was sky-high and that of Catulus' soldiers was shaky at best. Therefore, any sensible strategy would have given a greater role to the more experienced troops with a better record.

In fact, the same thought seems to have occurred to the Germanic generals. No description exists of the battle from a tactical standpoint, but later events make sense if the Germans decided to concentrate their forces into a huge wedge. This wedge would ignore the wings and drive straight for the army of Catulus in the centre. With that army broken into rout, the Cimbri would then wheel and dispose of each Marian wing in turn. Once again, the strategy involved a sensible concentration of force which would defeat the enemy in detail.

Consequently, on that hot July afternoon, Marius led his wing of the army into the huge dust cloud created by a quarter of a million men on the move across dry fields. He proceeded briskly to where the opposing wing of the Cimbric army would have been had it not formed part of the wedge attacking the centre. Not finding the enemy where they were supposed to be, Marius and his men passed by the shortened battle lines. They eventually emerged from the dust cloud to find themselves alone on the plain with the battle happening somewhere behind them. It took a certain amount of aimless wandering before they were able to find out where the event was currently located.

It turned out that Marius had not been missed. Skilful deployment by their commander had allowed the Roman cavalry to catch their opposite numbers off-balance. The Cimbric cavalry were, in any case, fewer and more poorly equipped than the Roman horsemen. Consequently, after a quick action, the barbarian cavalry were swiftly routed and driven back on to the main body of the Cimbri. The Roman horsemen moved quickly to exploit the disruption this caused and Catulus, seeing his opportunity, threw his men forward to follow up this initial success.

The Cimbri never had the chance to drive home their wedge, and now presumably had the other wing of Marius' army closing in on their flank. The battle became a rout that was stopped by the waggons drawn up (as was customary among Germanic and Celtic peoples) at the rear of the battle line. At this point the rout became a massacre that stopped only when the Cimbri began to surrender *en masse*.[9]

As overall commander, Marius was entitled to the kudos for the victory, however lacking in glory his own part might have been. However, he was forced to concede that the actual fighting had been mainly done by the army of Catulus. It is less certain whether Marius was able to bring himself to admit that the battle had turned on the crucial role of the Roman cavalry commander. That commander was the same man who had organized the army supplies from the Alpine tribes and the same man who had stolen Marius' thunder with his daring capture of Jugurtha in Africa – Lucius Cornelius Sulla.

It is once more almost certain that Sertorius was present at this battle, and once again any description of the part he played in the salvation of Rome is curiously muted. Possibly he was with Marius while the latter had literally not the foggiest idea of the enemy's location. Perhaps he did indeed fight both successfully and heroically. If the latter, he would by now have known his commander well enough to shut up about it. Marius had very clear ideas about who was deserving of glory – i.e. Caius Marius – and was spiteful towards others who gained it. And as his later career was to show, Sertorius was nothing if not an astute politician. We are told explicitly that he earned his general's trust, and with the jealous and suspicious Marius, succeeding in that achievement involved playing down any other ones.

It would be natural for Sertorius to return to Rome to gain political advancement while his general's star was in the ascendant. However, the political waters of what Cicero once brutally (but accurately) called 'the sewer of Romulus' were at that time even more polluted than usual. Reasonably certain that even saving the city would not cause the aristocracy to love him, Marius allied himself with an extreme demagogue called Saturninus.

Currently tribune of the plebs, Saturninus was a canny political operator. He had a talent for pushing self-serving legislation through the constitutional process by a mixture of guile, demagoguery, threats and riots. At least one man who dared to challenge Saturninus died, beaten to death by his thugs. However, the Roman aristocracy were not above violence either, and once Saturninus had gone too far the senate used public revulsion at his tactics to organize a mob of their own. Despite Marius' attempts to protect his ally, Saturninus and his henchman Glaucia were briskly lynched.

Under the circumstances, it seemed best for both Marius and Sertorius to get out of town. During his ascendancy, Marius had succeeded in having Metellus, his former commander, driven into exile. Now the senate arranged to have Metellus recalled. It was the turn of Marius to leave in disgust before he had to observe in person the triumphant return of a rival. Marius set off for Asia Minor, ostensibly in fulfilment of a vow he had made during the Cimbric wars, and Sertorius headed for Hispania, back with the legions as a military tribune.

He was posted to Castulo, a town which the Romans had regularly garrisoned since at least the time of the Hannibalic War. The town, in modern Andalusia, was wealthy due to its highly productive lead and silver mines. This wealth had more than somewhat corroded the moral fibre of the garrison, who (Plutarch assures us) 'in the midst of such abundance, had abandoned all pretence of discipline and spent most of their time getting drunk.' The urgent need to get the garrison back into shape might have been why the provincial commander sent Sertorius there in the first place.

Urgency was needed, because the local tribesmen had noted that their Roman oppressors could barely hold their own against the local vintages, let alone against more serious opposition. The misbehaviour of the garrison almost certainly extended itself to the property and womenfolk of the town, and either Sertorius was too inexperienced at sole command to stop the rot, or he arrived too late to do so. The latter presumption seems more likely, since when matters came to a crisis, Sertorius showed that he could be both decisive and brutal.

The locals decided that they could not take out the garrison on their own, and invited their neighbours from a nearby city to help with the enterprise. (Note that the term 'city' was sometimes used by contemporary writers to describe what a modern historian would refer to as a fortified village of a few thousand inhabitants at most.)

Getting by what passed as a gate guard proved no challenge for the newcomers. Thus, as the garrison settled down to its nightly bout of debauchery, the men discovered that the evening's diversions included annoyed and murderous Spaniards bearing swords.

It is probable that the troops were not quartered in the actual houses of the townsfolk – as was the practice in some parts of Asia Minor, for example – for had they been so quartered, most of them would have been hung and drawn as well. In fact, most of the garrison escaped, which makes it likely that they had a separate barracks at the edge of town. (Garrisons defending a town might have a citadel in the centre, just as the Capitoline had once served as Rome's fortress of last resort, but those garrisons occupying a town are more sensibly situated at the edge, making it easier to deal with hostile townsfolk and enemy attackers separately.)

Most of his men had not only escaped, but done so with much of their arms and equipment. This allowed Sertorius to coldly set about restoring order in the traditional Roman fashion, which the imperial historian Tacitus later memorably described as 'creating a desert, and calling it peace'. The exits from the town were secured, and once the occupants could not escape, the Romans methodically killed every man of military age without enquiry as to each man's role in the uprising.

Then, once he had ascertained the origin of the extra corpses, Sertorius set out for the town they had come from. He ordered his men to wear the armour of the slain, so the citizens of the town happily opened their gates to what they mistakenly believed were their returning warriors bearing booty. Those who were not slaughtered in the process of being brutally disillusioned about this became booty themselves, as the surviving townsfolk were sold into slavery.[10]

This episode is a microcosm of Hispania at the time. Guile and ambuscade were employed by both sides, along with generous helpings of brutality and massacre. Sertorius, by his studied ruthlessness, showed both the local tribesmen and his own men that he was capable of coping very well in such an environment. The rest of his tribuneship consequently passed without serious incident. Young Sertorius was making a name for himself.

Chapter 2

From the Tiber to the Tagus

aving a reputation for boldness and brutality did not harm Sertorius' status with the Roman electorate. Neither did his association with Marius, who was still a hero to the common people of Rome. Consequently, at some time around 91 BC, Quintus Sertorius gained the first step on the career path to becoming a Roman senator. He was elected quaestor, the lowest rank of Roman magistrate.[1]

A quaestor such as Sertorius would usually work closely with his commander. This commander would be a provincial governor and consequently a senior senator. His quaestor's role would usually be logistical and financial – for example arranging supplies for the troops and payment for those supplies. Generally, quaestor and commander formed a close bond with the senior expected to take a benevolent interest in his subordinate's future career.

This did not always work out according to the convention. For example Marius closely followed the career of his former quaestor Cornelius Sulla, but his interest was anything but benevolent. Even after his victory of Aquae Sextae it had chagrined Marius that part of his army's supplies arrived courtesy of Sulla's good work with the Alpine tribesmen.[2] The fact that Sulla had helped to win the climactic battle of Vercellae for him likewise caused Marius much more pain than gratitude. Sulla maintained his friendship with the king of Mauritania who had kick-started Sulla's career by handing the Numidian king Jugurtha over to him, so finishing the African war.

Now this king paid for the erection of statues in Rome which depicted in a tableau gilded with gold, the handover of Jugurtha to Sulla. Marius was wild with jealousy, and demanded the statues be removed, apparently on the grounds that they glorified someone other than himself. Sulla stubbornly refused, and the people of Rome squared off for a round of civil commotion, with the senate mainly backing Sulla, and the common people generally favouring Marius.

The coming fight was averted, but by no benign means. The talent for misgovernment which the later Roman Republic had already demonstrated to such great effect in Spain by now extended to the people of Italy. As Roman power grew, so did the city's domination of the people of Italy. These people were now largely allies of Rome, whether they wanted to be or not. As allies, their young men served alongside the Roman legions, sharing the same risks but getting fewer of the spoils. At home, wealthy Roman senators enlarged their estates at the expense of local farmers who had none of the protection which the law allowed even the poorest Roman citizen.

The Italian people demanded to share in Roman citizenship. Not because they were great fans of Rome, but because this would allow them to serve in the legions on an equal basis, and allow them some protection from the rapacious Roman aristocracy. In early years, Rome had become great by granting citizenship to almost anyone who asked for it, and sometimes imposing it on people whether they wanted it or not. As Rome had expanded through Italy, entire communities, including Sertorius' home town of Nursia, had been made Roman citizens against their will. But with Rome wealthy and hegemon of the known world, its citizens had become more selective about whom they allowed into their ranks.

Roman senators would have even more rivals from among ambitious rural aristocrats of the type that Sertorius already represented. Besides, when a Roman landowner had illegally misappropriated his neighbour's lands, the last thing he wanted was that neighbour appearing in the courts asking for redress as a Roman citizen. So the aristocracy stirred the voters into rejecting all initiatives to broaden the franchise, claiming that hordes of new citizens would steal their corn dole, and take all the best seats at the public spectacles. The idea of foreigners getting citizenship and then moving in, stealing their jobs and marrying their daughters was enough to persuade Roman voters to turn against the tribune Livius Drusus, the main advocate of votes for Italians.

Then someone assassinated Drusus in the courtyard of his own home, and all hell broke loose. The squabble between Sulla and Marius was forgotten as the Italian people rose in a concerted rebellion. The Italians had numbers, and the same military training and equipment as the Romans they had so long fought beside. The very survival of Rome was again at risk, and men and materiel were urgently needed.

Sertorius was just wrapping up his term as quaestor. He had been stationed in Cisalpine Gaul, the Gallic province on the Italian side of the Alps. From surviving accounts, it seems that Sertorius had also not had a typical quaestorship. Instead of working closely with the governor of the province, he had been running the province more or less by himself, while the actual governor was across the mountains tidying up the military and civil chaos left by the Cimbric invasion.[3]

The violent outbreak of civil war – and given the closeness in culture, language and armies, the Italian revolt was to all intents and purposes a civil war, suddenly highlighted the role of the quaestor of Cisalpine Gaul. For over a century this province had been a prime recruiting ground for the legions, and with much of the rest of Italy lost to Rome, it suddenly fell to Sertorius to meet the urgent need for men and materiel.

This was a task requiring a certain delicacy, for a maximum of men, money and supplies had to be extracted from the provincials. Yet that extraction had to be accomplished from a people who had no great fondness for Rome, and a choice of which side they picked. If Sertorius was too energetic in his exactions, he might alienate the people he was administering and end up as a recruiting sergeant for the enemy. (It was probably this consideration which gave pause to many other provincial administrators in Sertorius' position, rather than the 'slowness and idleness' of which Plutarch accuses them.)

If he was not energetic enough, Rome would lose the manpower and supplies she so desperately needed. Sertorius was not to know it, but this task which combined logistics with the politics of diplomatically extracting resources from a restive population was superb training for his later career. The contemporary historian Sallust briefly acknowledges this early effort of Sertorius with the remark 'He made a valuable contribution to the war against the Marsi by supplying recruits and arms'.[4]

The following year Sertorius abandoned his support role and got personally involved in the fighting. Since he had certainly fought at Arausio and had probably also contributed to the victories at Aquae Sextae and Vercellae, he was by now an experienced warrior and a valuable addition to any military staff. His rank at this time is unknown, as Sallust goes on to explain.

Much was achieved under his command, but this has gone uncommemorated; firstly because of his [relatively] humble birth and secondly because of the ill-will of those writing [on the topic].

(Sallust, *Histories*, frag 1.88)

Sallust, as a pro-Marian and anti-aristocratic historian, is one of the few near-contemporaries who is favourably disposed towards Sertorius. Sadly not much of his *Histories* has survived.

It is quite possible that Sertorius served once again under the same commander whom he had served in Spain, T. Didius – who later in the war came to a sticky end under the walls of the Etruscan town of Volterrae. It is also very possible that Sertorius had a semi-independent command, either of a unit of cavalry or even as legate in charge of a legion. After all, Sallust specifically refers to '*ductu eius*' – Sertorius' 'command' or 'leadership'.

It is also quite possible that towards the end of the war Sertorius served under the father of his later opponent, Gnaeus Pompey. A bronze tablet has been discovered which lists the staff officers of the elder Pompey (who is usually called Pompeius Strabo). Three of the officers in Strabo's staff later joined Sertorius in Hispania, a number high enough to suggest an earlier association. Another officer who served with the elder Pompeius Strabo also later joined Sertorius in Hispania – but as one of his most mortal enemies. This was Metellus Pius, whom we last met as a youth in the tent of his father, Metellus Numidicus, the former commanding officer of the insubordinate and scheming Marius (p.9).

By now something of a pattern is emerging of young Sertorius at war. The early years of one of Rome's greatest generals are obscure not through a quirk of history, but through deliberate obfuscation. In the eyes of the near-contemporaries who recorded events, Sertorius was a traitor, and the deeds of traitors were not to be immortalized. The only reason why the subsequent history of Sertorius could be reconstructed by later more impartial historians such as Plutarch was because those against whom Sertorius struggled were more favoured sons of the Republic. The achievements of these generals were recorded, so those of their opponent Sertorius went on the record also, in a sort of negative image.

The war against the Italian allies gave little for Roman historians to cheer about. In the opening phases of the war the Romans were regularly thrashed by the people they had so despised, and for a while the actual survival of Rome itself was in doubt. Roman historians never relished describing defeats, nor trumpeting the achievements of their enemies. Therefore, we have no record of the achievements of the future traitor, Sertorius, against the current traitors of the rebel movement in a war the latter were winning.

Predictably, Sertorius was quite prepared to put his body in the way of the rebel tide, and he was considerably injured in the process. He took a number of wounds ('to the front' Sallust assures us). In the course of taking one too many wounds to the face, Sertorius lost an eye.

Now this is something of an on-going theme among the great opponents of Rome. Hannibal was one-eyed, having lost the other to infection while crossing the swamps of Etruria. So too, in later years Julius Civilis who led the Batavian revolt of AD 70 made much of the fact that he was missing an eye for the very reason that two of his antecedents in the struggle against Rome had suffered the same handicap.[5] Despite the idea that one-eyed opponents of Rome were a 'shamanistic mythologem' (to use the wonderful expression of one academic) there seems little reason to disbelieve that Sertorius did in fact lose an eye. After all, so did Philip II of Macedonia, the aptly named Antigonus Monopthalmus and indeed the heroic Horatius Coccles of early Republican history. It was an inevitable risk on an ancient battlefield where sharp objects and edged pieces of steel were flying about in considerable quantities.

> Sertorius used his wounds as personal propaganda. Being scarred in the face had its advantages. 'Other men, he used to say, could not always carry about with them the evidence of their heroic achievements. Their tokens, wreaths and spears of honour must at some times be set aside. His proof of valour remained with him at all times.'
>
> (Plutarch, *Sertorius*, 8)

Rome won her war by surrendering. After all, when all your enemies want is to join you, surrender is a relatively painless option. So once they had their backs to the wall, the Romans magnanimously announced that they were prepared to offer Roman citizenship to everyone who would stop killing them to get it. This immediately split the ranks of the rebels into those who were fighting for equality with Rome, and those who wanted, at heart, to destroy the place. Since those who were fighting to become citizens got their wish, they automatically became Roman legionaries and, in that capacity, turned upon their former allies.

By giving the majority of their enemies what they had wanted, the Romans now had the larger army and the war swung dramatically in their favour. This gave renewed prestige to the Roman commanders of the time, which included the consul for 88 BC, Cornelius Sulla. Sulla had distinguished himself in the war, whereas Marius had retired early to Rome in a sulk after he felt that his mediocre performance to date had not been sufficiently honoured.

Sertorius too emerged from the fighting as a popular war hero. When he returned to Rome, the people recognized him with shouts and applause when he attended the theatre. It was time to take the next step up the political ladder and become a tribune of the plebs. To his bafflement and fury, Sertorius failed to get elected. It did not take him long to work out why.

With the war approaching a successful conclusion, the old enmity between Sulla and Marius had resurfaced. Sertorius had not only served under the command of Marius, but – unlike Sulla who had done the same – he had been both loyal and trusted. Given the very substantial powers of a tribune to make the life of a consul awkward (keeping consuls in check being in fact one of the purposes of the tribunate), a firm Marian supporter was the last thing that Sulla wanted on the tribunes' bench during his year in office. Consequently Sulla and his aristocratic colleagues made a considerable effort to foil the hopes of Sertorius. Marius, on the other hand, never particularly cared to see his subordinates do well, and made no commensurate effort in support.

Sertorius lost the election not because of any personal failing, but as collateral damage in the struggle between two more powerful men. It was, as a later Italian might have put it, 'just business, nothing personal', but Sertorius took it very personally. He became a committed enemy of Sulla, though thanks to the tepid support he received from his former commander, he now distanced himself from Marius as well. On the bright side, the intent was only to stop Sertorius from becoming a tribune. With that achieved, his relative unimportance meant that Sulla and friends had little objection to Sertorius being enrolled in the senate on the strength of his earlier quaestorship. Consequently, probably late in 89 BC Quintus Sertorius became a senator of Rome. This meant that Sertorius could now look for allies among a better class of Sulla's enemies. Sulla had plenty of these, and was soon to collect more by the bucket-load.

The same political shenanigans that had cost Sertorius his tribunate developed into something far greater and more sinister. In Asia Minor, Mithridates VI, king of Pontus had been provoked into war by Roman administrators too blinded with greed to recognize that their timing could have been better. Mithridates proved a remarkably competent commander. (The fact that Rome was loathed for its extortionate greed and maladministration across the Greek east did not harm Mithridates' cause either.) With Rome paralyzed by the Italian revolt, no supplies or reinforcements could be sent east and Mithridates swiftly ousted Rome from Anatolia and a good part of Greece. Only in 88 BC, with the Italian war on the wane, was Rome finally able to mount a response.

Naturally enough, command of the army to be sent east fell to one of the current consuls, in this case Cornelius Sulla, a man who had also previous experience in campaigning in Asia Minor. However, Marius was not going to let his upstart rival reap yet further glory. For some weeks he had been forcing his aged body into public demonstrations of youthful vigour on the Campus Martius 'and showed himself still competent with arms and on horseback despite his age [Marius was approaching seventy years old] and his corpulence'. (Plutarch, *Life of Marius*, 34)

The point of these exercises became clear when Marius used his connections with the tribune Sulpicius to pass legislation removing Sulla from command of the coming campaign against Mithridates. Aged and fat he might be, but Marius wanted this war for himself anyway. The senate and Sulla's supporters did not take this political coup quietly, but Sulpicius had prepared his ground well. Sulla was forced to abandon attempts to block Sulpicius' legislation by a mob that killed his fellow consul's son in the course of a series of violent riots. These same riots forced Sulla into humiliating himself by seeking protection for his own life beneath the roof of Marius.

Anyone who knew the proud and viciously vindictive nature of Sulla would have known immediately that Sulla would not stand for this – and more importantly nor would the army which Sulla had already mustered for the campaign. The officers whom Marius sent to take command of that army were lynched by the men, and when Sulla arrived soon afterwards all 30,000 soldiers fell in behind him to 'restore order' in Rome.

This was a decisive moment in Roman history. Never before had a Roman general led a Roman army against his own city. However he tried to prettify his actions with phrases such as 'restoring civil order' and 'preventing mob rule', Sulla was essentially conquering Rome for himself. His officers fully understood the enormity of his actions and deserted him, but Sulla was implacable. All the more so once he discovered that the Marians had started killing his friends in Rome in revenge for the officers whom Sulla's army had lynched.

Marius tried hard to mount a defence, but all he had on his side were the common people of Rome. Sulla had six veteran legions. He took the city without any casualties other than those his men suffered from being pelted with roof tiles by the indignant citizenry. Once in charge, Sulla immediately set about reorganizing affairs to his liking. He was officially restored to command of the army. Sulpicius and all who had worked with him were condemned to death, and Marius along with them, although the latter made his escape with the aid of a very considerable body of sympathizers. At this point Sertorius' earlier alienation from Marius probably saved his life, as his new-found disdain for Marius had kept him aloof from the machinations of Sulpicius. Sertorius was not therefore among the casualties of Sulla's subsequent vengeance.

The consular elections for the following year were due, and to show that order had been restored, Sulla presided over these elections as an outgoing consul normally would. Despite Sulla's attempts to appease them, the Roman voters showed their disapproval of his conduct by unanimously rejecting his candidates and choosing those who most dared to voice their opposition. Given his animosity towards Sulla, it is no surprise that Sertorius was among the most enthusiastic supporters of Lucius Cinna, the most anti-Sullan candidate on the ballot. It is also very possible that Cinna was also on the staff of Pompeius Strabo during the Italian war, so Sertorius might have already known the man.[6] It likely that Sertorius lost little sleep over the fact that his former commander Marius was now a public enemy and an exile.

Sulla made both of the new consuls swear an oath that they would adhere to his policies, and then departed with his army to fight Mithridates. It soon became clear that Cinna had no intention of keeping his promise, whereas his fellow consul intended to do so. This consul was a man called Octavius, a man who appears to have believed that peace was best maintained by keeping the prevailing *status quo*. This drove Sertorius yet more firmly into the camp of Cinna, as Octavius made it plain that any former subordinates of Marius would not prosper under his administration.

Relationships between the consuls deteriorated to the point where Cinna was eventually driven from Rome, along with him his firm supporter Sertorius. This was one of the turning points in the young officer's life. Had Sertorius abandoned Cinna and opted for neutrality in the coming struggle he may well have survived to become an aged nonentity in his home town of Nursia. Instead, Sertorius used his recent fame as a war hero to help Cinna to recruit ex-legionaries back to the Marian standard. The son of Marius had joined Cinna in his flight from Rome and this undoubtedly helped the recruiting process.[7] There were many of these discharged soldiers scattered around Italy, and, as is often the case with military veterans, some had found it hard to re-adjust to civilian life. They gladly once more took up arms in their former commander's name, and before long Cinna had an army.

There was only one problem. The army had been raised in the name of Marius, and now along came Marius himself, out of exile in Africa and proposing to join the anti-Sullan cause. Sertorius was appalled. The army he had raised for Cinna was more than enough to restore his faction to power in Rome. The two 'legions' that Marius had raised for himself on his way to join Cinna were ex-slaves, shepherds and opportunists. Their addition did little for Cinna's forces. But it did add a horde of ill-trained and undisciplined troops and a man with a spiteful character and a very long list of grudges that he intended to settle as violently as possible. Sertorius knew his former commander of old and 'feared his harsh nature, and that at the moment of triumph he would cause chaos with a limitless vindictiveness that would overcome the limits of justice.' (Plutarch, *Life of Sertorius*, 5)

Of course, in his telling of events Plutarch has the advantage of perfect hindsight and knew already the walking disaster that Marius would become. However, there is no reason to disbelieve that Sertorius was opposed to his former commander joining the cause. As pointed out already, Marius was not needed and the few advantages of having him along were vastly outweighed by the flaws of the man himself – flaws of which Sertorius was very well aware. However, Cinna was eager to have Marius with him and could not be dissuaded.

When pressed, Cinna claimed that Marius had actually joined the army at his invitation, something which Sertorius could hardly dispute without calling his commander a liar. However, Plutarch has Sertorius doing something pretty close to that.

> Oh, really? Here I was thinking that Marius had decided for himself to come to Italy, and so I was trying to decide what good it would do. But it turns out there's nothing to discuss. Since after all, you invited him, then you have to receive and employ him. There's no question about it.
>
> (Plutarch, *Life of Sertorius*, 5)

Once again, we get little detail of the role of Sertorius in the civil war which followed. We know the dispositions for the final attack on Rome – Cinna was east of the city ('opposite' it) and Sertorius commanded the force immediately to the north. Here he faced troops commanded by Pompeius Strabo, which may not have been a coincidence, if – as has been alleged – Pompeius Strabo had worked with Sertorius before, and was negotiating a change of sides. When negotiations fell through Pompeius attacked Sertorius' positions but without success.

Marius went west, and gave an indication of his future conduct by pillaging Ostia once his supporters within had betrayed the city to him. Sertorius had already stopped food barges from reaching Rome by throwing bridges across the river to block them, so Marius' action was probably intended as an act of terrorism aimed at the people of Rome, and to appease his own unruly troops with plunder.

If Marius had terror in mind, it worked, for the people of Rome worried about starvation, and forced Octavius to negotiate a surrender. A cowed senate agreed to rescind the banishment of Marius, and to allow Cinna to re-take control of the city. Cinna vowed that he would 'not willingly be the cause of anyone's death', but he willingly received the head of Octavius, his former fellow consul, when his troops presented it to him, and he allowed the head to be displayed on the forum.

> Now the victors sent informers to seek out their enemies ... disrespect for the gods and the horror of men moved them as little as fear of disgust for their crimes. Godless sights followed savage deeds. They

killed remorselessly, and severed the necks of those they had killed.
These horrors they flaunted publicly so as to inspire public fear and
horror. ... The slain were not allowed to be buried, but lay where they
fell, to be torn by dogs and pecked by birds.

(Appian, *Civil Wars*, 1.71–73)

Lutatius Catulus, who had shared in Marius' victory at Vercellae now paid
the price for having obtained greater glory in that battle than his fellow
general. A jealous Marius accused him of insipid support for his cause
when Sulla had him banished. Catulus, seeing what was coming next,
anticipated his inevitable arrest and execution by committing suicide.

This was not what Sertorius had expected. It was one thing to re-take
Rome back from the minions of Sulla, the usurping general who had
overthrown the constitution. It was another to blatantly abuse a position
of power to persecute enemies – real or imagined – and leave their bodies
in the street. Sertorius had dreamed of being among the leaders of Rome.
Now he was in that position, people cowered from him or fled in horror.
It has been seen that Sertorius was a hard man, and indifferent to a bit of
massacre when necessary, but he felt Marius was going too far – and it is
probable that Cinna agreed with him.

As a military man, Sertorius would have been particularly disgusted
with the undisciplined conduct of the men that Marius had recruited
on his return to Italy. 'His allies during the war and body-guards under
his tyranny, these men had become rich and powerful. Sometimes with
Marius' orders, and sometimes while Marius looked the other way, they
killed men who were once their masters, slept with their wives, and raped
their children' says Plutarch.[8] Appian adds 'They plundered houses, and
killed men at random on the street, even when he [Cinna] had forbidden
it.'

Finally Sertorius had seen enough. The ex-slaves had an encampment,
probably an amphitheatre, though the forum itself is another possibility.
In any case, they needed somewhere they could gather at nights for mutual
security against the by now outraged populace of Rome. One night, regular
troops surrounded this camp and rained enough javelins down upon it to
turn everyone within into a very dead pincushion. Plutarch claims that
Sertorius was behind this mass execution; Appian says Cinna, but it is
significant that Appian allows that Cinna used Gallic soldiery – probably

those commanded and recruited by the ex-quaestor of Cisalpine Gaul, Quintus Sertorius.

The question of whether Rome was currently a democracy or a military dictatorship ruled by the Marians and Cinna was partly sidestepped when Marius insisted on, and naturally enough obtained a record seventh consulship – more than any man before or since held this office in the Republic. Fortunately for Rome, Marius died before he had settled into the second fortnight of his consulship, his body and mind worn out by the stresses of recent years. He was seventy years old. For better or worse, in his struggle with Sulla, Marius had dramatically altered both the course of Roman history and the life of Quintus Sertorius.

If, during the Cimbric wars, chance had left Sertorius under the command of Catulus or Sulla himself, there is every possibility that Sertorius would have gone east with Sulla to fight Mithridates, and enjoyed perhaps as successful a career within mainstream Roman politics as his contemporary, the equally brilliant general Licinius Lucullus. However, Sertorius ended up with Marius, and because he was a loyal and competent subordinate to Sulla's enemy, Sulla naturally stymied Sertorius' political career when Sertorius' advancement might hurt his. This drove Sertorius into the ranks of Sulla's enemies, and the rest of his life was shaped by that enmity.

For though in January of the year 86 BC Marius left the scene for the underworld and a reckoning with the ghosts of those whom he had slain, his rival Cornelius Sulla was very much alive. Not only alive, but coming home. Deeply disturbed by reports from Rome (including one received in person from his wife who had been driven from the capital), Sulla patched up a peace with Mithridates. The Pontic king agreed to abandon those of his conquests he had not already lost to Sulla, and in return Sulla agreed to let Mithridates remain king of Pontus, despite his execution of Roman magistrates and the slaughter of tens of thousands of Roman civilians in Asia Minor.

Terrible as that slaughter had been, it was the on-going slaughter of his friends and allies in Rome that concerned Sulla, and barely had peace been agreed in the east than he and his veteran legions headed west for Italy and vengeance. Plutarch claims that it was the thought of Sulla's return which helped to drive Marius to his grave. This is uncertain. Marius had considerable military resources of his own and faith both in his own leadership and that of Cinna and Sertorius. Sulla would have not found it so easy to take Rome a second time with Marius in command, and indeed, even with Marius dead, his followers did not go down without a fight.

The problem was that even before Sulla reached Italy the successors to Marius fought almost as hard with each other as they would with the approaching enemy. The command of Rome's forces was split among generals of varying competence who could agree only on the fact that if Sulla was not stopped their necks were certainly on the line. But how and where to fight, and who should lead that fight was something the fractious allies had difficulty in agreeing. The problems at the top percolated down through the ranks, and led to uncertainty and mistrust among the common soldiers in the legions – an uncertainty which strongly contrasted with the determination and clear purpose of Sulla's men.

Plutarch sums up events thereafter in one long sentence which is still pretty terse, given that it sums up three years.

> Cinna was murdered and against the wishes of Sertorius, and against the law, the younger Marius took on the consulship while [ineffectual] men as Carbo, Norbanus, and Scipio had no success in stopping Sulla's advance on Rome, so the Marian cause was being ruined and lost; cowardice and weakness by the generals played its part, and treachery did the rest, and there was no reason why Sertorius should stay to watch things going from bad to worse through the inferior judgement of men with superior power.
>
> (Plutarch, *Life of Sertorius*, 6)

Cinna was murdered in 84 BC, lynched by his own troops, who were none too keen on fighting the Sullan legions in a war which promised a great deal of pain for little profit. Cinna tried to force the issue at an assembly of his soldiers, and his attempt to restore discipline by force went very badly wrong. Sulla had opened tentative negotiations with Cinna while still in the east. When he learned of the latter's death, he broke off negotiations, probably in the well-founded belief that no-one remained in the ranks of his enemies with the status or reputation to mount an effective defence against his return.

It is probable that Cinna died in the same year that Sertorius took the next step with his own career and became praetor. Although there is no direct evidence that Sertorius ever held this office, the assumption that he was a praetor is based on the fact that (though his exact age at this time is uncertain) this was about the time when a successful politician of his age would have been eligible to stand for the position. His record gave Sertorius high standing within the group currently ruling Rome. His personal authority was strong, and the electorate knew that – unlike most of his colleagues – he had not killed any of his fellow Romans out of malice or greed. Altogether it is unlikely that Rome's squabbling generals could have stopped Sertorius from becoming praetor even if they had wanted to, and there is no sign that they did want to. In his later actions, Sertorius behaved as though he was a high-ranking ex-magistrate of Rome, and this is because he probably was.

A man with the experience and level-headedness of Sertorius was needed, and needed in Italy. Normally, after his year in office, a praetor would take up command of one of Rome's lesser provinces as a propraetor. However, in an emergency an ex-praetor might be needed in Italy, and the return of Sulla certainly counted as an emergency. The middle of the decade of the 80s BC has been described as spent 'Waiting for Sulla'.[9] In 83 BC that wait was well and truly over.

Nor was it only Sulla whom Sertorius and his colleagues had to face. A young man called Gnaeus Pompey, son of Sertorius' putative former commander Pompeius Strabo, raised a pro-Sullan rebellion in the countryside of Picenum (a region once described as being 'in south-west north-eastern Italy'). Also one of the top Roman generals of the war with the Italian allies in 90 BC went straight over to the side of Sulla as soon as the latter landed in Italy. This was Quintus Metellus Pius, the son of that Metellus who had been Marius' commander until Marius had successfully replaced him in Africa. Now Metellus Pius was a formidable general in his own right, not only because he was a skilled commander, but because his personal prestige was considerably higher than that of any of the mediocrities who commanded the Marian forces.

These commanders did not include Sertorius. In the years after Marius' death a number of senators had jumped on the Marian bandwagon, either because they truly believed in the wrongness of Sulla's cause or because they mistakenly believed that enthusiasm for the Marians was their best chance for survival. Sertorius was now an ex-praetor. He was outranked, not only by the serving consuls, but also by the ex-consuls of recent years. All of these men were well aware of Sulla's ruthless and unforgiving nature and insisted on personally commanding armies in the hope that they could prevent Sulla from exercising these qualities.

Among those who outranked Sertorius as the fighting went on into the year 82 BC was the younger Marius, who now became consul. Marius junior had held none of the offices which a candidate for the consulship might be expected to have held, and at 27 years old was too young for a post for which neither experience nor the law qualified him, especially at a time of major crisis. Sertorius, who probably was by then qualified for the consulship, objected strenuously but his opinion was ignored – something which in his opinion happened all too regularly and generally with disastrous results.

> As the last straw, Sulla set up his camp near Scipio. He acted in a friendly manner as though wanting peace, and all the while proceeded to subvert Scipio's army. Sertorius bluntly warned Scipio about this but could not make him understand.
>
> (Plutarch, *Life of Sertorius*, 6)

Plutarch is wrong here, as the testimony of Appian demonstrates. In fact this incident occurred before the younger Marius became consul, but it well demonstrates the sort of thing which caused Sertorius to finally throw up his hands and storm out of Italy.

Cornelius Scipio Asiaticus was of the family of the great Scipio Africanus, the conqueror of Hannibal in the Carthaginian war of over a century before. He was also an experienced general in his own right, having campaigned with some distinction in Illyria. He was not however, a natural leader of men. Not only did he lose his army to Sulla (as described below) but later he led another army against the young Pompey which kept on going right past him and joined the ranks of the enemy.

In 83 BC Scipio was camped near Capua, with Sertorius in his entourage. Despite a recent defeat for his side, Scipio had reason to be cheerful. Sulla was now caught between two substantial Marian armies and facing defeat. It seems Scipio was keen on getting the glory of finishing the war, but preferred to do so without risking a battle. Firstly he would have then had to share the glory with Norbanus, the general of the other army, and secondly battles were always chancy affairs. Scipio would rather Sulla did not add to his already well-proven reputation for fighting his way out of a tight corner and so happily took Sulla up on his offer to negotiate.

Sertorius quite rightly did not trust Sulla, and advised Scipio to force a decisive action. Instead he was sent to Norbanus to explain to Scipio's colleague that an armistice was in force and negotiations were under way. Probably with the express intention of breaking that armistice, Sertorius made a small detour along his way and captured the town of Suessa which until then had been held by Sulla's faction. When Sulla complained of this breach of trust, Scipio sent back the hostages which Sulla had given as a sign of his own good faith.

This wimpish behaviour outraged Scipio's troops, who were already upset that Sertorius had taken Suessa and exposed them to the risk of having to face Sulla's formidable legionaries in battle. Consequently the men (which probably means the senior centurions) made a secret deal that they would go over to Sulla as soon as he approached their camp. This duly happened, though out of respect for the ceasefire which was still in force Sulla allowed Scipio to leave, unharmed apart from a substantial dent in his pride. Ever optimistic, Sulla then approached Norbanus and proposed taking up peace talks where Scipio had left off. Norbanus did not deign to reply. However, he undoubtedly had strong words with Sertorius, whose impetuous actions had played a large part in Scipio's undoing.

Shortly thereafter, Sertorius left Italy, whether in high dudgeon at the constant disregard of his advice, as Plutarch states, or, as Appian implies, kicked out before he could do any more damage. Sertorius intended to return to Hispania, the province where he had served with distinction as a quaestor, and intended to do so again as a propraetor.

> At last, therefore, completely giving up on the city [of Rome], he set out for Hispania. His plan was to see if he could establish a firm power base there. If so he would have a place of refuge to offer his friends once their cause had been defeated at home.
>
> (Plutarch, *Life of Sertorius*, 6)

After years caught in the travails of Italy, Sertorius was off to meet his destiny – but more than a few pitfalls and setbacks lay on the way to getting there.

Chapter 3

A Beginner's Guide to First Century Iberia

bout twenty years after the death of Sertorius, Julius Caesar wrapped up his conquest of Gaul to complete a series of campaigns which had begun eight years previously.[1] Later Caesar would fight in Spain. Here, the Romans had started campaigning over a hundred years before Caesar's birth, and would keep doing so for a half-century after his death. Compared to Iberia, Gaul was easy.

To understand the career of Sertorius in Hispania, one has to understand the history of the Romans in the peninsula, and indeed the history of the Iberian peoples living there. As will be seen, this was not a land of peace. War had been more or less a constant since the start of recorded history in the province. Iberia was packed with a number of different tribes, each more warlike and bloodthirsty than the next. When there had been no foreigners to fight, the locals had fought each other with skill, energy and enthusiasm. The early military history of Rome in Hispania was not that of a bullying oppressor subduing a peace-loving, gentle opponent, but rather that of someone unwarily sticking a hand into a hornets' nest. Historians have debated ever since why Rome chose to do this, and what Rome thought it would get from the province that was worth the two centuries of pain needed to conquer it.

Like many an invader over the ages which followed, the Romans first got involved in Iberia by claiming to protect the very people they were later to attack. The year was 218 BC, one hundred and thirty-six years before Quintus Sertorius came to write his own bloody chapter in the peninsula, and Rome was worriedly watching the activities of that other one-eyed enemy – Hannibal Barca.

At that time Hannibal had both his eyes and was not (not officially anyway) an enemy of Rome. On the other hand, not many Spaniards counted Hannibal as a friend. Hannibal wanted the Iberian Peninsula for Carthage. Rome had just won the first in the series of three wars which the city was to fight with Hannibal's native city, and the loss of that first war had cost Carthage control of her lands in Sicily and drained the coffers of the state. In the early years of the peace which followed, Rome took Sardinia from Carthage as well, with blatant disregard for both justice and treaty agreements.

Hannibal's family, the Barcas, decided that Iberia would make good Carthage's losses. The gold their city had lost would be replaced by Spanish silver, and land lost to Rome would be reclaimed from Iberian tribesmen. The Barcid intentions in the peninsula were made clear by the name of the base they had established there – Quart Hsdasht – which the Romans called 'New Carthage'. (Actually, the Romans translated the Carthaginian meaning better than the actual name, which in Phoenician means 'New City'. The original Carthage had the same name, and even the unimaginative Carthaginians quailed at naming their Spanish colony 'New, New City'.) The intention behind the name was clear – Carthage would be born anew in Iberia, and regain her ancient power.

Thus, we come to the first reason why the Romans became interested in Hispania. They did not want anyone else to have it. This was rather tricky, since by the time the Romans had worked out what the Carthaginians were doing, the Barcids already had about a third of the place under their influence. Rome's first step was to limit the damage. It was first agreed with the Carthaginians that Hannibal's armies would not advance beyond the river Ebro. The Carthaginians had no problem with that, since the Ebro is not that far from the Pyrenees, and Carthage had not yet expanded half that far. However, this was merely Rome's first move in the containment game.

Though they had persuaded Carthage to set an outermost limit on its Iberian expansion, there is no record that the Romans agreed not to interfere within that limit, and they promptly did so. They made a defensive pact with the city of Saguntum (modern Sagunto) which is situated about halfway between New Carthage and the Ebro. At the same time Rome strengthened its ties with Massalia, a Greek colony in what is today southern France, but a city which had a strategic colony of its own – Emporion in Spain.

In due course, Hannibal attacked Saguntum and the Romans had their excuse for attacking the Carthaginians in Iberia. There was also, as it transpired, the unforeseen and far from minor matter of Hannibal attacking the Romans in Italy. However, even as the Romans struggled with this unexpected and nearly fatal extra development, they never abandoned their original intention. The war with Carthage was fought not just in Italy but also in Spain. Even as Hannibal rampaged through southern Italy the Romans continued to send armies west to the Iberian peninsula.

These armies had no easy time of it. Hannibal had left armies under the competent command of his younger brother Hasdrubal and his close relative Hanno. The Romans were quickly caught up in a three-sided war with Iberian tribesmen choosing one side or another in a fast-changing struggle. There were very few armies in the ancient world that could stand up to the Roman legions in a fair fight, but this did not greatly worry either Carthaginians or Spanish, since neither had any intention of fighting fairly. They knew each other and the terrain very well and used both for ambush and double cross.

After a promising start, Scipio Calvus (the uncle of the great Scipio Africanus[2]) was joined by his brother Gnaeus. The pair recruited a host of mercenaries and advanced confidently against the Carthaginians. Their opponents promptly bribed the Spanish mercenaries to go home and fell upon the now outnumbered Romans as they desperately tried to retreat across the inhospitable terrain. Both Scipios were killed and the Romans were left penned up by the Ebro, which is where they could have been even without a war and the cost of having to deal with Hannibal in Italy.

Things changed in the next decade, when Rome tried again with a new army and another Scipio. This Scipio was the great Scipio Africanus, the greatest general of his era. On his arrival, the young commander immediately displayed a tactical genius that was not to be seen again in Iberia until the arrival of Sertorius just over a century later. Scipio started with the successful capture of Carthago Nova. He went on to give Hasdrubal a beating at Baecula, but Hasdrubal was quitting the peninsula anyway – he and his men were urgently needed by Hannibal in Italy.[3]

This left yet another Barcid brother, Mago, in command of Spain. Scipio promptly took on Mago and the combined Carthaginian forces at the Battle of Ilipa in 206 BC, and by his victory won Rome a presence in Iberia that was to last for over half a millennium. A presence which, in fact, has never completely gone away.

The Roman occupation was initially along Spain's eastern seaboard. It was not a happy experience for the Spaniards living there, and they made sure that the occupying legionaries did not greatly enjoy it either. Rome had decided on a permanent military presence of at least a legion in Spain, and these legionaries were back in action against rebel tribesmen almost before Scipio had departed from his Spanish conquests to take the war to Carthage in Africa. Apart from the eastern coast Rome also had to defend the southern colony of Italica, where Scipio had settled wounded and discharged legionaries after the battle of Ilipa. The two Roman provinces into which Spain was to be divided did not come into being for another decade.

These two provinces were created in part to regularize the position of magistrates whom the restive tribesmen of Iberia kept busy campaigning in the region. The Roman occupation had acquired a dynamic of its own. The Roman senate quickly discovered that keeping legions in Hispania was a relatively painless business (for Rome as a whole, rather than for the legionaries). Spanish tribute in money, materiel and corn meant that troops there could be maintained without much expense, and the troops had to be maintained there because the tribesmen resented paying tribute. Command of the army in Hispania provided another outlet for the martial ambitions of Rome's warrior aristocracy. In fact the division of the peninsula into two provinces was less for administrative purposes than to determine where people of what rank were allowed to campaign.

At that time the peninsula was known to the Greeks as Iberia and to the Romans as Hispania. Both of these descriptions were purely geographical. Pre-roman Hispania was not a single entity politically, socially or culturally. Some forty tribes and sub-tribal groupings jostled for space on the peninsula, trading and making war with one another as circumstances dictated. As a very rough guide, the region could be divided into Iberians on the east coast, and Aquitanian peoples in the far North West. At some indeterminate point in previous centuries a huge influx of Celts had disrupted tribal settlement in the interior, and most of central Spain was occupied by tribes with Celtic-based languages, such as the Celtiberians, the Carpeti and the Vaccaei.

However, the Iberian terrain made it possible for some groups to resist Celtic expansion, so the rough broken land of the interior just off the west coast was home to the Lusitanians and Vettones, pre-Celtic peoples who had managed to hold their homelands against the invaders. The Celts had also failed to penetrate the far south of the peninsula, which was held by a people called Turdetani.[4]

The reason so many different people could simultaneously exist in the one peninsula was due to its geography. Iberia is dominated by a huge central plateau, which in Roman times was largely occupied by Celtic peoples. This plateau slopes gently downward to the west, and consequently five large river systems flow west across the peninsula into the Atlantic, while only three shorter rivers discharge east into the Mediterranean. Because the central plateau is surrounded by mountains, the river valleys were essential passages into the interior, and these had considerable strategic significance.

We have already met one of these east-flowing rivers, the Ebro. This is watered from the Pyrenees and is the largest river in Spain by volume, a fact which made crossing the Ebro something of a feat, especially for an ancient army. The city and military base of Tarraco, north of the Ebro was Rome's fall-back position in Hispania. It was easily supplied from Emporion to the north, or Gaul beyond that, while an enemy marching from the south could be held at the few possible crossing points of the Ebro until reinforcements arrived.

Further south two rivers wind their way eastward from the mountains in Celtiberia, the Turia and the Sucro, which rivers reach the Mediterranean within fifty miles of each other. Saguntum stood just north of the Turia until Hannibal knocked it down, while the later Roman settlement of Valentia (modern Valencia) was founded on banks of the Turia in 138 BC on the site of a pre-existing Iberian town.

Even further south, the Idubeda mountain chain gives up being the only major Spanish range that runs from north to south and swerves eastward, separating Carthago Novo from the north-west. For the Romans the next significant water feature on the way southward was the headwaters of the river Baetis, which flowed in a south-westerly direction through Turdetanian country. Here, upriver from Gades on the coast, the settlement of Italica was founded. (A settlement which, centuries later, was to count the emperor Trajan as a favourite son.)

In keeping with the tradition followed by later colonial powers elsewhere in the world, the Roman division of Iberia was based on geographical convenience with little consideration for who actually lived on either side of the division. Very basically, Hispania Citerior (literally 'the closer bit of Spain') was the area north of Carthago Nova, and Hispania Ulterior ('further Spain') was the south-western part including the strategically important Baetis valley and Italica. This division endured for the remainder of the Roman Republic. Citerior spread westward and southward along with Roman expansion in those directions, while Ulterior grew in a north-westerly direction, taking up the lands of the Lusitanians until it met with Citerior in the north-west of the peninsula with the west-flowing river Duoro forming the north-south boundary.[5]

Roman expansion through Iberia was a slow process which the natives resisted every step of the way. In the 190s the Romans faced a series of wars and rebellions that basically forced them to re-conquer their provinces from scratch. One of the generals sent to do this was Marcius Porcius Cato, better known as 'Cato the Censor', a man famous for his moral rectitude. Yet even Cato was not above reproach. He was disappointed that his predecessor had won a convincing victory in the south, and so sought an equivalent victory in the north around Emporion.

The problem was that, although the tribesmen in that area were unfriendly, they were not actively hostile. Cato overcame that problem by descending on local villages for a brisk series of plundering raids for profit and provocation. He soon had the countryside up in arms against him, and was able to crush the 'rebels' when they attacked his camp.

Cato was far from the exception among Roman commanders in Iberia, and possibly more honest than most. However, like the rest of the Roman nobility he saw in Rome's new provinces the potential for plunder, slaves and military glory. A peaceful, prosperous province might benefit Rome greatly, but it was of no use to Cato personally. With his colleagues getting rich and famous by campaigning in the lands of the eastern Mediterranean, Cato had to keep up as best he could with the wars on hand, even if he had to start them himself.

Another feature of Cato's campaigns which became a standard feature of Roman campaigns in Iberia was the use of local rivalries between tribes. The Romans would ally with a tribe such as the Suessetani and help them to crush their hated enemies, in this case the Lacetati. With the Lacetati enslaved and their town plundered, the Romans informed the Suessetani that they were now under Roman protection and should surrender their weapons and break down their town walls, as these were no longer required.

When the inevitable 'rebellion' resulted, the Suessetani joined the ranks of the conquered.

The Romans kept up this game of divide and conquer for the next two centuries, and even when the tribesmen could clearly see what was happening, it often worked nevertheless, so powerful and enduring were local feuds. Often, and especially in the early years of Rome's conquest, the Romans were seen as just an extra enemy on an already crowded tribal military agenda. The idea of ceasing internecine warfare to unite against the invader was one which only a few exceptional leaders managed to drum into tribal skulls, and the idea never firmly took hold.

The exception to Iberian pugnaciousness was the mercantile and notoriously unwarlike tribe of the Turdetani in the south. Roman generals had to work hard to provoke them, and won the consequent battles easily. When the Turdetani refused to get into the spirit of things and hired Celtiberian mercenaries to defend them, the Romans simply offered the Celtiberians more. Cato defended such offers of payment saying that they took the Celtiberians out of his campaign. If he was defeated anyway, the Celtiberians would have no-one to get payment from. If the Romans won the payment would come out of Turdetanian plunder and so not cost Rome a single denarius.

Roman conquests yielded not only plunder but the opportunity to strip ownership of valuable iron and silver mines from the locals. Under new management the profits boomed, both because of superior Roman engineering skill, and because of the wealth of manpower supplied by the previous owners, who now worked the diggings as slaves. From the start of the second century BC onwards the silver mines of Iberia supplied the Roman mint, except on those occasions such as the Sertorian era, when they financed Iberian rebels instead.[6]

For the next thirty years after Cato, Roman 'policy' consisted of commanders arriving in Iberia and looking for the nearest source of enemies and booty. Provincial governors spent little time governing, and indeed were quite happy to wander into their neighbouring governor's part of Iberia if the fighting looked more promising there. Because there was no systematic program of conquest, and because the local tribesmen did not take Roman oppression lying down, we find Roman sources reporting campaigns and battles in places which were originally 'pacified' decades previously.

It was only in the 160s that warfare in the peninsula became anything less than endemic. Even then there are suggestions that although the locals had finally got the message about the futility of taking on the legions in face-to-face combat, this had merely caused them to change their tactics. Instead of full-scale battles and the chance for plunder and glory, the commanders of the 160s had to deal with grinding and profitless guerilla wars of petty ambuscades and large-scale banditry. There are a number of cases from this period where generals appointed to command in Hispania simply said 'no thanks' and found excuses to remain in Rome.[7]

Such efforts at organizing a provincial administration as actually took place were by the energetic Sempronius Gracchus, governor between 180 and 178. While doing the usual amount of campaigning, Gracchus took the unusual step of drawing up proper treaty arrangements with the tribes he defeated. These defined what tribute was due to Rome, and in at least a few instances also shifted the people to new towns – presumably these new towns, in keeping with later Roman policy elsewhere, being better suited for commerce than defence.

Gracchus' efforts laid the foundations for the relative stability of the 160s but the treaty terms were abused by unscrupulous governors who constantly found new ways to enrich themselves. (For example by persuading the Roman senate to allow governors to assess the value of farmland for which they would demand the percentage of tax specified in a treaty. Naturally each governor found the land increasingly valuable and raised taxes accordingly.)

In 153 the Celtiberians of Segeda decided they'd had all they could take of exploitative Roman rule and began re-fortifying their town in direct violation of agreements signed under Sempronius Gracchus. These were very good fortifications, as the praetor Fabius Nobilior discovered when he attempted to take them down. Nor did the Celtiberians stay behind the walls. Nobilior lost over 10,000 men in his campaign. Admittedly some of these were due to an ill-advised attempt to overawe the Celtiberians with elephants. In battle the elephants excitedly rampaged through the Roman ranks, creating chaos which the Celtiberians gleefully made the most of.

Nobilior's successor resumed the war, which by then included a number of Celtiberian tribes. After the usual succession of skirmishes, treachery and broken promises on both sides, the Romans put together a serious army with the intention of subduing the Celtiberians once and for all. Just the news of the proposed assault was enough to convince the Celtiberians to seek terms. Therefore when the new commander, Licinius Lucullus arrived with his army, he found that the war was already concluded.

However, Lucullus was a typical Roman commander. 'Greedy for glory and desperate for money'.[8] Therefore he did what a typical Roman commander in Iberia would do under these circumstances. He attacked a neighbouring tribe which had been neutral during the war and had done nothing against either Lucullus or Rome. The tribe, a people called the Caucaei, were beaten in battle and forced within the walls of their main settlement.

The next day the elders of the city asked Lucullus what they should do to make peace. Lucullus demanded hostages, 100 talents of silver, and a contingent of horses to serve with the Roman army. All these demands were complied with. Lucullus then demanded that a Roman garrison enter the city.

> The Caucaei assented to this, so he ordered 2,000 carefully-chosen soldiers to enter the city and occupy the walls. This being done, Lucullus brought in the rest of his army. A trumpet blast was then the signal for the soldiers to kill all the adult males of the Caucaei. These men ... were cruelly slain. Only a handful of some 20,000 victims escaped by leaping down the sheer walls at the gates. Lucullus then sacked the city.
>
> (Appian, *Iberia*, 52)

Not altogether surprisingly, this was the last time anyone in Iberia trusted Lucullus. And the plunder was limited, because the attack was on a part of Spain poor in precious minerals and occupied by a people who cared little for them. Consequently Lucullus had trouble thereafter even in provisioning his army. He was low on funds, no-one would sell supplies to him anyway and Celtiberian horses constantly harassed his supply lines and his army's attempt at foraging.

It would have been cold comfort to Lucullus to know that his colleagues elsewhere in the peninsula were having an even worse time. Though the Romans had done nothing to the Lusitanians, this fierce mountain people launched an unprovoked attack on Roman territory and killed some 15,000 Roman soldiers in a series of battles which also saw the Romans lose their legion standards.[9] In fact so overwhelming were the Lusitanians that once they had swept down as far as the strait of Gibraltar, they crossed over and started plundering the territory on the other side. This over-enthusiasm was their undoing, for the Romans followed, and caught the Lusitanian army spread out in search of plunder.

The crushing defeat which followed caused the Lusitanians to fall back on their homeland, where Lucullus advanced, methodically depopulating the country by massacre as he went through. His current colleague Sulpicius Galba did the same on the other side of the country, but at least in Galba the Lusitanians had found a man who understood them.

'Your poor soil and poverty forced you to this' he told them. 'If you want to be friends with Rome, I will move you to richer land.'

So the Lusitani left their homes and gathered where Galba directed. He divided the people into three parts, and took each division to a separate area of open country, and ordered each to remain there until they were assigned their land grants.

Then he came to the first division ... When they had yielded him their weapons he surrounded them with a ditch. Then he sent in soldiers with swords who killed them all ... thereafter he hastened to the second and third divisions and destroyed them while they were still ignorant of the fate of the first.

(Appian, *Iberia*, 59)

The concept of the Romans as an honourable people never had many followers in Iberia, though Sempronius Gracchus had done a fair bit towards cultivating the idea. Galba and Lucullus between them comprehensively quashed it thereafter, and their successors did very little to restore it. Neither Lucullus nor Galba was punished in Rome for their flagrant violation of the rules of war, even though the pair had accomplished the near impossible by uniting most of western Iberia against Rome.

The result was a war which lasted for the next eight years and cost tens of thousands of Roman and Iberian lives. The Iberians found a leader in the person of Viriathus, a Lusitanian shepherd who had escaped the massacre perpetrated by Galba. Viriathus understood the nature of the Iberian terrain, and used it as an ally in his war against Rome. Time and again, the Romans felt that Viriathus had finally over-extended himself, only to see their opponent escape through his knowledge of the land and superior cavalry. The Romans helped the Iberian cause by mismanaging the war and sending a succession of mediocre commanders whom Viriathus made appear totally incompetent.

The Roman conduct which had provoked the war meant that the battle for hearts and minds was over before it was begun. Those Celtiberians who had signed treaties of allegiance to Rome felt unabashed about tearing these up, since Roman promises were evidently worth less than the tablets they were inscribed upon. Viriathus himself was less cynical. When he had a Roman army trapped and at his mercy he allowed the men to go free in exchange for a peace treaty with Rome. The treaty was signed, ratified by the senate and Viriathus was declared a friend and ally of the Roman people. This disgusted one senator, a certain Quintus Servilius Caepio, who thus lost the chance for glory as the next governor in Hispania. By a combination of provocations to the Lusitanians and misrepresentations to the senate, he had the treaty abrogated and the war renewed. It is unlikely that anyone in Iberia was deeply surprised by this further display of Roman bad faith. Despite this, some tribesmen continued to display a touching faith that next time the Romans made a promise they would keep it.

A further demonstration of this triumph of hope over experience came when, after months of unproductive warfare, Viriathus sent envoys to negotiate peace with Caepio. Caepio received the envoys generously, and bribed them to assassinate his elusive enemy. Once that had been accomplished, and the war won, Caepio again reneged on his promise and the killers did not receive the money they had expected. However, flushed with victory, Caepio generously allowed the men to escape with their lives.

This just left the far-from-minor matter of the Celtiberians. These held out in the fortified town of Numantia, (giving this campaign the name of the Numantine war) and from there they launched a series of stinging attacks on the Romans. A consul called Quintus Pompeius was sent to sort things out in 141, and after he proved totally ineffectual at fighting, Pompeius instead made peace in return for thirty talents of silver as tribute from the Numantines. Pompeius kept the money, and denied in Rome that any treaty had been made. He suffered no punishment, and in fact his son was consul with Sulla in 88 when the Marian-inspired riots provoked Sulla's march on Rome (see p.24). The war went on.

The next commander of note in the inglorious succession of generals who attempted to subdue the Celtiberians was Hostilius Mancinus. He was resoundingly defeated, and was forced to surrender his army. Fortunately, one of his officers was Tiberius Gracchus, the son of Sempronius Gracchus. The Spanish had fond memories of Sempronius Gracchus as they considered him about the only trustworthy Roman to set foot in Iberia. Therefore, they were prepared to give the son the benefit of the doubt. Tiberius Gracchus negotiated a treaty in good faith, only to have it rejected by the Senate in Rome as soon as Hostilius' army was out of danger. By way of consolation to the Celtiberians, the Senate ordered Hostilius stripped of his rank and his clothing, and he was handed naked to the Numantines. The somewhat nonplussed Numantines contemptuously refused to accept this scapegoat, and the war resumed again.

Subsequent Roman commanders avoided defeat by maintaining so low a profile that hostilities practically ceased. By now the war had become something of an embarrassment to Rome, and in 134 a large army of some 60,000 men was sent to finish things once and for all. This army was commanded by another Scipio, Scipio Aemilianus, and in his retinue, as has been noted (p.8) was the young Gaius Marius.

The Numantines literally fought to the end. Their city was comprehensively enclosed with siege works, and Scipio let famine and disease do his work for him. When the defenders had become too weak to resist an assault, most committed suicide rather than fall into Roman hands.

Though the Numantine war was the last of the major wars fought in Iberia over the next half-century, the provinces were far from settled. Our sources become poorer at this point as Roman historians turned their attention first to the war in Africa against the renegade Numidian king Jugurtha (who was, incidentally, yet another of Scipio Aemilians' protégés during the Numantine war), and then to the Cimbric threat faced by Marius.

However, we discover that various commanders celebrated triumphs over the Lusitanians in 107, 102, 98, and 93 which suggests a long-running war fought in the west of the peninsula. The last of these triumphs was celebrated by T. Didius, Sertorius' commander during the latter's first stint of service in Hispania (p.16–17). Didius kept up the old Roman tradition of massacre and betrayal. He first wiped out the population of a town called Kolenda, and then invited a truculent nearby Celtiberian tribe to take their land. Apparently unaware that Roman promises of land could be lethal, the Celtiberian tribesmen duly mustered in a ravine which Didius blocked off before sending in the legionaries for the standard massacre.

Despite the background of violence, ambuscade and low-intensity guerilla warfare which made up everyday life in first-century Hispania, the second part of the first century also gave some hints of the settled and prosperous provinces later to arise in the peninsula. This began as Iberian tribesmen in conquered areas were introduced to the amenities of Roman towns – amenities which compared very favourably with the highly defensible but somewhat crude Iberian hill-forts.

A number of cities were founded in the 130s, including Valentia and Brutobriga, the latter somewhere in southern Spain while Cordoba was settled even earlier in 152.[10] These were followed in the 120 by the new cities of Palma and Pollentia. Cities such as Asta, Urso and Gades, which had been settled independently of Rome now began to take on a somewhat more Roman appearance. A population of Roman and Italian merchants took up residence in the coastal cities, the better to process the flow of silver and slaves coming from the campaigns in the interior. It is uncertain how many of the inhabitants of the other cities were Roman, though the sources indicate that most populations of new settlements were 'selected' by the governors who established them.

Another force which got Iberians and Romans used to each other was the constant presence of legionaries in the peninsula. When not actually fighting the locals, a good number of legionaries got into liaisons with the womenfolk. Many of the soldiers who retired in Hispania took Spanish wives or sometimes regularized already long standing partnerships. Consequently the peninsula began to develop a population of 'Hybridae', half-Roman Iberians, with a foot in both Roman and Iberian cultures and acting as a unifying influence between the two.

Iberian women had a reputation for courage and hardihood rather than beauty. The Romans have several accounts of these women fighting beside their menfolk when their town was attacked, and if the town was taken they might kill themselves and their children to escape capture. The geographer Strabo adds the following colourful tale to illustrate his point.

Poseidonius says that his host... narrated to him how he had hired men and women together for ditch-digging. One of the women, upon being seized with the pangs of childbirth, dropped out of the work-gang, and took herself to somewhere nearby. As soon as she had given birth she immediately returned to her work, since she did not want to lose her pay. He [the narrator] saw that she was in pain as she worked but only found out why late in the day. Thereupon he paid her and sent her off. She carried the infant out to a little spring, bathed it ... and took it home.

(Strabo, *Geography*, 3.4.27)

Thus, by the time of Sertorius Iberia was something of a mix. There were some areas that were occupied by wild tribesmen who only interacted with Romans while carrying sharp objects and other areas, such as that around Baetulo (near modern Barcelona) where the villa farmsteads typical of Roman rural life were already dotted around the landscape in their hundreds.

Likewise many towns were a mix of Iberian and Roman culture. It is possible that such towns had separate Roman and Iberian quarters, but in any case a certain amount of cross-cultural fusion took place. Column drums have been found in the Roman style but with the markings of Iberian workers. A grim example of the different currents pulling at the peoples of the peninsula comes from the pro-Roman senate of the small town of Belgida in a tale related by Appian.

Later the Celtiberians revolted again. Flaccus was sent against them and slew 20,000 of them. The people of the town of Belgida were eager for revolt, but their senate was hesitant. So they set fire to the senate house and burned the senators inside. When Flaccus arrived there he put to death the criminals responsible.

(Appian, *Iberia*, 100)

It is quite probable that the Romans were using the technique which they had perfected by the start of the imperial era. Once a tribe had been moved (forcibly or otherwise) to a Roman-style settlement, the chieftain discovered that he was now the local magistrate, and the tribal aristocrats became the senate. Magistrates and senators were generally treated with considerable respect by the Roman authorities and as their clients these men received favours and protection. Consequently it was normal for local elites to take the lead in Romanizing their people, although as the case of Belgida proved, those who romanized too quickly risked leaving the general population alienated and hostile.

Also those 'bindings of empire' – Roman roads – had begun to appear in the Iberian provinces from around 100 onwards. The Romans had long had an established road running from Italy through Gallia Transalpina (later the province of Narbonensis) past the Pyrenees to the Ebro. Over a century of experience had taught them that large numbers of soldiers might be needed in Iberia at very short notice, and no-one would risk transporting that army by sea if an alternative could be made available.[11]

However, once the road reached Hispania our understanding becomes more fragmentary. This is partly because the archaeological evidence for the first Roman roads in the peninsula is poor, as most routes were repaved over the next 500 years, but also because the Roman road building was piecemeal and fragmentary. There seems to have been no strategic plan behind the construction of the various roads of the peninsula. Rather, individual governors built roads where and as they felt these were needed. Sometimes this was to expedite commerce – for example with the transport of minerals from the silver mines – but more often the intent was that troops heading for trouble-spots need fight only rebels rather than the terrain as well.

The military situation continued to vary from tense to dire, but, as one historian puts it by the time of Sulla and Sertorius, for the Romans 'Hispania ... was more than just the name of a battlefield'.[12] For one thing some provincials had found that it was possible to make money out of the Romans. Although Rome had no policy of systematically setting up trade with conquered provinces there were plenty of enterprising souls both among the conquerors and the conquered who quickly grasped the economic benefits of a newly-expanded market. For one thing, the population of Rome was already too large and sophisticated to be able to get by on the supplies from the city's own hinterland. The trade web that was eventually to stretch halfway around the world, bringing silk from China and sandalwood from India had already extended its tendrils to Hispania. Roman palates discovered a taste for a highly spiced-fish sauce called garum that rapidly became a staple at Roman dinner tables. The Spanish climate was ideal for the processes needed to produce the sauce, and by the time of Sertorius, the first of what were to be millions of amphorae of garum had already made an impression on the Roman market.

Another culinary speciality which quickly found a place on Roman tables was the *Thrushes* (Turdes) which gave Turdetania its name. The Romans appreciated these birds for both their song and their taste, and the people of Baetica prospered from the export of what they had formerly viewed as something of a pest. Coins from the early first century BC have turned up in archaeological digs where other signs indicate that the former inhabitants of the site were native Iberians, which is a strong suggestion that the people of Hispania were coming to appreciate the value of Roman cash and commerce, even if most still did not care very much for the Romans themselves.

Romanization was not uniform across the Iberian provinces. Decades of Roman rule had largely pacified the eastern seaboard, and there are records which show that the tribes there had understood that land disputes should now be taken to the law courts rather than the battlefield. Nor had the misbehaviour of Rome's misgovernors gone unnoticed, especially as the perpetrators of some of the worst injustices were now senior senators and well aware of the sort of misdeeds their successors would be up to.

A series of laws had been passed (called the *repetunda* laws) which gave provincials the novel experience of following a bad governor back to Rome at the end of his term of office and demanding their money back in the courts. Naturally, the endemic corruption in which the contemporary senate was steeped meant that the guilty governors were generally able to bribe their way out of trouble. Nevertheless, the laws put an end to the most flagrant abuses, and meant that the east of Iberia, where the Roman presence was most firmly and longest established was generally peaceful.

The south, which in any case contained the least warlike people in Iberia, was also calm. However, the Celtiberians were still far from subdued. Some of them had served as mercenaries with Roman armies abroad, for both the Celtiberian people and their horses were excellent over broken terrain, and a match for cavalry anywhere. This service came at a price higher than silver to the Romans, for it meant that by the 80s BC there were a goodly number of warriors in Iberia who were intimate with how the Roman army operated, and exactly what its weaknesses were.

The Lusitanians and Carpeti of the west had still not been persuaded that the only good Roman might not be a dead Roman. More than most, they had suffered betrayal and massacre at Roman hands, and they had a penchant for taking out their resentment with bandit raids on their more Romanized neighbours.

By now it was plain to all the occupants of the peninsula that the Romans had done the Iberians no favours by ejecting the Carthaginians. One set of exploitative foreigners had been replaced by another, and the new set were getting more entrenched every year. Hispania was now firmly within the bounds of Rome's growing empire, but its people had not yet resigned themselves to the fact. Much of the peninsula was bitter, disillusioned and cynical but far from resigned to subjugation. It was a land where the prevailing mood perfectly matched that of the bitter, disillusioned but far from resigned Sertorius who now came to govern it.

Chapter 4

The Fall and Rise of a Roman Governor

Sertorius was a conscientious officer, albeit a headstrong and outspoken one. He demonstrated both of these qualities before his departure to his province, by first conscientiously going to Etruria and there recruiting some forty cohorts of troops to fight for the Marian cause. Then he bitterly criticized his leaders for inertia, unconstitutional conduct, and incompetence. He pointed to the illegal election of the young Marius to the consulship as a prime example of what he meant. Whether or not Plutarch is right in saying that one of Sertorius' purposes in going to Iberia was 'that he might provide a refuge to his friends once they had been beaten at Rome', it is also reasonably certain that his departure was given further impetus by the fact that by now he and the top management of the Marian cause could no longer stand the sight of each other.

Currently holding Iberia (and a good chunk of Gallia Transalpina) for Rome was a man called Valerius Flaccus. The Marians had some doubts about how closely Flaccus was allied to their cause, and these doubts caused them some concern since Flaccus commanded the substantial veteran army which in one way or another was always present in Hispania. These doubts would certainly have intensified if the Marians had known that one of their hundred most wanted, M. Licinius Crassus· was currently in hiding in Hispania, with Flaccus (probably wilfully) ignorant of the fact.[1]

The good thing was that no-one had bothered to relieve Flaccus since the entire political situation in Rome had slipped into civil war. Since he had been in sole command in Iberia for over seven years, the only complaint that Flaccus could legitimately make about being replaced was that the authorities had taken so long to do it. Nevertheless, complain Flaccus did. It is highly probable that he saw Hispania as a bargaining chip which he could surrender to Sulla in exchange for his own safety. Flaccus would also know that Sulla would take a dim view of anyone who tamely handed over two complete provinces to his enemies. And by now it was becoming clear that the disapproval of the ruthless and vindictive Sulla was a very serious business indeed.

As a result there were certain practical difficulties for Sertorius as he tried to enter his province. Plutarch tells us

> First they ran into severe weather in the mountains. Then the [mountain] barbarian tribes demanded tribute from him, and a price for allowing his passage. His companions indignantly claimed that it was outrageous for a Roman magistrate to give in to extortion by poxy barbarians; but while they considered it disgraceful, Sertorius simply commented wryly that he was buying himself time, and if a man had a lot to do, nothing is more precious than time. So he paid off the barbarians with cash and hurried on to take command of Hispania.
>
> (Plutarch, *Life of Sertorius*, 6)

We know from Strabo that, whenever they thought they could get away with it, the tribesmen of the Pyrenees were in the habit of shaking down Romans trying to get into Iberia.[2] Quite often – as was currently the case with Sertorius – the situation in Hispania was simply too urgent for delay. Rather than have to fight their way through a succession of difficult and easily-blocked passes, the Romans often paid up. This was particularly the case when the coastal road to Emporion was blocked – and this was quite possibly the case on this occasion, courtesy of the army Flaccus had put there so as to prevent Sertorius reaching the Peninsula.

It is uncertain which of the two Iberian provinces was officially allocated to Sertorius, and the question has little practical significance. The ructions of the previous decade had done considerably more than merely decimate the Roman ruling class, and the few men still standing who were capable of running a province were mainly focussed on killing each other in Italy. Basically Sertorius was free to help himself to as much of the peninsula as he could wrest from Flaccus. There was no other competition for either governorship in Hispania.

Sertorius had brought a substantial force with him, and knew exactly where he could get more men. He went straight to the Celtiberians, a warlike people still seething from the defeat at Numantia a generation before. Here, despite his previous history of massacre, Sertorius was well received. He must have given considerable thought as to how he was going to approach the Celtiberian leaders, and as we have seen, Sertorius was not above bribery when he felt it was necessary. However, cash was probably not required. Given the larcenous incompetence of the average Roman administrator in Iberia, it is highly likely that Sertorius merely presented the tribal chieftains with a shopping list of the most egregious Roman injustices and asked which of them they would like righted first.

'With the army he had [brought] from Italy itself, and that raised from the Celtiberians he drove out the officials who had refused to give the government to him because they wanted to give it to Sulla' says Appian.[3] Our other source for current events, the biographer Plutarch, now takes up the story.

> The province proved to have a numerous supply of fighting men. The rapacity and arrogance of the Roman officials periodically sent to take charge had made them hostile to everything Roman, so he [Sertorius] had to win them over. He charmed the chiefs in personal interviews and the general population by cutting taxes.
>
> (Plutarch, *Life of Sertorius*, 6)

Sertorius might have been able to afford to be generous with his tax rebates for the simple reason that he stopped any of the revenue due to Rome. Since he regarded the war in Italy as lost, there was little point in sending revenue that would eventually end up swelling the coffers of his enemies – all the more so when that money could be better spent making Hispania a redoubt for his cause.

> All Roman settlers in the country of military age were conscripted and he undertook the construction of assorted engines of war, including triremes. He kept the cities well under control by the mildness of his civil administration, but showed himself powerfully well-prepared against his enemies in the military sphere.
>
> (Plutarch, *Life of Sertorius*, 6)

'Mild civil administration' notwithstanding, nothing endeared Sertorius to the city-folk more than the abandonment of the perfidious practice of billeting the army in cities. A city on which an army had been billeted was forced to provide food, lodging – and probably entertainment – for the soldiery in the houses of its citizens. There were manifold forms of abuse which a soldier could visit on the home upon which he had been forced, and the legions in Hispania had mastered most of them. Sertorius would have been well aware of these abuses, since they are the most probable grievance which provoked the murders and subsequent massacre in his first Spanish posting at Castulo (p.16–17).

His army from Italy was not yet accustomed to literally making itself at home among Iberian townsfolk, and Sertorius was determined that they would not start. He himself was the first to pitch his tent in winter quarters (*hibernia*) set up outside the city, and his men followed his example. The technique of sharing the everyday discomforts of the men as a means of endearing himself to them is something which Sertorius probably learned from Marius, who also made a point of publicly demonstrating that he did not feel himself above any privation his men had to endure.

Of one thing Sertorius was sure – the army he had raised would soon be tested. Not by Spanish tribesmen, though this was also a possibility, but by his fellow Romans. It was inconceivable that the Sullani, once they had taken control of Italy, would not attempt to take control of the remainder of Rome's empire. Paradoxically, this was where Rome's history of arrogance and misgovernment would come to the current governor's aid. The people of Iberia had not greatly enjoyed the experience of being under Roman rule. Under Sertorius it appeared that for the moment they had slipped the leash, and they were quite happy to make the most of someone who, for once, appeared to be governing the country in the interest of its inhabitants.

Nevertheless, while the Celtiberians and Lusitanians might be counted on not to rebel, they had no intention of fighting on either side in a war which was strictly Roman business. Even the loyalty of Sertorius' countrymen in Iberia was suspect. Some Romans, especially the merchant class, could see clear benefits to being reconciled with Rome, and if Sulla was not loved, he was certainly feared.

The Roman civilian population of the peninsula was, at a very rough estimate, some 15,000 men. The emphasis is on 'men' as there was something of a frontier feel to Hispania at this time, and many of the new arrivals had left their families to make their fortunes in this new land.

It has been postulated that many of the 'Romans' whom Sertorius armed were Italians who had never reconciled themselves to Rome's victory in the

Social War of 90 BC.[4] These men had either voluntarily exiled themselves to Hispania or in some cases had left Italy before they could be captured. Neither group would have had a great deal of affection for Sulla and the old Roman aristocratic party which he represented, but again, they did not care greatly for the Marian cause either. So though Sertorius had a base to build upon, the foundation was shaky, and there was not a lot of time to shore it up.

A steady flow of refugees came to Sertorius bringing news of the war in Italy. The tidings were unsurprising, but nevertheless grim. Sulla was proving every bit as competent and ruthless as his reputation made him out to be. The struggle for Italy came to its climax in November of 82 BC outside the Colline Gate of Rome itself. Here two separate groups combined in a desperate effort to deny Sulla mastery of Italy. These were the Marians and those last hold-outs (mainly Samnites) still grimly fighting the tail end of the Social War.

They nearly managed to beat Sulla, too. The younger Marius had Sulla's full attention at nearby Praenestae when the troops coming to relieve him instead made a sudden dash for Rome. Sulla only just managed to disengage and get to Rome in time to forestall the taking of the city, but he still had to fight some 70,000 Marians and Samnites to keep it.

The actual battle lasted well into the night, and Sulla found his army disintegrating before him. He was on the verge of acknowledging defeat when he got a message from Marcus Crassus – the same man whom we last heard of taking refuge from the Marians in Hispania. With Sertorius in Iberia and Sulla in Italy, Crassus had quickly decided on a change of scenery, and after joining the Sullan army in Italy he had become one of its foremost commanders. In the battle Crassus had taken command of the right wing of Sulla's army and had comprehensively crushed the enemy before him. Now Crassus wanted to know, did Sulla need a hand, or could his men stop for supper?

News that they had the battle at least partly won stiffened the resolve of the rest of Sulla's army, even as news of the collapse of one wing of their army became known to the opposition. Slowly the tide of battle turned. The Samnites did not give in easily, but by the next morning Sulla was master of Rome. He made this point very clearly in his address to the senate, while in the background the last cries of some six thousand prisoners brought into Rome and massacred on his orders still lingered in the air.

Sulla then turned on his enemies among the Roman aristocracy, and showed that he was every bit as cruel as Marius had been in the same situation. He had published lists of his enemies, known as 'proscriptions'. Those on the list – the proscribed – could be killed with impunity, whereas anyone who helped the condemned in any way would have his own name appended to the list. Many of the proscribed seized whatever portable assets they could and fled to inform Sertorius that his own name featured prominently on Sulla's list. Others fled to Africa. There they were followed, defeated and executed by another of Sulla's young generals, Gnaeus Pompey the son of Pompeius Strabo (p.21). Gnaeus Pompey was later to be known as Pompey the Great, but in those years his nickname was *carnifex adulescens* – the young butcher.

Soon only Sertorius and Hispania stood alone against an empire controlled by Sulla, who had awarded himself the ancient title of dictator. As soon as Sertorius heard that Sulla's army had returned from its grim work in Africa, he prepared to defend himself.

In due course, a Sullan army, led by an obscure general called Caius Annius Luscus set out for Hispania. Sulla had not wanted to give Sertorius until the spring to make himself yet more secure in Iberia, so this army was despatched in the last weeks of winter. This gave Sertorius a clear advantage, because he knew for certain where the enemy would be coming from. Sending soldiers on troopships was a chancy business for the Romans even in summer. If Annius had even attempted to make the crossing by sea in January or February, he would be killing his army as surely as Sulla had massacred the Samnites. Not for nothing did the Romans know the wintry Mediterranean as the *mare clusum* (the closed sea). Annius would have to come by land, and Sertorius sent a legion to make sure that he could not do that either.

It is certain that the Sullan army greatly outnumbered the men whom Sertorius had sent to stop it, but the terrain more than made up the difference. Sertorius' men were well familiar with the landscape, and knew exactly where the defensible choke points were. Having fortified these, they left no access to Annius. 'Seeing that Julius [Salinator, the commander of the Sertorian force] could not be assailed, he had no idea what to do, and remained idly encamped', having decided that he would probably have to wait a few weeks until spring after all.[5]

At this point, and not for the first or last time, treachery and stealthy murder played a part in the military affairs of the peninsula. One Calpurnius Lanarius took it on himself to kill Salinator, almost certainly to get himself into Sulla's good books. Taking prompt advantage of the confusion in the enemy camp, Annius launched an attack on the leaderless enemy army and scattered it to the winds. The road to Hispania lay open.

This dramatic change of fortune immediately changed the mind of the cities of the east coast as to which side they wanted to support. Roman legions in Hispania were noted for neither their gentleness nor their understanding, and those cities in their path knew that the only way to mitigate the damage was to surrender as early and enthusiastically as possible.

Sertorius was heavily outnumbered at this point because he could not persuade enough of Iberia to fight for him. His tenure as governor had been too short to build a personal following, and the people of the peninsula quite reasonably considered neither the Sullan nor the Marian cause worth dying for.

This left him in Carthago Nova with three thousand men and the question of what to do next. Surrender was out of the question. Since he was proscribed, any battle Sertorius fought would be a battle to the death. And given that he was outnumbered by somewhere around five to one, it was reasonable to assume that the death it would be.

If Sertorius could neither surrender nor stand and fight, the only remaining option was flight. Accordingly, Sertorius informally abdicated as governor of Hispania and adopted the role of rebel-at-large, the condition in which we found him at the start of this history. Even for the man who had swum the Rhone to escape the Cimbric massacre of the rest of his army and who had been acrimoniously turfed out of Italy after watching his elders and inferiors mismanage the war, this was one of the low points in Sertorius' career.

Nevertheless, Sertorius embarked his men and fled. The fact that he made his escape by water tells us that the weather was good, it was now early spring, and that Sertorius was desperate enough to risk the Mediterranean weather before the start of the sailing season. He crossed to Mauritania in Africa and discovered that he was not welcome there either. While his men were getting water after their sea crossing, the locals mustered enough warriors for a devastating surprise attack. Sertorius took heavy losses and decided that there was nothing for it but to re-embark for Hispania.

Exactly what Sertorius hoped to accomplish by this is uncertain, and the most probable reason for his actions is that he was basically at a loss as to what he could usefully accomplish in whatever span of life remained to him before the Sullani hunted him down. Unsurprisingly, the return to Hispania went badly. Whatever target Sertorius had in mind, he failed to attain it. Plutarch merely states baldly 'he was repulsed'.

This further cloud over Sertorius' progress came at least with a silver lining, for his activities brought him to the attention of a group which made a speciality of attacking cities from the sea – namely Cilician pirates.

These pirates were another of those plagues which, like corruption and civil war, the Romans managed to continually inflict upon themselves during the last decades of the Republic. Piracy had been a constant of Mediterranean life since before the days of Homer almost a thousand years before. It had generally fallen to whatever naval power which was at a given time in the ascendant to keep the pirates in check. Athens had been good at it, and after Athens fell, the burden fell to the island of Rhodes. A mercantile people who depended on sea-trade, the Rhodians were skilled mariners. They kept piracy in check until the Romans came along. The Romans were not a seafaring people, and they feared and distrusted those who were. The Rhodians were accused of thinking of collaborating with Rome's enemies and stripped of all but a token fleet.

This suited Rome's enemies down to the ground. Chief of these enemies was the wily Mithridates, who had indirectly triggered Rome's current civil war when Sulla and Marius had come to blows about who should go to fight him (p.24ff). Mithridates had seen the damage that pirates were doing to trade and the Roman economy, and he gleefully subsidized their efforts.

With few natural predators, pirate numbers expanded exponentially. Single ships grew in number to small fleets which attacked cities and terrorized shipping in the eastern Mediterranean. (One victim was the young Julius Caesar who was captured while travelling to Athens and ended up paying a huge ransom.) With shipping in the eastern Mediterranean becoming scant and wary, the pirates started moving west, striking deep inland into Italy, and sniffing around the coast of Iberia, which is where a group of them fell in with Sertorius.

Now advised by pirates expert at that sort of thing, Sertorius attacked the most southerly of the Balearic isles, the island of Pityussa. He easily displaced the Roman garrison there, and was once again master of at least a patch of Spanish soil. It was to be a short return, for Annius efficiently set about dealing with the Sertorian menace as soon as he learned of his opponent's whereabouts. The Sullan governor had a major advantage in that Sertorius had worked hard to bring his province up to a high standard militarily, and part of that work included a fine set of battle-ready triremes.

It is unlikely that Sertorius, with his lighter sea-going transports and unreliable pirate allies appreciated seeing the triremes he had brought into being now taking to sea against him. Since these now-hostile triremes were acting as escorts for almost a full Roman legion, Sertorius had no choice but to attempt an engagement at sea. The odds against victory were high, but the chances of his severely depleted and demoralized troops defeating a legion on land were even more so. Even the gods seemed to have turned against Sertorius, for the weather chose this moment to turn.

Sertorius had hoped that his lighter and faster vessels would outmanoeuvre the heavier triremes in open water. Instead, a stiff gale left his fleet struggling for sea room between themselves and the lee shore against which they were being blown. All the heavier triremes had to do was turn upwind and use oars to hold their station. Then they watched as the wind did their job for them by smashing the lighter enemy vessels on to the rocks. Sertorius managed to extract around half his ships from the debacle, but he was on the run again.

The next ten days demonstrated the inadvisability of going to sea before the official sailing season. Sertorius could not take to open water, because his ships would promptly be capsized by the wind and waves – a fate that not a few had suffered in the abortive naval battle. On the other hand, capture and death awaited him the moment he set foot on land. The only choice was a miserable struggle westwards along the coast.

The powerful wind had at least one benefit – it would enable Sertorius to get through the Pillars of Hercules (as the strait of Gibraltar was then known). Usually ancient vessels struggled to leave the Mediterranean, as there is a powerful inward current pushing ships the other way – a rowing boat has to be propelled at faster than a brisk walking pace just to stand still. Having a stiff wind in the right direction allowed Sertorius and his battered little fleet to run before it, with the evident intention of at least getting away from the more Romanized part of the peninsula.

Landfall was finally made north of the river Baetis, the river which gave the later province of Baetica its name. Here, perched at the edge of the known world, the exhausted and disillusioned Sertorius seriously contemplated going over that edge and striking out for the Isles of the Blessed. There was not, he would have thought, a great deal to keep him where he was. He and his handful of ships and men were all that remained of the Marian cause. Italy was firmly in Sulla's control, and it appeared that Hispania was going that way as well.

Given that his proscription was effective through all the known world, Sertorius had three options. He could join Rome's enemies. (Several of his former colleagues had found refuge at the court of Mithridates.) He could take to sea and strike out for the west in the hope that there was indeed easy living to be found over the horizon. Or he could seize somewhere within the known world, and hope that this time around he could succeed in the strategy which had failed in Hispania, and create a defensible position by the time the Sullan army found him.

Deciding which option to exercise was partly resolved by the pirates. They and Sertorius had a falling out, probably because the pirates had decided to sail to Africa and put a man called Ascalis on the Mauritanian throne. The aforesaid Ascalis (p.1) appears to have been a client of Sulla, so Sertorius would have taken a dim view of his new associates fighting on the side of the enemy. On the other hand, Mauritania seemed to fit many of the criteria for Sertorius' option number three.

The kingdom could be made defensible, and the largely unexplored and trackless region beyond the mountains could serve as a bolt-hole if things went wrong. Mauritania could become the Marians' final redoubt. And then, given the fratricidal nature of politics in Rome, it would just be a matter of hanging on until the next political upheaval. This would produce someone looking for support, and none too fussy about who supplied it, and he would find a ready supplier in Sertorius. In exchange, Sertorius would look to return to mainstream Roman politics. He might have been down, but he was not yet out, and he had a reasonably clear roadmap to get himself back in the game.

Part one of the master-plan went like clockwork. The Mauritanians were none too enthusiastic about having a Roman puppet foisted on them, so this time around they not only refrained from massacring Sertorius' watering parties, but gratefully accepted his offer of help. Sertorius' little army had been badly depleted by its recent travails, but even if we assume losses of two-thirds, he still had around a thousand men. These were Roman regular soldiers, veterans of the Social War and more than a match for several times their number of Cilician pirates and Mauritanian irregulars.

A more serious challenge came in the form of Paccianus, a commander sent out by Sulla himself once word arrived in Italy of a setback to the Sullan plan for Mauritania. It is quite possible that this commander was not accompanied by many legionaries. The Romans quite often sent out only a single man with orders to make use of native troops once he got there. In fact, in his younger days Sulla himself had been sent to Asia Minor with just such instructions. Since his opponent was the canny Mithridates Sulla did not fare too well on that occasion, nor did Paccianus this time around.

Sertorius saw the arrival of the Sullan commander as an opportunity rather than a problem, and the men whom Paccianus had brought with him as a resource rather than a threat. If these troops were native Mauritanians then they were probably unenthusiastic warriors to start with, and if they were Italian soldiers, they might have been ex-Marians unhappy with their new management. In either case, once Paccianus had been killed in a brief but decisive battle, Sertorius recruited the entire army.

From there the next stage of the plan unfolded smoothly. Sertorius now had the only significant military force in the country, so the fall of the country's major city (Tinga, today's Tangier) was a matter of course. We are not told what happened to the unfortunate Ascalis who had fled there, but we can safely assume it was something terminal.

With the land of Mauritania under his control, Sertorius set about winning the hearts and minds of its people.

All those who appealed to him, these he did no wrong, and nor to any who had put their trust in him. Instead he restored them to their lands, and to the government of cities. In return he accepted only such gifts as it was right and proper to receive.

(Plutarch, *Life of Sertorius*, 9)

At this point Plutarch offers a strange but interesting digression. Local legend had it that one of the characters of Greek myth was buried in Mauritania. This was Antaeus, the son of Poseidon and Gaia, and the husband of that Tinge whose name is still recalled by that of Tangier today. Antaeus, like much of the contemporary Mediterranean population, was slain by the homicidal hero Hercules, and his tomb apparently preserved into the time of Sertorius. It was commonly believed that the men of the heroic age had a stature to match, and Antaeus was several times the size of a normal modern man, a fact which accounted for the size of his grave. Sertorius was deeply sceptical, but had to see for himself.

> Sertorius had the tomb excavated, since it was so large that he could not believe the Barbarians. But when he came upon the body and found it to be sixty cubits long [ninety feet].[6] That's the story, and he [Sertorius]was dumbfounded by what he saw. After performing a sacrifice, he filled up the tomb again, and thereafter was among those promoting its traditions and honours.
>
> (Plutarch, *Life of Sertorius*, 9)

Whatever Sertorius actually found in the tomb, it was certainly not the skeleton of a seven-storey human. However, the man set on winning the trust and loyalty of a nation was not going to go about it by smashing one of their favourite myths. So for us, the interesting aspect of the tale is the extent to which Sertorius had grasped the importance of embedding himself into a native people's culture and not only identifying with its legends but weaving himself into them. He was to use very much the same techniques again in his later career.

Just as Mauritania seemed to be shaping up nicely, fortune presented Sertorius with a pleasant dilemma. The Iberians wanted him back. Or at least the Lusitanians of Hispania Ulterior did. So should Sertorius remain and build on his auspicious beginning in Africa, or return to the travails of Hispania? In the end, one suspects, the deciding issue was one of duty. Sertorius was, and never ceased to think of himself as being, the Roman proconsul of Hispania. Like Aeneas, he would have to abandon a promising position in Africa and follow the path of duty and destiny.[7]

The interesting question is why did the Lusitanians want Sertorius back,when they had been relaxed enough about his being kicked out of his province in the first place? Plutarch assures us it was because word had finally reached them of Sertorius' sterling character, and after confirming this by questioning his close associates they decided that 'he, and only he' was the man to lead them.

However, the real reason is betrayed by the preceding sentence, in which Plutarch tells us that the Lusitanians 'faced the terror of Roman arms'. There were a number of reasons why the Lusitanians could be worried about being attacked by the soldiers of the man who was supposed to be governing them. The first was the obvious one: the new governor of Hispania Ulterior was continuing the long and dishonourable tradition of enriching himself with booty from making war on Rome's enemies in Hispania – even if those he plundered had only become Rome's enemies because he was making war on them.

Secondly, it is improbable that the Lusitanians had not given this governor (one L. Fufidius) plausible excuses for his planned campaign. The absence of Sertorius' army on other business was a temptation which young Lusitanians would find hard to resist. One can assume that local grudges had been settled or reinforced, cattle had been stolen, and neighbouring tribes outraged in various ways. In short, the Lusitanians had taken advantage of the prevailing uncertainty and disorder to act like Lusitanians. It has further been suggested that those Marians who had been unable to embark for Africa with Sertorius had been trapped in a suddenly-hostile province, and these found at least a grudging welcome among the Lusitanians.[8] If so this would be another excuse for the governor to make war on them.

So Fufidius had motive, means and opportunity to attack the Lusitanians. In consequence, the Lusitanians logically concluded that if the Sullan governor was hostile, they would be better off with the Marian one, and made their choice accordingly. Thus, although Plutarch assures us that the Lusitanians wanted Sertorius as their general because 'they were totally without anyone with reputation and experience to command them' it is unlikely that they offered, or that Sertorius would accept the position of tribal war chief. Sertorius returned as a Roman governor, and the Lusitanians prepared to fight as loyal Roman subjects to expel the governors of the rebel usurper Sulla.

So, at some point well into the year 80 BC, Sertorius set out for his province. He tried to evade detection by crossing on a moonless night but was detected nevertheless. He pushed aside the attempt to stop him at sea by a feeble naval force from the coastal town of Mellaria, and returned to Iberia for the third and final time. He was never to leave the province again. The Lusitanians had dispatched a small force of 4,700 men to meet Sertorius when he landed at the little fishing port of Baelo, near the Pillars of Hercules (Gibraltar).[9] There is a small mountain near the town, and Sertorius took up station there while waiting for the Lusitanian contingent to arrive. While ensconced in his defensive position, Sertorius no doubt took the chance to size up local opinion.

That Sertorius had landed so far south suggests that support for the Marian cause extended beyond Lusitania, and certainly included many elements in the Romano–Italian population. The reasons are not hard to guess at. With governors representing the central power firmly back in charge, the Roman administration in Hispania had gone back to business as usual. All the abuses which Sertorius had checked had now returned with a vengeance, as presumably did the pre-Sertorian taxes to Rome. People whom Sertorius had given a taste of what it was like to be fairly and honestly governed had decided that they rather liked it, and were prepared to use force to get it back.

Sertorius shared his mountainside with a motley band. There were 700 North Africans in his mini-army, presumably mercenaries or adventurers. It is highly likely that these were horsemen or light infantry, and therefore could work closely with the Lusitanian skirmishers and 700 cavalry who were waiting for him. There was also the hard core of Sertorius' army; twenty-six hundred 'Romans', some the veterans he had taken along in his evacuation of Carthago Nova, and others he had picked up from the unfortunate Paccianus after the latter's defeat and death. Add to this various disaffected local Romans, Turdetani and some Celtiberians (who were always up for a fight), and Sertorius had a handy little army of some 8,000 men.

The chronology of what happened next is uncertain, but it would appear that the first victim of this army was Fufidius. As the governor in charge it would fall to Fufidius to deal with the sudden resurgence of the Sertorian menace, and as he was planning an attack on the Lusitanians anyway, he had an army ready to do it with.[10] Sertorius knew full well that a victory would strengthen support for his revolution like nothing else, so this was one of the few occasions in his career when he actively sought an open battle. Fufidius would also have been keen to engage his enemy before Sertorius crossed the river Baetis and raised further support from the Hispanian interior.

We do not know how large an army Fufidius had, since his was a scratch force gathered in haste. Much depends on how much of the army he was preparing for the invasion of Lusitania was at hand and how well-prepared it was. We can assume that his army outnumbered the Sertorians, and that Fufidius would have reckoned he had a good chance of crushing the uprising in the bud. After all, Fufidius was no stranger to warfare. It is generally believed that he was a former centurion who had become a confidante of Sulla and had been at his general's side throughout the latter's re-conquest of Italy. However, he was new to a country that the enemy army knew intimately.

The Baetis estuary was a swampy maze which favoured those with local knowledge, and though Fufidius did not know it, he was facing one of the best generals of his day. When the two sides met in battle, the Sullan army was crushed. The only fragmentary description we have of the battle confirms that local knowledge of the terrain gave the Sertorian force a decisive advantage.

> Afterwards, Fufidius arrived with his legions. He discovered that the banks of the river were steep, and if they had to fight, the ford would be hard to get across. Everything favoured his enemies more than his own side.
>
> (Sallust, *History*, frag 1.95)[10]

Fufidius lost two thousand men, and the greater part of southern Spain along with them. Fufidius survived the battle but the aristocrats in Rome had never forgiven the fact that a former centurion had attained a provincial command ahead of many of their own. Sulla had either just resigned his dictatorship, or was about to do so and was less able to protect his favourite than formerly. Fufidius vanishes into obscurity, remembered today and probably by his contemporaries mainly as the man who lost Iberia to Sertorius.

This was not completely correct. The west was Lusitanian and therefore already allied to Sertorius, and the south had been conquered. However some on the eastern coast still needed convincing. A rumour swept through the cities that Sertorius had landed with a massive force of fifty thousand gigantic cannibals from the coast of darkest Africa, and the people of the cities were uncertain whether the Sertorian army wanted them as allies or lunch.

Also a remnant of the Sullan army remained in the peninsula under the command of one Cotta.[11] He was in the north-east, possibly but not certainly the governor of Hispania Citerior. It was he, rather than Fufidius who had been behind the failed attempt to stop Sertorius at sea off Mellaria.

By now Sertorius had a lot to sort out in the lands he had newly reconquered. Therefore, he dispatched one of his close subordinates, his 'quaestor' (though officially this man's term of office had long expired) Lucius Hirtuleius, to deal with Cotta. This was not the last time that Sertorius was to show such faith in his fellow Roman commanders, and generally this faith was justified. This, even though some of these men, including Fabius Hispaniensis and Tarquitius Priscus first appear in the historical record on the side of the Sullan commander Annius. These men served loyally once they had switched to the Sertorian side – this being the disadvantage of Sulla's inability – and that of his successors – to forgive and forget. Those who betrayed his cause were of necessity enemies for life.

In fact, continuing political ructions in Italy meant that a steady flow of refugees from losing causes in Rome fled to Sertorius for sanctuary. These men became Sertorius' officer class. Because Sertorius never stopped thinking of himself as a Roman, he acted as a Roman governor would in appointing Romans to positions of command. The idea that the Lusitanians and Celtiberians should have their own generals was unpalatable, because this would make these nations allies rather than Roman subjects.

As he travelled north, Hirtuleius discovered that he no longer had Cotta to worry about. Command had been passed to another Sullan, Domitius Calvinus. And there was no need for Hirtuleius to go north to deal with him. Domitius and his army were preparing to come south. It would appear that when he was updated on events, Hirtuleius changed his plans and set about preparations to give the new Sullan commander a warm welcome when he arrived. It was already late in what had been a busy year. Winter was closing in fast, and this signalled an end to the campaigning season – not so much because the Iberian winters were too harsh for combat, but because until the winter wheat had been harvested there were not enough ready supplies of grain to keep armies in the field.

It was a good time for all sides in the conflict to pause and take stock, so the protagonists of the war temporarily turned their attention from fighting. Hirtuleius had defences to prepare, and Sertorius had troops to train, supplies lines to set up, and a province to govern. The Sullani had to re-arm and regroup before returning to the offensive. A replacement for the unfortunate Fufidius was required. The new appointee was Metellus Pius, a man who had matured considerably since we last met him as one of the officers of Pompeius Strabo (p.21), and before that in Africa in the company of his father Metellus Numidicus (p.9).

Metellus was among the very first to join the Sullan cause. In fact, it might be said that the Sullans joined his cause, since Metellus became a committed anti-Marian well before Sulla. The 'Pius' (meaning loyal and faithful) part of his name was bestowed upon him because once Marius succeeded in getting Metellus Numidicus exiled, his son had dutifully and unremittingly campaigned for his father's return.

Metellus served with Strabo at the outbreak of the Social War of 90 BC, but after being elected praetor in 88, he took up an independent command. He fought the Samnites and captured the town of Venusia, while in his civil role he played a major part in managing the transition of former rebel Italians into becoming the Roman citizens they had fought to become. As the political situation deteriorated, Metellus proved again that his cognomen of Pius was well deserved when he refused a demand by his men that he take over command from the consul Octavius. Thereafter, for a while his career paralleled later developments in the life of Quintus Sertorius.

Not wanting to get tangled up in affairs in Italy, Metellus went to his province as a propraetor. With Metellus, the province was Africa. But as with Sertorius, the government in Rome fell to the enemy party (in Metellus' case the Marians). The new group in power invalidated his command and sent out a replacement with enough force backing him to make sure he got there. Although Metellus had done his best to prepare his province militarily for this eventuality, he was driven out and forced to flee to Mauritania.

However, Metellus had one major career advantage over Sertorius. He had chosen the winning side. Ever since the fall of Rome to his enemies,

Sertorius was gloomily aware that it was him against the world. But Metellus had Sulla. So while Sertorius would have no-one to turn to but Cilician pirates, Metellus joined Sulla's veteran army, and capably assisted in the re-conquest of northern Italy. Though he remained a loyal supporter of Sulla for the rest of Sulla's life, he played no part in the atrocities which accompanied Sulla's return to power, and was probably the most respected of the Sullani thereafter.

Metellus was consul in 80 BC, the year that Sertorius returned to Iberia. The swift collapse of the Sullan cause in the peninsula convinced the senate to upgrade Hispania from a praetorial to a consular province, and sent Metellus and a substantial army to join Domitius Calvinus in restoring order. Neither Metellus nor Domitius intended to leave the initiative with the enemy, so as soon as Metellus arrived, the Sertorians would be under attack on two fronts.

If the year 80 BC had been a busy one in Iberia, 79 promised to be even more so.

Chapter 5

The White Fawn

As Sertorius well knew, it was one thing to gain control of Iberia and quite another matter to keep it. The Roman legions might at times be poorly generalled, but the men themselves were the finest warriors in the world. And they were all the more formidable because the ructions in Italy over the past fifteen years meant that much of Rome's military manpower was composed of hardened veteran soldiers. Sertorius also knew that as well as being very good at what it did, Rome's army seldom stopped until it had done it. As Jugurtha and the Cimbri had been among the most recent foes to discover, the Romans were seldom discouraged by setbacks and generally considered that peace talks were to discuss how best to accept an enemy's surrender.

If a military victory was out of the question, Sertorius could still hope to hold off the legions until there was a chance of a political settlement. After all, there was the precedent of the Italians. They had persuaded Rome to negotiate, albeit by pushing Rome's back to the wall and holding a knife to its throat. But even at that point negotiations only happened because the Romans regarded most Italians as practically family anyway, so it was not as though they were making concessions to a barbarian foe.

This latter point was important, and was certainly one reason why Sertorius stressed that he was a Roman leader rather than an Iberian one. There might be a violent change of government in Rome at any time. (Attempted military coups in the Sullan style were a recurring theme for the remainder of the life of the Republic.) A new government might be prepared to reach a settlement with a rebel Roman governor, but it would never negotiate with a Spanish renegade. So Sertorius' best chance was to hold out against the legions, and insist to the world that he was just as Roman as Domitius or Metellus, and rather than leading a rebel province, he was still fighting Rome's civil war. Nor was this a pretence. As far as we can determine, this is actually what Sertorius believed. However, so successful was Sertorius at managing his public persona that virtually nothing is known about the private thoughts and plans of the man behind it.

Plutarch debates whether Sertorius was a relatively gentle character (for a first-century Roman, that is – by modern standards they were all a brutal lot) or whether the mildness with which Sertorius punished transgressions was a deliberate act of policy to encourage loyalty. The people of Castulo might have an opinion on the matter, since it will be remembered that Sertorius had cold-bloodedly massacred the adult male population there after an attempted uprising (p.16). Even Plutarch admits that on occasion his hero could be savage and vindictive, though he adds that by and large Sertorius was a remarkably level-headed individual.

> He did not easily fall prey to pleasure or fear, and it was not in his nature to feel fear when faced with danger. He handled prosperity with moderation ... and was generous in rewarding the brave deeds of others. ... He never drank to excess even when he was relaxing, and he was easily able to endure hard work, and long journeys with little sleep. He was content with mediocre food, and not much of it either ... He behaved better toward women than Philip [of Macedon, father of Alexander the Great], he was more faithful to his friends than Antigonus [another great Macedonian general] and was more merciful towards his enemies than Hannibal. He was inferior to none of these in ability, but he had worse luck than all of them put together.
>
> (Plutarch, *Life of Sertorius*, 10, 13 & 14)

From the sources a picture of the man begins to form. Sertorius was decisive, outspoken and self-assured. He had 'strength of body and shrewdness of mind'.[1] He was a rather serious character, with all the rural conservatism of an Italian country lad. His dinner parties were formal, rather stilted and very decorous occasions. Sertorius could certainly be bold, imaginative and unconventional, but he saved these attributes for the military sphere. Few of his jokes or *bon mots* have survived, because he uttered few in the first place. He was energetic, and though unscrupulous, he was careful never to let his pleasures slip into becoming vices. And he missed his mother.

Above all, Sertorius was a great general – and not least because, far better than did his opponents, he understood that man-management was an essential part of his job. Although through choice and aptitude he was a military man, 'he convinced many that he was a mild soul, best suited to a quiet life, whose enemies had driven him to take up arms in his own defence, and practically forced him, against his will, to become a soldier'.[2]

This improbable feat of propaganda was achieved because Sertorius had charisma. It was not the easy charisma of a Julius Caesar or even the young Pompey – Sertorius had to work at it, and he did so with the same mix of assiduous hard work and genius which he brought to other aspects of generalship. Gifts and favours were reciprocated with interest. He performed small kindnesses, and made sure that everyone got to know of them. He took an interest in his men and led by example. Indeed, leadership in battle came easily enough, for Sertorius was naturally hardy, energetic and genuinely fearless.

Had there currently existed in Hispania a manual called 'How to make your men love you enough to follow you to the Gates of Hell' one suspects that Sertorius would have read the book from cover to cover, made copious notes, and then improved on it. Instead, Sertorius had to learn from the example of others, and one of his tutors in that respect was the great Scipio Africanus. It will be remembered (p.36) that Scipio had started his career with the capture of Carthago Nova.

This capture was a tricky feat, because the walls of that city were considerably higher than the morale of the Roman legions at the time. Scipio's daring plan was to take part of his army through the waters of the lagoon beside which Carthago Nova was built, and attack from an unexpected direction. It was a risky manoeuvre, yet the men executing it were reassured by the fact that Scipio had spent much of the preceding day in prayer. Sure enough, a mixture of wind direction and low tide made the northern walls of the city vulnerable at just the right moment. Scipio had told the men that it would be so, and he credited the plan in its entirety to inspiration from Neptune (rather than, say, careful reconnaissance and close questioning of local fishermen). The success of the operation assured his men that Scipio had the gods on his side, and this carried them on to further victories which in turn reinforced this belief.

We have already seen from Sertorius' hearty endorsement of the myth of Antaeus in Africa that he had the ability to weave himself into local legend. It is certain that from the moment he arrived in Iberia Sertorius was looking for some way to identify himself as a favourite of the gods, and make his leadership as much a cult as a matter of pragmatic faith in his ability. The opportunity came early.

Plutarch tells the tale:

Spanus, one of the commoners who lived in the country came across a doe trying to escape from hunters. The doe fled faster than he could pursue, but the animal had newly given birth. He [Spanus] was struck by the unusual colour of the fawn, for it was pure white. He pursued and caught it.

As it happened, Sertorius was in the area, and it was known that he amply rewarded those who brought him game and produce. So Spanus gave the fawn to Sertorius, who at that time felt only the usual pleasure of one who receives such a gift.

After a while the animal became so tame and well-trained that it came when he called it, and followed him on his walks without minding the crowds and bustle of life in camp. [That the fawn did this tells us something more about the character of Sertorius.] Eventually it occurred to him that the barbarians easily fall into superstition, so he started to give the fawn religious significance.

He announced that the doe had been sent by [the goddess] Diana, and solemnly claimed that through the doe she revealed hidden information to him. He helped the idea along by various tricks. If he heard of an enemy raid into his territory, or of an attempt to subvert a city from its allegiance to him, he would claim that the fawn had told him of this in a dream, and tell his men to prepare.

Or when his commanders sent him messages of a victory, he would hide the messenger and bring out the fawn wearing celebratory garlands. He would sacrifice to the gods, and tell his men to celebrate, because they would soon learn that something good had happened.

By such stratagems he persuaded his people that they were guided not by the fallible wisdom of a foreigner, but by a divine power. So the people were made tractable and all the more ready to help with his plans, and consequently the extraordinary growth of Sertorius' strength led to events which reinforced their belief.

(Plutarch, *Life of Sertorius*, 11)

Though some cities on the eastern coast and inland (for example Consabura and Contrebia Leucade) remained loyal to the government in Rome, Sertorius had persuaded most of the people of Iberia to either unite behind his cause or remain neutral. The winter was spent in politics of this sort and mustering and training an army to face the assault of the legions in spring. For an army Sertorius had his North African adventurers, and his core of veteran legionaries, but the rest of his forces would be composed of Iberian tribesmen. Despite the record of Roman military success in the peninsula, these tribesmen were no rabble which the legions easily outclassed.

At this time Roman legionaries were heavy infantrymen, clad in chain mail. Their helmets were of what archaeologists today call the Montefortino type (after the place where an early example was discovered). In comparison to the more rounded 'jockey cap' of the later *coolus* and imperial helmets, the Montefortino helmet was higher and had sides which sloped somewhat more. This was for the same reason as the double layer of mail on the shoulders – barbarians were fond of attempting to split skulls with a savage downward slash, and steeper helmets deflected such blows – usually onto the aforesaid shoulder pads.

The legionaries preferred to fight in close formation, which prevented extravagant gestures with the sword. Their optimal killing stroke was a stab delivered underhand, up under the ribs to the heart. Naturally their opponent would try to block this with his shield, so the Romans generally preceded any swordplay with a brisk shower of the heavy spears they called *pila*. The point of the pilum was to concentrate maximum penetrative power right there at the point. So while the spear was large and heavy – over eleven pounds (5kg) and six feet (2 metres) long, the all-important point was a narrow little pyramid less than an inch wide at the base.

This arrangement gave the pilum tremendous penetrative power. As the later writer Vegetius remarks, a pilum thrown with force and skill is easily capable of piercing a shield, and unless he is particularly well-armoured, the man behind the shield as well.[3] Even if the pilum failed in its primary task of stapling an enemy warrior to his shield by the abdomen, a shield that stopped a pilum now had the thing stuck through it, making it more than somewhat unwieldy for defensive purposes. And it is known that on occasion Roman generals would weaken one of the pins attaching the long iron shank behind the spearhead to the main wooden shaft. Once the pin broke, this made *pila* embedded in shields even more droopy, and the shield an encumbrance which was best discarded.

Of course, the legionaries were well aware of this, and at this time they generally carried a second, even heavier pilum for a second try at their now shield-less opponents. It was only after the enemy had been battered by *pila* that the Romans closed to melee. In that melee their close formation meant that whatever the number of warriors in each army, five Romans stood shoulder to shoulder, stabbing underarm at a maximum of three sword-swinging barbarians. The remaining barbarians had to wait their turn to fight the Romans, for trying to get more warriors into the battle-line at one time would merely lead to a combatant getting decapitated by his own side.

Yet in Hispania not all the advantages were on the Roman side. Firstly, it must be remembered that not only the Roman helmet, but also Roman shields were based on the same design as those of their Celtiberian opponents. And the legionary sword was called the Gladius Hispaniensis, precisely because it was adapted from the weaponry of the enemy there. So many Iberian warriors were armed and equipped in much the same style as the legionaries themselves.

Such warriors were called *scutati*, from their shields, which were larger than the small, round *caetra* carried by lighter infantry. Like the Romans, *scutati* used heavy spears, though in some cases these were *solifera* – weapons which lacked the subtlety of the Roman spear design but got their penetrative power with sheer heft, being made completely out of iron. There are reports that on occasion the warriors using these would tie bundles of pitch-soaked grass to the shaft, and ignite them just before throwing – a tactic that would work particularly well at causing confusion among the tight-packed Roman ranks.

While some *scutati* wore metal armour of scale or chain mail which was not dissimilar to that of their Roman counterparts, many wore corslets of stiffened linen or hardened leather. These were less impermeable to sharp objects than Roman armour, but on the other hand they were lighter – a valuable consideration in a hot country where there was a lot of marching to be done.

In part, the structure of the legions is believed to have evolved in response to combat with Iberian tribesmen. The Romans originally had a phalanx structure – a solid block of spearmen in a style adopted from the Greeks and Etruscans. However, this just did not work against a mobile enemy who hit the battle line in concentrated groups and from all directions. Consequently, the Romans broke their phalanx into smaller handfuls of men – and this is just what the word for these groups means: the new formation – the 'maniple' – translates as a 'handful'.

More recently, Roman experiences against the Cimbri had demonstrated that in larger-scale actions, individual maniples were easily overwhelmed. So around 104 BC Rome had adopted the formation that was to last for the next 300 years – the cohort of about 500 men.[4] What formation the Romans used when campaigning against Sertorius is unknown. It is possible that the proven utility of the maniple formation against Iberian tribesmen meant that this was used long after it was phased out in the rest of the empire. The legions now had the option of combining three maniples to form a single cohort whenever the situation called for it.

It is also clear that Sertorius – a man who had on several occasions seen the legions in action – was reluctant to let the legions show what they could do in a set-piece battle. His support base was enthusiastic, but morale was fragile. Putting a large number of men through the Roman meat-grinder would demoralize his troops, since even if they won a victory the casualty list would be frightening. Fortunately there were other ways to beat the Romans, and Sertorius had just the troops for the job.

Like the conscientious commander he was, Sertorius had undoubtedly studied the campaigns of Viriathus, the great Lusitanian commander whom the Romans had been unable to defeat in the field, and had finally vanquished through treachery (p.44). Sertorius was in the unique position of being able to get feedback on that war from the children of those who had fought on either side. He noted that Viriathus was, like himself, leery of taking on the legions head on and instead used his light troops to remove anything edible from the area around the Roman armies, his cavalry to cut down foragers, and his knowledge of the terrain to produce his heavy *scutati* unexpectedly from ambush. The Romans might not see many Iberian warriors, but they would not see much Iberian food either, and their supply lines were terribly vulnerable to the fast-moving and superb Celtiberian cavalry.

It appears that not just the Celtiberians, but most Iberian tribes were not merely skilled cavalrymen, but literally revered their horses. Shrines have been found – for example at Mula north east of Carthago Nova – where the central deity appears to have been in horse form.[5] In the mountains horses were sacrificed to the god of war. Strabo has this to say of the wild mountain tribes which gave many newly-arrived Romans their first experience of war before they were properly into the peninsula.

> Like women, they let their hair fall in thick tresses, though they tie it around their foreheads before battle. To Ares they sacrifice a he-goat and also the prisoners and horses... They also hold contests for light-armed and heavy-armed infantry and cavalry, in boxing, in running, in skirmishing, and in fighting by squads.
>
> (Strabo, Iberia, 7)

Strabo also quotes another writer (Poseidonius) to tell us that 'The Celtiberian horses resemble the Parthian, and not only are they faster than others, but they also run more smoothly.[6] He adds that the horses, though only medium in stature were excellent in mountain terrain, and had superb stamina. It was very common for warriors to ride to battle two on a horse, and then fight as a cavalryman and an infantryman in a mixed unit. Such units could deploy and retreat considerably faster than any Roman legionary unit could move to catch them, making a hypothetical issue of the damage the legionaries might have been able to inflict if they had managed to come to close quarters.

Parts of Hispania's terrain, such as the plains of Baetica, were well suited for the rearing of horses. So well-suited in fact that the horses often managed without human intervention. Wild horses could be found through much of the country, but particularly in the south. The abundance of horses translated to plentiful cavalry – up to a quarter of most Iberian armies was mounted. This means that, if the warriors doubled up on the saddle as was their wont, half an army could be moved around the countryside at speeds that not even legionaries on forced marches could match.

Contemporary pictures show that some cavalrymen wore spurs, but stirrups were unknown, both in Iberia and the rest of the contemporary Mediterranean world. Saddles were regarded by Iberian cavalry as an effete Roman luxury, and most rode while seated on a thick felt saddle blanket, often covered with an animal-skin. The same thick felt seems to have been used by the non-Celtic element for their helmets. Sculpture shows these helmets as fitting close to the head and gaudily decorated with feathers and mini-sculptures, but – such being the nature of felt – no examples have survived to the present day.

For combat, the Spanish cavalry preferred the *falcata*, this being the modern word for a heavy somewhat curved sword which resembles something between a cavalry sabre and the *kukri* of today's Ghurkas. Cavalry shields were the light *caetra* type, slung on the horse's side when not in use in battle. Like other *caetra* users, cavalrymen were enthusiastic and skilled flingers of javelins. The Romans were both exasperated and reluctantly admiring of talents such as those demonstrated by the Cantabrians from the north east of Iberia.

These galloped in a fast-moving and flexible circle in front of an infantry unit, bombarding the infantry with javelins at the closest point, and reloading when furthest away. The result was an unending stream of missiles which continued whether the long-suffering infantry advanced, retreated or just hunkered under their shields and waited for nightfall. And if overwhelmingly powerful relief troops turned up to save the infantry from their misery, the Cantabrians would vanish like smoke before re-materializing elsewhere to torment another unit. The only ways to really suppress such activity was to have a huge number of infantry covering all exits from the fray, or superior cavalry to drive off the Iberian horse. The Romans of the Sertorian war seldom had the troops for either option.

It is evident from the results that the winter spent training Sertorius' army was by no means a one-way process. Sertorius in turn learned much about his men. Fortunately he found the Iberian character compatible with his own. 'Sertorius armed Hispania, for a brave man easily unites with other brave men; and the energy of the Spanish soldiers never appeared to better advantage than under a Roman leader' remarks the later historian Florus.[7]

Sertorius was a highly intelligent commander, and he was well aware that there was no point in trying to make the Iberians into copies of the legions which they would be fighting. The copies would always be inferior, and would negate the inherent strengths of the Iberian way of war. So even as he taught them how the Romans manoeuvred and fought, Sertorius was busily learning exactly what his new recruits could do, and working out ways for them to do it better.

One of these moments of instruction is preserved in the works of that indefatigable collector of anecdotes, Valerius Maximus.

The Lusitanians were keen to take the legions head-on by attacking en-mass. Sertorius tried to persuade them against this, but his words were having no effect. So he tried the following cunning teaching aid.

He had two horses brought before [the council] one a powerful steed, the other a weak nag. He put a wizened old man at the tail of the powerful beast, and set him to plucking out the hairs of the horse's tail one by one. He also put an exceptionally strong young man at the nag's tail, and ordered him to rip out the tail by main force.

The old man accomplished his task, while all the muscular youth was able to do was tire himself out. The assembly had watched the proceedings, and now asked Sertorius to make his point. Sertorius explained that the Roman army was like a horse's tail. Take it on piecemeal and you can overcome it, even though relatively weak yourself. Try to take on the whole thing at once, and you would be handing over the victory you are trying to win.

So a rough barbarian nation that had the inclination to rush ungovernably to its own undoing saw with its eyes the usefulness of an idea which had escaped its ears.

(Valerius Maximus, 7.3.5)

What Sertorius strove to attain was an army which combined the best of native and Roman military tradition. He needed men who were highly mobile, who could operate semi-autonomously when required, and who could fight ferociously when required. These traits were native to most Hispanian warriors, and as was his wont, Sertorius developed and improved upon them. As we have seen, he also worked hard to eliminate negative traits such as the heroic but suicidal tendency to rush headlong into battle without consideration of the odds or of what everyone else was doing.

By introducing Roman formations and signals, and dispensing with courageous and frenzied outbreaks of heroism, Sertorius made an army out of a conglomeration of bandit groups, and the barbarians loved him for it.

(Plutarch, *Life of Sertorius*, 14)

Metellus was less able to prepare for the coming conflict, as he was currently consul of Rome, and as such he had other matters on his mind.

1. Bust believed to be of Caius Marius now in the Munich Glyptothek. The fateful decision of Sertorius to support Marius in his feud with Sulla lay at the root of the entire Sertorian war in Iberia. (*Picture: Geoffrey Faldene. Used with kind permission*)

2. Bust of Gnaeus Pompey now in the Munich Glyptothek. Brash, vain and occasionally foolhardy, the young Pompey learned a number of hard lessons from Sertorius in Iberia; lessons he applied in later life to become one of the most successful generals of his generation. (*Picture: Adrian Goldsworthy, used with his kind permission*)

3. The Roman theatre at Zaragoza, Spain. This city was founded as Caesar Augusta on the banks of the River Ebro to establish Roman dominance of the area where Sertorius made his last stand. As this theatre shows, Roman Hispania eventually because a peaceful and prosperous province of the empire. (*Picture: Philip Matyszak*)

4. Bolskan silver denarius. Bolskan was the native name of Roman Osca, headquarters of Sertorius (modern Huesca). Abundant finds of Bolskan coinage from the first quarter of the 1st century BC is probably due to this being used to pay Sertorius' troops. (*Copyright: Museo de Teruel; used with kind permission*)

5. Aerial view of La Caridad, Caminreal, Teruel, Spain, during the 2002 excavation. The remains show that for a while Roman and Celtiberian culture co-existed within the town. However, around 74 BC, the city was violently destroyed during the Sertorian wars. (*Copyright: Museo de Teruel. Used with kind permission*)

6. Excavations at Clunia. Founded by the Romans in Celtiberian territory, this city was a key Sertorian strongpoint which Pompey besieged unsuccessfully. At the end of the war the city was totally destroyed, and was only refounded in the Imperial era. (*Picture: Felix Paulinski, used with his kind permission*)

7

8

9

Finds from La Caridad, now in the Museo de Teruel (Spain).

7. Spear points, probably belonging to spears which were in use when the town was violently destroyed circa 74 BC.

8. Remains of a *scorpio*, c. 74 BC, discovered in the so-called 'House of Likine'. The iron frame (*capitulum*) and the four *modioli*, made of copper alloy, were in the original position, suggesting that the bolt shooter was ready to be shot when destroyed.

9. Lead slingshot ammunition. These *glandes* were just being smelted when the city was destroyed. Some of them are still joined, fresh from the mould.

10. Iron shield boss, c. 74 BC. This winged shield boss (*umbo*) would have been attached to a warrior's oval shield (*scutum*), protecting the hand grip and securing the shield's wooden spine.

10

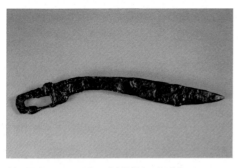

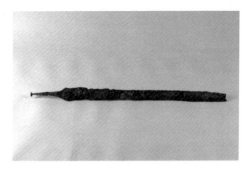

11. Falcata sword, c. 74 BC in the Museo de Teruel (Spain). The falcata was a typical Iberian weapon, most common in the eastern coastal regions of Spain. The falcata was suitable for slashing and thrusting, and its length made it ideal for close combat (*Copyright: Museo de Teruel. Picture: Jorge Escudero; used with kind permission*)

12. Spanish sword now in the Museo de Teruel. The Roman republican *gladius hispaniensis* was probably derived from the Celtiberian adaptation of La Tène I Celtic swords, such as this example. (*Copyright : Museo de Teruel. Picture: Jorge Escudero; used with kind permission*)

13

14

Bas reliefs of Iberian warriors from Osuna in Southern Spain.

13. A *caetratus*, a light infantryman named after his shield, the *caetra*. Though unable to match legions head-to-head, Sertorius used such soldiers with devastating effects in ambushes and surprise attacks.

14. An Iberian heavy infantryman. Until he was reinforced by the regular Roman legionaries of Perpenna, these were the only troops Sertorius had that were capable of standing up to Roman legionaries, but they were relatively few and were used sparingly.

(*Pictures courtesy of Fernando Quesada Sanz, Director. Dpto. de Arqueología, Facultad de Fil. y Letras Universidad Autónoma de Madrid*)

15. Montefortino helmet of a Republican soldier, now in the British Museum. Note the knob at the top for affixing plumes, and the steeper sides so that sword strokes sweeping downward were deflected onto shoulders armoured and padded for the purpose. (*Picture: P. Matyszak*)

16

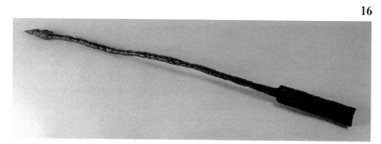

17

Iron *pilum* shanks now in the Museo de Teruel (Spain).

16. The first version is normally referred to as the 'light pilum'. The socketed head and a needle-like point gave this standard Roman infantry weapon huge penetrative power.

17. Is the 'heavy pilum'. At the bottom of the head is a flat tang riveted into the widened top of a wooden shaft. The pyramidal point was designed to break through a shield and thereafter be difficult to retrieve.

(*Copyright: Museo de Teruel. Pictures: Jorge Escudero; used with kind permission*)

18

A Roman legionary of the first century BC doing drills.

18. The attacking strike used the shield as an offensive weapon, with the armoured boss thrust into an opponent's face even as the sword disembowels him below.

19. Legionary in defensive stance. Note the padded shoulders which take the impact of downward sword slashes, and the fact that when in this position the legionary exposes virtually no vulnerable body parts.

(Pictures of re-enactor Jean-Luc Féraud used with his kind permission)

19

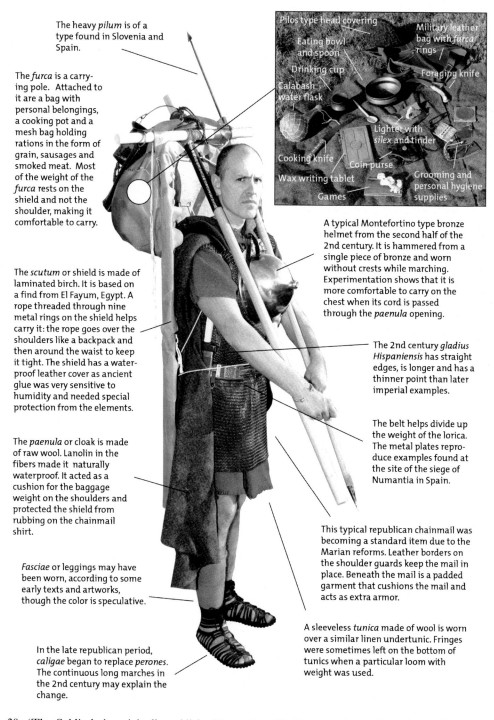

The heavy *pilum* is of a type found in Slovenia and Spain.

The *furca* is a carrying pole. Attached to it are a bag with personal belongings, a cooking pot and a mesh bag holding rations in the form of grain, sausages and smoked meat. Most of the weight of the *furca* rests on the shield and not the shoulder, making it comfortable to carry.

The *scutum* or shield is made of laminated birch. It is based on a find from El Fayum, Egypt. A rope threaded through nine metal rings on the shield helps carry it: the rope goes over the shoulders like a backpack and then around the waist to keep it tight. The shield has a waterproof leather cover as ancient glue was very sensitive to humidity and needed special protection from the elements.

The *paenula* or cloak is made of raw wool. Lanolin in the fibers made it naturally waterproof. It acted as a cushion for the baggage weight on the shoulders and protected the shield from rubbing on the chainmail shirt.

Fasciae or leggings may have been worn, according to some early texts and artworks, though the color is speculative.

In the late republican period, *caligae* began to replace *perones*. The continuous long marches in the 2nd century may explain the change.

Pilos type head covering

Military leather bag with *furca* rings

Eating bowl and spoon

Drinking cup

Foraging knife

Calabash water flask

Lighter with *silex* and tinder

Cooking knife

Coin purse

Grooming and personal hygiene supplies

Wax writing tablet

Games

A typical Montefortino type bronze helmet from the second half of the 2nd century. It is hammered from a single piece of bronze and worn without crests while marching. Experimentation shows that it is more comfortable to carry on the chest when its cord is passed through the *paenula* opening.

The 2nd century *gladius Hispaniensis* has straight edges, is longer and has a thinner point than later imperial examples.

The belt helps divide up the weight of the lorica. The metal plates reproduce examples found at the site of the siege of Numantia in Spain.

This typical republican chainmail was becoming a standard item due to the Marian reforms. Leather borders on the shoulder guards keep the mail in place. Beneath the mail is a padded garment that cushions the mail and acts as extra armor.

A sleeveless *tunica* made of wool is worn over a similar linen undertunic. Fringes were sometimes left on the bottom of tunics when a particular loom with weight was used.

20. 'The Soldier'. As originally published in *Ancient Warfare* magazine, and used with their kind permission.

22

21

23

Roman soldiers from a contemporary sculpture now in the Louvre, Paris.

21. Roman legionaries. Note the plumed helmets and chain-mail armour. It is not known what colour the tunics were, but historians no longer believe they were always red.

22. Roman cavalryman. Roman cavalryman of the type who fought in Hispania. Though smaller than modern cavalry steeds, Spanish horses were prized for their speed and toughness.

23. Roman officer. Roman officer of the late Republic. It is probable that Sertorius looked very much like this when dressed for battle.

(Pictures: Adrian Goldsworthy, used with his kind permission)

We know from a comment by Cicero that Metellus was still in Rome in the August of 80 BC, so even if he left soon afterwards he would have had mere months to prepare for the coming struggle.

Sertorius had no such distractions, and if we accept the implications of a fragmentary piece of text from Livy, he used the extra time to practise military manoeuvres on those areas of Iberia that still remained loyal to the Sullans in Rome.[8] It was probably at this time that he used force to persuade the Celtiberian city of Contrebia Leucade of the error of its ways, and made the survivors reluctant converts to his cause. There would also have been problems with the Carpeti, a tribe in central Hispania that had long been loyal to Rome – probably because their perpetual rivals and enemies the Vettones and Celtiberians were not.

One city which adamantly refused to have anything to do with Sertorius or his cause was Lauron, a city situated on the coast about half-way between Carthago Nova and Saguntum. Sertorius would have made representations which combined dire threats and blandishments, but here he had no success. The people of the east coast knew well that not one but two Roman armies would be arriving in the spring, and Sertorius was likely to fall back to the interior to deal with them. A premature defection to the Sertorian cause would leave the people of Lauron as a warm-up for Metellus' army before it proceeded toward the main event in the interior. Nevertheless Lauron lay directly across the main north-south Roman line of communication, so Sertorius kept a predatory eye on this strategically important city and waited for his chance to strike.

It was Domitius, the Sullan propraetor of Hispania Citerior, who kicked off the campaigning season by advancing south-west. As previously, Sertorius left Domitius to his capable subordinate Hirtuleius while he kept watch for the arrival of Metellus. Hirtuleius met Domitius in battle on the banks of the 'duck river', the Anas (the modern Guadiana). This battle was significant, as it reveals something of the Sertorian strategy for taking on the legions.

One distinctive feature of this battle is that it was fought deep in the interior of Hispania. This confirms that the Sertorians intended to fall back before the legionaries, and then make their lives as interesting as possible with ambuscades and raids, all while the Romans journeyed inland far beyond their comfort zone. Domitius was pushing for Consabura in Carpetian territory, with the intention of demonstrating that Rome stood by her allies, and from there was drawn by the elusive Iberians ever deeper into the hinterland.

Given the greater mobility of the Iberians it is a reasonable bet that Hirtuleius would have been content to run rings around his relatively static opponents. He would not have taken on the Romans in direct conflict until he was good and ready. The future governor of Britain, Frontinus, tells of an incident which probably relates to this time, and shows the sort of difficulties that the Romans had in getting to grips with the Iberians.

> Hirtuleius, a lieutenant of Quintus Sertorius was taking a handful of cohorts up a long narrow road between two steep and impassable mountains. On being told that a substantial enemy force was approaching he dug a ditch between the mountains, and set a wooden rampart behind that. He then set fire to the rampart and made his escape with the enemy cut off [on the other side of the flames].
>
> (Frontinus, *Stratagems*, 1.5.8)

By the time he got Domitius on the banks of the Anas, Hirtuleius was ready for battle, which means that Domitius was not. By then the Roman army was probably hungry, harassed and demoralized. From close examination of a fragment of text known as 'the Vienna Fragment' the modern scholar C. E. Konrad has concluded that at least a part of Domitius' army surrendered, and Domitius was either handed over to Hirtuleius for execution or was killed by his own men as a peace-offering to the Sertorians.[9] In either case, it is improbable that any but a small percentage of the army which marched out with Domitius ever made it back again afterwards.

Next up was one Thorius, a subordinate of Metellus, and a man possibly sent to start operations in Hispania while his boss tied up the loose ends of his consulship in Italy. (The consul who succeeded Metellus in Rome was an aristocrat with a somewhat anti-Sullan bent, an individual called Marcus Lepidus. Indirectly, this election was to have a decisive effect on Hispanian affairs.)

To Thorius Sertorius gave his personal attention. Though 'Thorius' is identified in the Plutarchian manuscripts as 'Thoranius' this man is clearly identified in other sources as Lucius Thorius Balbus, of whom Cicero says 'he operated on the principle of enjoying to the full the most exquisite pleasures he could find. ... yet he was so lacking in cowardice that he died for his country in battle'.

It is not certain where Sertorius was based at this point. We know that in later years, he set himself up at Osca, a town just on the Hispanian side of the Pyrenees, all the better to beat up Roman armies wearied by their passage through the mountains.[10] (Operating on the same principle, the emperors in later Rome moved to Milan to do the same to invaders crossing the Alps.)

Once Hirtuleius had beaten Domitius in the south, the Sertorian position was strengthened (as testified by a number of coin hoards buried in Baetica by terrified Sullan supporters and retrieved in modern times). Action shifted northwards where the unfortunate Thorius had discovered that he no longer had the army of Domitius to support him. Help was expected from Gaul but if he was already at Osca, Sertorius was ideally positioned to prevent any army already in Hispania from joining with one from Gaul.[11] Without help, Thorius was outclassed, outmanoeuvred and defeated. His name became the latest in the list of commanders killed or disgraced in the attempt to dislodge Sertorius from Iberia, and yet another Roman army was lost.

It was time for Metellus himself to enter the fray. Metellus was a solid if unspectacular general. Sertorius was a genius. Plutarch describes the unequal campaign which followed as a contest between the two generals, with all the advantages on the side of Sertorius. However, he does give a glimpse of the different tactics of the armies involved.

He [Metellus] was accustomed to regular warfare with heavy infantry. He liked to command a solid, ponderous bloc of infantry. This formation was superbly trained to push back and vanquish the enemy in combat at close quarters. For constantly chasing men who floated like the wind over the mountains he had to climb, for enduring – as their enemy did – constant hunger without either tent or camp-fire, his army was useless. The light armour and consequent agility of his Iberian warriors meant that Sertorius was constantly shifting the focus and changing the situation, until Metellus was at his wits' end.

Metellus was no longer young, and after the many heroic contests of his youth he was now somewhat inclined to ease and luxury, while Sertorius was full of mature vigour. ... When Sertorius challenged

Metellus to single combat, Metellus' men cheered and urged him to fight it out, general on general, and they mocked him when he declined.

(Plutarch, *Life of Sertorius*, 12–13 passim)

In fact Sertorius was himself coming to his fiftieth birthday by this time, and Metellus could hardly have been more than five years his senior. However, the energetic and daring Sertorius acted as though he were younger than his age, the cautious and uninspired Metellus as though he were older. Sertorius contemptuously called Metellus 'the old woman'.[12]

If Sertorius was master of the countryside, a number of cities were still loyal to the government in Rome. 'With one army [that of Metellus] intent on devastating the countryside and the other [Sertorius'] to the destruction of the cities, unhappy Hispania was punished for Rome's quarrels by Roman generals' remarks the later historian Florus, with some accuracy.[13] It was usual practice for Rome to establish colonies which served as secure bases in unfriendly territory – a practice which had served the city well in the Social War of the previous decade, when Roman colonies had been strong-points of resistance to the Italian insurgency.

Lacking such strong-points in central Hispania, Metellus set about creating them, and in so doing he indelibly left his imprint upon the province. Five of these forts are known today – Medellin (originally Metellinum) in the central north of Spain was originally intended to serve as a springboard for attacks into Lusitania, and finished by giving its name to the second largest city in modern Columbia. Cáceres further to the south-west was an ancient village which Metellus fortified as Castra Caecilia, which in later years went on to become one of the great cities of Roman Hispania. The Viccus Caecilius was intended to hold down the mountain people living in the hills above the Duoro River, while Caecilina was intended to do the same for the Celtiberians.

Such fortifications were reasonably secure from all but a sustained Sertorian siege, and Sertorius was too canny to try to attack a Roman legion in its marching camp – though he was ready, willing and able to keep the occupants of those camps awake all night by constant alarms.

Metellus knew he was exposed to hit-and-run attacks and ambuscades in the open, and consequently was reluctant to operate far from a secure camp, which was another reason why he established them across the country. His caution made his army's drive north to the river Tagus a slow, cautious affair that exasperated the men. Sertorius did his best to exacerbate the situation.

> The methodical Metellus was too slow to follow up his opportunities and fast-moving events left him well behind. He commanded heavy and relatively immobile troops, and Sertorius attacked these like some sort of reckless bandit, with ambushes and raids on the flanks.
>
> (Plutarch, *Life of Pompey*, 17)

> For Sertorius would cut off his opponent's supply of water and prevent him from foraging. If the Romans attacked, he evaded, and if they dug themselves into a camp, he would constantly harass the camp. If the Romans surrounded his strong- points, he would cut off their supplies, so putting them under siege themselves. By the end of it the Roman soldiers were in despair.
>
> (Plutarch, *Life of Sertorius*, 13)

Metellus, like Thorius before him was forced to call for help from Gaul, and this time help was forthcoming. Sertorius was too busy making Metellus' life a misery to be distracted by this new threat, so he dispatched Hirtuleius to literally head the enemy off at the pass in the Pyrenees.

Galloping to the rescue of the Romans in Hispania was one Lucius Manlius, former praetor and now governor of Gallia Transalpina.[14] He brought with him a substantial force of three legions. Livy's summary of the period conflates this incursion with that of Domitius described above, but the later historian Orosius, certainly drawing on an earlier, unknown source clearly describes this as a separate confrontation.

> Manlius, the proconsul of Gaul crossed [the Pyrenees] to Spain with three legions and 1500 cavalry. He and the iniquitous Hirtuleius were joined in battle, and afterwards his camp was stripped and his sole refuge was in the town of Ilerda.
>
> (Orosius, *Contra Paganos*, 5.23)

Having suffered this major setback, Manlius pulled back to his own province. A fragment which has survived from a text by the historian

Sallust suggests that Hirtuleius did not let Manlius get away easily. 'He occupied the highest hill, and built many siege works around him and Ilerda.'[15] When Manlius did get back over the Pyrenees an already bad proconsulship was made worse by the warriors of the local Aquitani. These took advantage of the battered state of the Manlius' army to give it yet a further mauling. This effectively knocked Manlius out of the picture in Hispania where once again the only serious Sullan presence was the army of Metellus – and that was effectively pushed out of Hispania Ulterior for the remainder of the year.

In 78 Metellus decided to attack the one element of Sertorius' support which could not easily evade him – those cities which had joined in the insurgency. In fact as the war went on, cities – both on the Sertorian and Sullan side – gained in importance for just that reason. Though Sertorius was impossible to pin down in the countryside, he had to stand his ground when either attacking a city or in defending one from capture. Consequently the terrain around the cities were one of the few places in the war where Hispanian arms could be counted on to directly confront the Roman.

Langobriga (probably today's Laccobriga, not far from Lisbon in Portugal) seemed an easy target.[16] The town had a single well, which was nowhere near adequate for the needs of the population. This was not normally a problem, because there were springs that ran right alongside the city walls. Anyone in need of a refreshing glass of mineral water need only step outside the city gates with a bucket – unless there was a Roman army sitting in front of those gates.

Separate the town from its water supply, Metellus reasoned, and thirst would quickly force a surrender. And surrender would be highly significant, because it would demonstrate to the cities of Hispania that Sertorius could not defend them – even here in Lusitania at what was probably the furthest point that Metellus had managed to penetrate into Sertorian territory. Two days, Metellus estimated, would be enough to subdue the city. But his experiences in Hispania had turned him into an incorrigible pessimist, so he ordered his men to take supplies for five.

We hear little of the intelligence gathering operations of Sertorius, but from the results of its performance, we know that it was superb. Every town had its share of Sertorian sympathizers, and some of these worked as servants in the Roman camps, plied legionaries with wine in taverns and noted the Roman army's direction of march. Thereafter swift Iberian horses and local knowledge of short cuts carried the news to Sertorius or his lieutenants. It is quite probable that Sertorius was informed of Metellus' plans for Langobriga before some of Metellus' lieutenants.

Metellus eventually worked out this security problem for himself, and decided that the only way to keep a secret in Iberia was to share it with no-one. On a later occasion a young centurion asked him the intention behind the orders he had received. Metellus retorted 'If the shirt on my back knew what I have in mind, I would take it off and throw it in the fire'.[17]

Such wisdom came at a price, and part of this price was paid at Langobriga. Forewarned of Metellus' intentions, Sertorius was well and truly forearmed. In Roman Hispania silver mining had been converted from a desultory tribal activity to a full-scale industry, and Sertorius reaped the advantages of having control of that industry at peak production. He used some of the largess to lavish gifts on his men, and to award bonuses to those who carried out particularly tricky or daring operations.

So when he offered one such bonus for anyone prepared to transport a wineskin of water across the mountains to Langobriga there was no shortage of volunteers, allowing Sertorius to select the fittest and fleetest for the mission. Loaded with two thousand wineskins of water, the water-carriers arrived in plenty of time to forestall the Romans. In fact, they even had time to conduct all non-essential defenders safely out of the city, and to carry everything edible in the neighbourhood into it.

As ever, the Iberians made the Roman journey to Langobriga as arduous and frustrating as possible. Much of the five days' rations that Metellus had ordered the men to pack were consumed even before the army reached its destination, there to find a well-watered and strongly defended city sitting on a site denuded of anything useful outside the walls. There was nothing Metellus could do but detach a legion from his army and send it scouting for provisions. This legion was commanded by one Aquinus, who – since this name is not common among the contemporary Roman aristocracy – may well have been a Sullan loyalist of the equestrian class in Hispania. If so, he would have been given the foraging job because of his better understanding of local conditions.

Sertorius had expected this, and his agents kept him informed of where the forage party was at any given time. Sertorius had two options. He could precede the foragers and remove anything usable from their path or he could wait until the enemy wandered into a vulnerable position – the local terrain being such that at some point this was inevitable – and attack. By necessity foragers have to spread out in their search for food, and being dispersed across the countryside was not an easy option for the legionaries. After all, a light Iberian cavalryman with a sword could go a lot faster than a Roman forager with a sack of grain.

It is unknown what success the foragers enjoyed, but eventually they decided to rejoin the main army. The return route of Aquinus' legionaries took them past a shadowy ravine. Once the legion had passed this ravine, two thousand Iberians suddenly sallied out and hit the legion from behind. The vanguard of a legion on the march could easily be a mile ahead of those at the rear, so there was a certain amount of confusion as news of the assault was conveyed up the line and orders and reinforcements were sent back in response. Just as the legion had more or less got itself turned around to face the threat from the ravine, Sertorius popped up on the other side, and hit the legion in the rear once more.

After a day or two of harrowing work as foragers, the legionaries were in no mood to fight hard when unexpectedly assailed from front and back. Some were killed, many were captured and the survivors – including the unfortunate Aquinus – escaped by abandoning the supplies, their armour and their dignity by the roadside and heading back to Metellus in headlong flight. This left Metellus with nothing to feed his army and no choice but to retreat back along the route he had come. His total failure of a siege had achieved nothing. Nothing, that is, but to expose his men to the taunts of the Iberians who took every opportunity to gleefully point out how totally ineffectual their attempt had been. It was not the sort of treatment to which the conquerors of the known world were accustomed.

In 78 BC news arrived in Hispania which must have afforded Sertorius a certain grim satisfaction. Cornelius Sulla, the man who had put Sertorius on the infamous death-list of the proscriptions was himself dead, killed by a grotesque and lingering disease. Sertorius had at least outlived his would-be executioner. The Sullan faction still held power in Rome, but Sertorius now faced a lesser generation of enemies – the survivors of over a decade of warfare and political murder which had purged Rome's ruling class of its best and brightest.

Nor was the political instability in Rome at an end. Aemilius Lepidus, the consul who had succeeded Metellus in Rome, showed his colours by a violent dispute with his Sullan colleague over the honours given to Sulla at his funeral. That Lepidus intended to raise once more the standard of the Marians was clearly shown by his outright attack on some of the recently-dead dictator's more controversial legislation and by his eager efforts to recruit like-minded allies. Should Lepidus succeed in creating a coherent anti-Sullan coalition and bringing it to power in Rome, the Iberian war might be brought to a negotiated end without further bloodshed.

This thought seems to have influenced both sides in Hispania. In the previous year, Metellus had pushed as far as the mouth of the Tagus, and taken his army north towards Segovia in the mountains where Madrid is today. The pain caused by these adventurous excursions had outweighed any fleeting gains, for Sertorius had constantly harassed the Romans without ever allowing himself to be brought to pitched battle, and when dwindling supplies forced Metellus to withdraw, Sertorius simply re-occupied the lands the Romans had vacated.

So now Metellus adopted a more cautious strategy, intending only to hold the line along the Baetis River in the south while he awaited the results of the political struggle in Rome. He was left alone by Sertorius, who concentrated instead on subduing those tribes in the interior that had not yet yielded to his authority. The Sertorian strategy had two benefits. Firstly, by not taking the war to the Romans, Sertorius could justifiably claim to a new administration in Rome that he, the legitimate Roman governor of Hispania, had done no more than defend himself against aggression by the Sullans. Secondly, in subjugating the wild tribes of the interior Sertorius was doing no more than his gubernatorial duty, in a tradition made hallowed by generations of Roman generals in the peninsula before him.

On the other hand, if Lepidus failed in reviving the anti-Sullan cause in Italy and the war flared up once more in Hispania, Sertorius would have consolidated his base in the interior and have fewer potential enemies at his back, while inaction would have served to debilitate the already somewhat demoralized army of Metellus. Overall, the coming year looked more hopeful for Sertorius than had many of those previously, and certainly things looked a great deal better than when Sertorius had been a refugee washed up on the beaches of Lusitania, contemplating a desperate flight across the western ocean.

Chapter 6

Pompey Enters the Fray

Things were looking promising for Sertorius in Rome. Lepidus had pledged to rescind the acts of Sulla and to restore some of the lands which Sulla had confiscated from rebel Italians who had sided with the Marians. Since this brought him into conflict with the Sullans who still dominated the senate, Lepidus took himself on a tour of Etruria – a tour which was a barely concealed fact-finding mission to discover how much support he would get if he raised an insurrection there.

Lepidus' fellow consul was Lutatius Catulus, a relative of that Catulus who had been general alongside Marius and had died because he failed to cede enough glory to Marius in the Cimbric wars (p.28). Not unexpectedly, this Catulus was a die-hard Sullan supporter who was bitterly opposed to Lepidus. Having lived through the agony of civil war between Marius and Sulla, most senators were desperate to avoid that conflict bursting out again between Lepidus and Catulus. Their combined pressure forced the pair to swear binding oaths to keep the peace.

At this time the senate allocated the provinces that the consuls would take over after performing their duties in Rome, but which consul got which province was literally left to chance. As it turned out, the lottery assigned Lepidus to Gaul, where the unfortunate Manlius was still nursing his army back to health after being beaten by both Iberians and Aquitani. Nevertheless, Lepidus now had an army, a fact which caused considerable apprehension in Rome, where many considered that Lepidus was actively working to punish the Sullans for their earlier atrocities and put his own faction in power.[1] To make things worse, Lepidus wanted to stand for a second consulship but refused to come to Rome to declare his candidacy. Had he done so, he would certainly have been pressed to renew his oath not to resort to arms, and there was a strong suspicion that Lepidus had decided not to come to Rome for exactly that reason.

Sentiment in the senate turned against Lepidus. The renegade consul was recalled to Rome, ostensibly to perform his duties in running the elections for his successor. However Lepidus had good reason for suspecting that charges of fomenting sedition would be brought against him when he arrived. Certainly violence had already broken out in areas where Italians had attempted to evict Sullan settlers from their land, and at the very least Lepidus had condoned this. Even now he had not gone to his province but was in north Italy. He was accompanied by an army, possibly intended to make up for recent losses suffered by the legions in Hispania but currently being used by Lepidus as an implicit threat against the senate. Gaul itself was governed for Lepidus by his lieutenant, M. Brutus, the father of the man later infamous for plunging a dagger into Julius Caesar.

So when recalled to Rome, Lepidus brought his army with him. He camped outside the city and issued a series of demands which, if accepted, would have led to a second consulship for Lepidus and cemented the dominance of his faction. For Sertorius this was a critical moment. He and the Sullans were sworn enemies, and his chances of making peace with them were remote. But Lepidus was a horse of a very different colour. There is no doubt that he and Sertorius could reach an accommodation, and it is very possible that Lepidus made the point to the senate that as consul he would be able to bring the Iberian war to a speedy conclusion without bloodshed.

The wild card in all this was Gnaeus Pompey, the son of the disreputable general Pompeius Strabo. At this time the younger Pompey rejoiced in the nickname of 'the teenage butcher' for his part in the Sullan purges, while his father had been designated by the historian Rutilius Rufus as 'the vilest man alive'. The gods had evidently agreed with Rufus' description of Pompey senior, who perished when the heavens smote him with a lightning bolt in 87 BC.[2] However, the young Pompey was still at large. He held no official position in the Roman state, but he had several legions' worth of veterans in the Picentine region of north-east Italy ready, willing and able to take up arms at his command. This, and the young man's fearsome reputation, meant that he could not be overlooked.

Though Pompey had served Sulla well, he had been a wilful subordinate. One of the ways in which he had gone against the former dictator's wishes was that he had thrown his support behind the initial bid of Lepidus for the consulship and had been instrumental in the latter's election. Now Lepidus was at the gates of Rome with an armed force, demanding a second consulship. Would Pompey support him again?

The senate, now that the threat of civil war was upon them, reacted decisively. Lepidus was declared a public enemy, and Pompey was offered the post of legate to the consul Catulus. This promotion was a major honour, as the position of legate to the consul usually went to a senior magistrate, and Pompey had not yet even held the junior office of quaestor. It may have been flattery, or a bribe, but it worked. Pompey came down on the senatorial side and the fate of Lepidus was sealed. Catulus took on his rebel colleague directly, while Pompey headed north to deal with Brutus, who had taken his army over the Alps into Italy.

This prompt military response swiftly defused the long-running political crisis which Lepidus had provoked. The army of Lepidus was defeated in a brisk military action outside Rome, and Lepidus pulled his forces back through Etruria to Sardinia. There he died, by some accounts of a broken heart – brought on not by his failed bid for political supremacy but by the accidental discovery that his wife had been unfaithful to him.

Brutus and his men reached Mutina (modern Modena in north-central Italy) where he was penned in by Pompey. The young general made the reasonable point that with his men disaffected and support for his cause rapidly dwindling across Italy, Brutus really had nothing to fight for. Brutus accepted the argument, and agreed to surrender on condition that he and his men would receive reasonable treatment. The 'teenage butcher' accepted the conditions of surrender, then promptly and dishonourably executed Brutus at the first opportunity.

Lepidus' rebellion was over before it had got properly started, but the implications for Sertorius in Hispania were profound. On the negative side, any chance of making peace with the government in Rome had gone. Even if the senate had any inclination to negotiate beforehand – and it had shown none – Pompey and Catulus had demonstrated that the judicious application of brute force could make negotiations unnecessary in any case. Now the question was not whether the rebellion in Hispania should be quashed but who should be sent to join Metellus to do it. The war would go on.

On the positive side, Sertorius was now better-prepared to fight that war than ever. His consolidation of the interior was going well, he had the wealth of the silver mines flowing into his war chest, and his programme to win the hearts and minds of the tribal nobility was working well. His army was gaining in experience, and he still had his hard core of veteran legionaries who had served with him since before his flight to Africa. These men had been few to begin with, and the attrition of the years had made them fewer still, yet they remained the only troops Sertorius had who were capable of taking on the legionaries of Metellus head-to-head. Fortunately for Sertorius that was about to change.

The army which Lepidus had taken with him to Sardinia was a substantial affair of fifty-three cohorts and thus (since at this time there were ten cohorts to a legion) five-and-a-half legions. A force this size mattered a great deal. In later years entire provinces were to be conquered with less. The question was who would get to command those men? At Mutina Pompey had assimilated Brutus' army into his own, and was finding ever more ingenious excuses for not disbanding it.

The army in Sardinia was by definition a rebel army, and there was no Pompey on hand to bring it firmly back under Sullan control. In fact, the most senior officer present was the aristocratic Perpenna Veiento, a committed Marian sentenced to die by Sulla and recalled from exile by Lepidus.[3] A return to exile was the best and most improbable treatment that Perpenna could expect from the Sullans if he surrendered, and with Pompey's treatment of Brutus as an example of the worst-case and most likely scenario, Perpenna was resolved to fight on.

In 76 BC Perpenna decided to take his rebellion to Liguria, in the north-west of modern Italy, but at that time a relatively remote area with several unconquered mountain tribes. The region also included the crucial road which linked Rome to Gaul and the Pyrenees, so by occupying Liguria, Perpenna was laying the foundation for a potential Marian empire combining Transalpine Gaul and Hispania.

One reason this measure might succeed was because the quality of the government in Rome was poor. The senate was packed with mediocrities, mostly because any outstanding figure in the previous decade had been on the death-list of one or the other of the warring factions. This meant that there were few generals of even Metellus' stature left to deal with the rebellion in the west – and Metellus himself was not exactly making spectacular progress.

Nevertheless, Rome was too large and inclusive for a dearth of talent to last. Others stepped forward to fill the huge gaps in the ranks of the established nobility. Previously neglected families – such as the Julii Caesares – found new prominence, and outsiders such as Cicero found their talents welcome. Unusual times meant that Rome's leadership had to pass quickly to a new generation. There was no-one in Rome willing or capable of taking on Perpenna or Sertorius. But, as the veteran senator Marcus Philippus pointed out, there was the very competent Pompey, still lurking around Mutina with an army he refused to stand down.

Why not, asked Philippus, invite Pompey to take on the rebels, not as proconsul, but *pro consulibus*? (That is, on behalf of the consuls who seemed unready and unwilling to do the job themselves.) There were all sorts of advantages to this plan. Pompey might kill Sertorius and Perpenna and thus bring the west back under the control of the central government. On the other hand, Sertorius or Perpenna might kill Pompey and so rid the state of a young man with a distressing disregard for authority and the disturbing habit of raising armies more loyal to himself than to Rome. And even if one failed to dispose of the other, Sertorius and Pompey might each debilitate the other to the point where the senate could send a properly-appointed general with a regular legion or two and tidy everything up.

In any case, Italy would be rid of a potential rogue general and his irregular army, while in Hispania, the flair and youthful energy of Pompey would complement the steadiness and experience of Metellus. In fact Metellus and Pompey had worked well together before, during the civil war against the Marians.

He [Pompey] was not only outstanding in his own performance, but he fanned the bold and warlike spirit of Metellus into new heat and flame which heretofore age had partly quenched. It was just as when molten and glowing bronze is poured about something cold and solid, it melts it into liquidity even more effectively than the original fire.

(Plutarch, *Life of Pompey*, 8)

News that Pompey was on his way somewhat rattled the army of Perpenna. During the civil war Perpenna had been in Sicily (where he had treated the natives brutally), until Pompey had arrived and thrown Perpenna off the island with barely a fight. Perpenna's men could see the same thing happening in Liguria, and they urged Perpenna to join his forces with those of Sertorius in Iberia. Perpenna had trouble stomaching this idea. He was wealthy and cultured, an aristocrat of Etruscan origins and impeccable pedigree. His family had been consuls of Rome in the previous two generations, and but for the civil wars Perpenna could have expected this same honour for himself. Yet his men seriously suggested that he put himself under the command of a boorish thug from the backwoods simply because the latter had shown he was good at ambuscades and impressing the locals.

Unfortunately, the constitutional position agreed with Perpenna's men. Perpenna and Sertorius were both ex-praetors operating *cum imperio*: that is, with the legal right to command armies (assuming of course that one recognized the legality of the Marians who had bestowed that right). However, Perpenna was a former consular legate and propraetor of Sicily. Therefore he was outranked by Sertorius who was a proconsul (Hispania being a proconsular province, which Sicily was not). Furthermore, Sertorius was operating in his own province, so Perpenna would be expected to defer to him if he went to Iberia. Perpenna knew all this, and it rankled. However it turned out that he could not stay in Liguria either, so circumstances forced his hand.

Reports came that Pompey was crossing the Pyrenees. This leads to the issue of how Pompey had got to the Pyrenees, and why he was now crossing back. We know from Appian that Pompey took his army across the Alps.[4] He made his way around the headwaters of the Rhone and built a new road through the Cottian Alps to outflank the truculent Salluvani tribe who were blocking his advance. In so doing Pompey must have inadvertently circumvented the Perpennan road-block in Liguria. Thereafter he took his army by sea from Massalia in Transalpine Gaul to Massalia's colony of Emporion in Hispania.

It was midsummer, and the sea was the optimal method of moving large numbers of men around quickly and easily. So it seems that until he reached Emporion, Pompey was actually unaware that Perpenna had planted himself across the land line of communication to his rear. Since five legions in Liguria posed a considerable threat to both Pompey in Hispania and to Northern Italy as a whole, Pompey rightly decided to deal with this threat before tackling that posed by Sertorius. After all, Metellus and his army were keeping an eye on Sertorius, but no-one was dealing with Perpenna.

> When they heard the news that Pompey was crossing the Pyrenees, the soldiers took up their weapons and lifted their standards [i.e. made ready to march]. They raised a clamour, demanding that Perpenna take them to Sertorius. If he would not do that, the men threatened, then they would leave him to his own devices and put themselves under the command of a man who could protect himself and his subordinates. So Perpenna gave in, and led his army to join Sertorius.
>
> (Plutarch, *Life of Sertorius*, 15)

At this point the Iberians under Sertorius' command also demonstrated a feisty disregard for the wishes of their leader. Perhaps their morale was boosted by the knowledge that substantial reinforcements were on the way. Perhaps also they were nettled by comments from the legionary regulars of Sertorius that their general would now have enough heavy, disciplined infantry to tackle the Romans head-on instead of by guerrilla warfare. In any case the Iberians now wanted to prove that they too could beat the legions in a stand-up fight. This rather worried Sertorius, because he knew both the legions and his own men, and he knew that they couldn't. However, as a war leader he could not refuse to lead his people into a battle they were determined to have. All he could do was to arrange things so as to mitigate the damage as much as possible.

Since they were determined to have their way, he let them take on the enemy in circumstances where he intended that they should not be crushed but roughly handled, and thus chastised to be more obedient in future.[5] From the scanty details of the engagement, whatever it was, it appears that Sertorius left leadership of the attack to the hot-heads among the Iberians, and turned up in time to save them from the worst consequences of their misjudgement. However, if a fragment of Sallust's history belongs at this point, the retreat to safety became somewhat more risky than planned.

The Iberians fell back on a strong-point, but the Romans were close behind. There was consequently a crush at the entrance which left Sertorius in danger of capture.

They were delayed by the mob crowding the gates. As generally happens when men are frantic, they paid no attention to either officers or orders. The servants of Sertorius carried him on their shoulders into the middle of the throng. From there the men standing above lifted him with their hands onto the wall.

(Sallust, *Histories*, frag 1.112)

Evidently no serious damage was done. In fact Sertorius benefited from the whole business. The Iberians were chagrined by their experience, and Sertorius had again risen in their estimation, both because he had been right, and because he had endangered himself to save them from the consequences of their error. The Iberians were now more prepared to accept a guerilla role, and to work as support troops for the legions which Perpenna was bringing.

Of course, there was also the matter of the legions Pompey had brought, and the matter of Pompey himself. Sertorius publicly derided the newcomer to the Iberian theatre of war as an insolent schoolboy badly in need of a spanking (Pompey was at this time in his mid-twenties). As a welcome, Sertorius' guerrillas delivered the first instalment of that spanking as soon as Pompey crossed back into Hispania. A legion apparently unaware that it was now in highly dangerous territory spread out to forage in the usual fashion of Romans on the march living off the land. As Aquinus had discovered at Langobriga, foraging in Iberia was a fraught business, and the discovery of this fact by Pompey came at the cost of a legion torn to shreds with the loss of its animals and camp servants.

We have this description of the tactics Sertorius used with the Iberians against the legionaries.

He put his skirmishers in the front line, keeping the best troops of his army in reserve. After they had thrown their javelins, the light troops were ordered to retreat through the main body of the infantry and rush to the flanks. There they would quickly re-engage so that as the enemy closed with the stronger troops their flanks were enveloped by the rest.[6]

(Frontinus, *Stratagems*, 2.3.10)

Yet despite his propaganda, Sertorius demonstrated considerable caution in handling his young opponent. 'Sertorius bestowed the greater praise upon Metellus, but it was Pompey he feared' remarked the ex-soldier Velleius Paterculus.[7] Sertorius could afford to be cautious. Pompey was indeed a brilliant general, but he was an inexperienced one. Given time and enough rope, it was inevitable that overconfidence would lead to misjudgement, and when Pompey made that misjudgement, Sertorius intended to hang him with it.

For the moment, Sertorius had a large complement of legionary infantry, and he aimed to use it. His target was the eastern city of Lauron, a strategic asset he had long coveted. Since the arrival of Pompey the acquisition of Lauron had taken on a new urgency, for Pompey's reputation had travelled before him, and many of the cities which had sided with Sertorius were now reconsidering their allegiance. So, just as he had demonstrated at Langobriga that Metellus could not take cities from him, Sertorius wanted to demonstrate at Lauron that he could take cities from Pompey.

Exactly where Lauron was located is uncertain today. There appear to have been several settlements in Hispania with this name. Yet from the prevailing strategic situation and from the fact that the city is identified as having a hill nearby (of which more later), and is situated on a river Lauron must have must have been one of two or three possible sites within fifty miles of Valentia, at a location which would have allowed whomever controlled the city to interfere with the juncture of the armies of Pompey and Metellus.[8] Therefore, since he did want to prevent Pompey and Metellus from joining forces, Sertorius would try to take Lauron, and Pompey would try to stop him. It would be not only a clash of armies, but a clash of generals, and the whole of Iberia awaited the outcome with interest.

This was a masterclass military action, so it has been recorded in detail by Frontinus, the later governor of Britain. The account below paraphrases the description given by Frontinus combined with incidental information from the very un-military Plutarch. Plutarch tells us that Sertorius arrived at Lauron first, and began to set up for a siege. Pompey came up against him soon afterwards 'with all his forces'. As mentioned previously, there was a hill just outside the town. As this was of considerable tactical importance both sides hurried to secure it. Sertorius had the advantage of being on the spot, and he quickly took the hill, and to make sure he kept it, he pitched his camp there.

Pompey, was delighted with the way things had turned out, for he now positioned his army so that Sertorius was, as he believed, caught between the city and the enemy's [i.e. Pompey's] army. So Pompey sent a messenger to the people of Lauron. He invited them to celebrate, and take their seats along the city wall to see how Sertorius enjoyed being besieged. Sertorius was told of this, and found it highly amusing. Sulla's pupil (as he jokingly liked to refer to Pompey) was due another lesson – this time from himself.

(Plutarch, *Life of Sertorius*, 18)

Pompey had a veteran army and was confident of the result should Sertorius want to try his luck in battle, so he made his camp close to that of Sertorius. Either his opponent would take the bait and try to fight out of his trap, or Sertorius would make it plain to his own men and the rest of Iberia that he was afraid to fight.

Sertorius was prepared to fight – but on his own terms. First, he intended to soften up his opponents. Though we do not know of the exact size of Pompey's army, we can assume from his readiness to engage it was at least comparable to that of Sertorius – at a rough guess, between twenty and thirty thousand men. That number of men need a lot of food, water and firewood, and on previous occasions Sertorius had already demonstrated in no uncertain terms that he could stop the Romans from foraging to get it. There were two areas where foraging was possible. One was reasonably close to Pompey's camp, the other more distant. Sertorius ordered his light troops and cavalry to make life hell for the Romans foraging in the nearer tract of land, and to let those foraging in the more distant tract to get on with it undisturbed.

Eventually, the Romans got the message, and tiring of the continual raids by Iberian skirmishers in the nearer tract, they transferred all their foraging to that further away. Eventually, when a large foraging expedition was due to go out, Sertorius made his move. Frontinus describes this with a military man's relish.

Sertorius dispatched ten infantry cohorts armed after the Roman fashion, and ten cohorts of light-armed Iberians under the command of Octavius Gracinus, along with Tarquitius Priscus (This is probably the Tarquitius Priscus of p.66) and two thousand cavalry to lay an ambush against the foragers. These men carried out their orders with enthusiasm. After studying the terrain, they moved by night to conceal the forces described above in a nearby wood. The Iberian skirmishers were posted at the front since they were most capable at warfare by stealth. The heavy infantry were positioned a bit further back, and the cavalry in the rear, so that the neighing of horses would not give the operation away. Then everyone was ordered to rest quietly till the third hour [i.e. around 9 am] of the following day.

(Frontinus, *Stratagems*, 2.5.31)

Pompey's men had also been out overnight, and were well loaded with looted supplies. They were starting to head back to camp, and everything looked so serene that some of the advance guard decided to slip away and rustle up some extra forage. Suddenly light-armed Iberians 'darting out with the swiftness characteristic of their people' (as Frontinus puts it) appeared as if from nowhere and began cutting down the stragglers at the rear of the main party. Bewildered by the suddenness of the attack, the foragers at the rear dropped everything and ran for their lives. Naturally, they ran straight at the main body of foragers who were desperately trying to form a battle line.

If having terrified Romans pushing frantically through their ranks was disruptive, this was as nothing compared to the Sertorian heavy infantry who charged from the woods hot on the heels of the routing men. They crashed into the already disordered enemy and broke them with a single charge. In minutes, the entire foraging force was a broken mass of men, each trying to save himself as best he could. That was when Tarquitius Priscus (from the name he was, like Perpenna, an Etruscan) unleashed his cavalry and turned the foraging area into a killing field.

There was to be no escape. Two hundred and fifty cavalry set off for Pompey's camp at the same time as the opening attack, and since they had scouted out all the short cuts they got there well before the first fleeing forager. Then the cavalrymen methodically worked their way back, killing everyone they met on the way. As a result, by the time Pompey discovered that his foragers were in serious trouble they had been wiped out almost to a man.

Unaware how grave matters had become, Pompey dispatched a legion to cover the retreat of his foragers, for not only were they a considerable body of men – in fact about another legion in strength – but they also had with them all the army's transport. The advancing legion speedily encountered the Sertorian cavalry, and forced it to fall back to the right flank, after which the horsemen dropped out of sight. However, the cautious advance of the legion failed to discover any surviving foragers, because there were, by now, no survivors. What they did encounter were the Sertorian heavy infantry and skirmishers. As the legion formed up to attack these, the Sertorian cavalry reappeared and executed the now routine manoeuvre of hitting the Romans from the rear. As the legion recoiled in shock from this unexpected attack, the enemy infantry hit their disordered ranks from the front. Like the foragers before them, the legion broke, and the massacre resumed.

Pompey did the only thing he could. He hastily formed up the rest of the army and prepared to take to the field to save whatever could be retrieved from the débâcle. As Pompey prepared to march to the rescue he discovered the army of Sertorius had also left its camp and was offering battle. It was a neat move. If Pompey ignored the plight of his legion and marched on Sertorius, his enemy would wait until he was committed to attacking up the hill. Then the offer of battle would be withdrawn, and Sertorius would retire to his camp, by which time Pompey's relief legion would be chopped to bits. It is also possible that with two legions shorn from his army, Pompey would be attacking uphill against an enemy who outnumbered him, and attempting to do this with men whose morale had been damaged by the loss of one legion and who could see another being cut down behind them even as they engaged. If Sertorius decided to stand and fight, he had an excellent chance of winning.

If, on the other hand, Pompey held to his original purpose and went to rescue the legion, then the rear or flank of his army would be exposed to Sertorius' main force, with catastrophic results.

The result was stalemate. As Frontinus comments grimly:

So by the same strategy that inflicted a double disaster [the loss of the foragers and transport, and the destruction of a legion], Sertorius also forced Pompey to be a helpless bystander while his own troops were cut down before his eyes. This was the first battle between Sertorius and Pompey. According to Livy, Pompey's army lost ten thousand men.

(Frontinus, *Stratagems*, 2.5.31)

Not just Pompey beheld these events. The people of Lauron, in the seats which Pompey had invited them to take on their city walls, beheld the humiliation of their would-be rescuer. Though the relevant section of Livy's text has not survived, there is no reason to disbelieve that Pompey had lost two complete legions – the foragers were probably a legion strong, and the failed relief force made up another legion. Add the legion which the Iberians (probably under Hirtuleius) had shredded as the Pompeian army entered the peninsula, and Pompey had lost somewhere around a third of his army without landing a blow on the enemy. The 'schoolboy' was learning his lessons the hard way – and class was not yet dismissed.

Pompey was now confined to his camp with his men on short rations. His position was too strong to be assailed, but Sertorius had him surrounded. All Pompey could do was watch as the citizens of Lauron reluctantly accepted the inevitable, and surrendered. The city had offended Sertorius in the past by refusing to ally with him, and with Metellus undoubtedly on the way it could not be held. Therefore the best use of the city was for demonstration purposes. After the judicious execution of those civic leaders who had rejected Sertorius' initial approach, the rest of the population was allowed to depart unharmed into exile in Lusitania on the other side of the country while the city was burned to the ground.

The demonstration was threefold. Firstly, the rest of Iberia saw that a city which Pompey had come to protect was destroyed right in front of him while he stood by impotently. 'He could not relieve the city, though he was near enough to warm his hands on the flames as it burned' Plutarch imagines the Iberians saying. Secondly, in sparing the population of Lauron, Sertorius demonstrated again that his war was with the Sullani and not the people of Hispania, and thirdly, by totally destroying the city, Sertorius gave grim warning to other cities that his advances were not to be lightly rebuffed.

Another warning, equally grim, followed the destruction of the city. This warning was not to enemies or potential enemies but to Sertorius' own followers. Perpenna's legionaries were veterans. Probably many had fought in the Italian uprising, and more in the civil war which followed. They were tough, and brutal. Sertorius had ordered that the people of Lauron should not be harmed, but we are told that one particular cohort actually prided itself on its savagery. Quite possibly as a deliberate test of their new commander's mettle, some soldiers decided to ignore orders and try a bit of rape and pillage.

This was the first time that some legionaries had met Spanish women at close quarters. These legionaries now discovered that the local ladies took their virtue very seriously. One would-be rapist ended up blinded when his intended victim tore out his eyes with her fingers. Yet worse was to come, for the entire cohort paid for their disobedience with their lives.

Sertorius had every man in the unit executed, though it was composed of Romans.[9] We hear that the condemned were 'addicted to brutality' and given the importance which Sertorius rightly attached to winning Iberian hearts and minds, such men were a downright liability. Sertorius turned the removal of this liability into an educational experience which so deeply impressed Perpenna's men that we hear of no further incidents of insubordination or unlicensed savagery.

Had Sertorius the time, Pompey's fate would have been sealed. If he left his camp to form up for battle, he would expose a vulnerable flank and the rear of his outnumbered army to those Sertorian forces waiting eagerly for him to do just that. If he protected himself against threats from all directions, Sertorius could concentrate his forces and overwhelm him with a frontal attack. In Sertorius' own words, 'the lesson is that a general must worry more about what is behind than what is in front of him'. The lesson had been learned, but Pompey was now too vulnerable to be able to offer battle. Retreat would be hazardous enough to border on the impossible. Pompey had no transport, and was in hostile territory. The risk of ambush was high, and surprise attacks and hit-and-run raids by Sertorius' highly mobile cavalry and infantry were a certainty. If he left camp at all Pompey would emulate the unfortunate Domitius whom Hirtuleius had killed on the banks of the River Anas at the start of the war.

So the only option was to sit tight. This was not a particularly comfortable option because Pompey had sent out foragers for a reason – his army needed supplies. Those supplies were now feeding the Sertorian army which certainly remained to make Pompey's men miserable for as long as possible before the arrival of Metellus forced them to withdraw. The reunion of Metellus and Pompey is not described, but it was certainly in circumstances different from what Pompey would have wished. Certainly the damage to Pompey's army was such that it was no longer effective as a fighting force for the remainder of the campaigning season. This season was drawing to a close anyway, so Pompey moved his army, probably back towards the safety of the Ebro, there to lick his wounds and prepare for the coming year.

This move presented him with another dilemma. His men would greatly prefer to be billeted on a city, and probably expected this. They were already demoralized after what might politely be described as a disappointing campaign to date, so spending a winter 'in camp, among the most savage of enemies' (as Pompey later described it in his own words[10]) would do nothing to lift their spirits.

On the other hand, Metellus would have stressed the point that Sertorius' strength lay in the fact that he had won over the native peoples of Iberia. Those people most likely to be won back to the Roman cause were those living in the cities, for they could see the commercial value of resuming trade with Italy and the rest of the Roman Empire. The city-folk were therefore the very last people whom Pompey should think of alienating. And billeting his army on an Iberian city would drive into the arms of Sertorius any city which considered that it might suffer a similar misfortune in future. Sertorius did not billet his men in Iberian cities. Therefore, however bitterly his men might resent it, Pompey could not do so either.

Lauron had not only been a body blow for Pompey's army, it had been a blow to Pompey's image which meant that neither Pompey nor Metellus were able to gain any traction in the diplomatic war to gain allies which followed the end of the campaigning season. Had Pompey done well, he would have built on an already formidable reputation and might have won over waverers to his side. As it was, Pompey's stock had fallen, while that of Sertorius had risen yet further.

Plutarch explains:

While he had to contend with Metellus, it was thought that much of his success was because his elderly and stolid opponent lacked the temperament to cope with the daring and energy of an opponent who used his light troops in a manner more suitable to a bandit horde than a regular army.

But then Pompey too came over the Pyrenees. Sertorius set up camp near him, and offered and accepted every challenge by which military skill could be tested. In this battle of ability he came out on top, both in frustrating the efforts of his opponent and in out-scheming him in the first place.

By now he was regarded as the most accomplished commander of his time, a reputation which had spread as far as Rome itself. For Pompey had no small reputation, as he had greatly distinguished himself in the wars of Sulla. From Sulla he won the name of Pompey the Great. He had risen so far as to the honour of a triumph before he ever needed to shave.

So many cities dominated by Sertorius were on edge of going over to Pompey until that great engagement which he conducted near the city of Lauron which turned out as no-one had expected, and this was yet [one great deed] amongst many others.

(Plutarch, *Life of Sertorius*, 18)

Sertorius spent the dregs of the campaigning season of 76 BC building on his success at Lauron by bringing yet more opposing tribes under his hegemony. Most of these tribes had nothing against Sertorius or his cause, but such was the nature of life in Iberia that if some tribes were loyal to Sertorius, then those tribes which were their hereditary enemies would automatically side with the Romans. Roman diplomats were renowned for their ability to 'divide and conquer', and they had spent generations in Hispania pitting one against the other tribes which had needed little encouragement in the first place. So Sertorius had not to contend with opposition to himself, but intractable tribal rivalries which generally succumbed to his patent mixture of cunning, assiduous diplomacy and brute force.

We have an example of one such tribal action, probably dating to before the arrival of Pompey, since at that time Sertorius was in Lusitania facing Metellus. (And we know that from 76 through the spring of 75, Sertorius left Hirtuleius to keep Metellus in check in the south-west while he concentrated on Pompey in the east of the peninsula.) But in early 76 or even 77, Sertorius was operating in Lusitania beyond the Tagus against a people called the Characitanians, probably in the area of modern Guadalajara.

Every tribe which Sertorius sought to bring under his control had its individual strengths and weaknesses. The strength of the Characitanians was that it was very hard to get at them. This was not simply because they were as mobile as only Iberian light infantry could be, but because instead of a central city, their strong-point was a huge hill riddled with caves. Not only were these caves inaccessible once defended, but the ground around the hill was so light and powdery that the least impact sent it flying into the air. Few would-be conquerors enjoyed the experience of standing in a dense cloud of dust which sawed at their throats and eyes and got in under their armour while their enemies mocked them from the safety of the caves. The experience was all the more annoying because the caves in the hill of the Characitanians faced north, allowing the tribesfolk a cool, refreshing breeze from the mountains while the opposition suffered in the dust below.[11]

Sertorius considered the matter as he munched dust like those who had tried to take the mountain before him. The next day he ordered his men to start getting the earth into a huge heap, which as a siege mound was so doomed to failure that it moved the Characitanians to tears of laughter. This laughter failed as the usual morning breeze picked up from the north. Sertorius had deliberately not packed down the earth of his mound, and the light, powdery soil was lifted by the breeze and wafted into the mountain caves.

As the wind grew stronger, Sertorius gave the dust-storm plenty of assistance, ordering his cavalry to ride back and forth across the remnants of the mound to raise further clouds of dust, while the infantry worked hard to break up any clods of earth. The next day, he did it all again. The Characitanians had never considered that warfare by air pollution might be used against them, so their caves had no defence as the wind 'rushed in upon them, quickly blinding their eyes and filling their lungs. They all but choked as they battled to breathe rough air mixed with dust and powdered earth'.[12]

After three days, the Characitanians conceded that Sertorius was deserving of his great reputation and offered their surrender. The value of this particular episode – and the reason it was singled out by Sertorius' biographer – was that it proved that those intending to defy Sertorius needed to contend not just with his armies, but with an ingenuity against which solid walls offered no protection.

The last people to discover this in 76 were the people of Contrebia Belaisca, a city in the modern Zaragosa province. This was a political and religious centre situated not too far from where Pompey had his winter quarters and the city's fall was probably one of the reasons why the newcomer felt that he spent his first winter in Iberia surrounded by 'savage enemies'. After all, there were friendly cities still available, not to billet soldiers on, but where a camp could be sited close enough to supply certain amenities. Pompey would not voluntarily put his demoralized and disillusioned army into the middle of unfriendly territory. Therefore, the territory must have become unfriendly after he had set up his camp there.

Chapter 7

Hearts and Minds

At the start of the campaigning year of 75 BC, Sertorius could regard the military situation in Iberia with some satisfaction. His repeated campaigns in Celtiberia had forced many of the tribes occupying that truculent region to acknowledge his authority. Nevertheless, fighting the locals took time and energy away from dealing with the more serious threat posed by the Roman armies. For example archaeological evidence from Contrebia Belaisca suggests that though Sertorius took the city just in time to deprive Pompey of a local ally, his forces had been besieging the place for some time before that.[1]

The peninsula was large in comparison to the size of the armies operating in it, and therefore we should not think of the situation as being similar to the Western Front 1916 with fixed lines drawn across Iberia where the Romans held one side and the Sertorians the other. Instead Iberia was a patchwork of cities and tribal confederations. Some of the patches were firmly attached to one side or the other, and the loyalty of others shifted depending on the proximity and affiliation of the nearest substantial army. Other patches – particularly in Celtiberia – were very firmly on their own side, and more interested in local battles with the neighbours than the larger war being waged across the peninsula.

None of the generals involved in the war controlled forces anywhere near enough to enforce their authority over a wide region, especially as their armies were largely engaged in squaring up to each other and so tended to cancel each other out. Even Sertorius, who was far more interested in gaining control over Iberian tribes than either of his opponents, tended to do this during intervals when the Romans were not pressing him too hard.

Perpenna had added fifty-three cohorts of legionary infantry to Sertorius' army. Even if the strict disciplinary pruning after Lauron had reduced the number to fifty-two this had given Sertorius the ability to match the Romans blow for blow on the battlefield. This legionary infantry was what had enabled him to push eastwards in the first place and destroy Lauron. At this time Valentia itself was under his control, though the record does not say when this happened. However, this meant that 75 BC started with the Roman forces divided by a wedge of Sertorian-held land that reached to the east coast.

Metellus was firmly encamped somewhere near the river Baetis in the territory of the unwarlike Turdetani, with loyal Roman colonies such as Italica to provide him with supplies through the winter. Thanks to his unremitting efforts, Sertorius held most of the land in the central interior just north of the Roman position. If there was such a thing as a front line here, it was the southern arc of Celtiberian hill-fortresses dignified by the name of cities which held to the Roman cause mainly because the Roman army was too close for an alternative affiliation. Whenever he could spare the time or the manpower Sertorius would pick off another of these places, but they were numerous and time and manpower were much needed for other matters.

The allegiance of the south-west was a shifting matter which seems largely to have depended on who had the larger army there at the time. Sertorius knew that if he could force Metellus out of Turdetania in the south-east, then the south-west would drop into his lap as a matter of course. Metellus knew that if he could push the Lusitanians over the Tagus in the north-west then Hispania Ulterior – including the south-west – would become his province in fact as well as in name.

Up in the north-east the difficult terrain of mountains and rivers meant that groups with very different views on the governance of Hispania could exist only a few miles apart. So Emporion was just one of a string of cities near the river Ebro that were unshakeably Roman, and Osca was but the leading city of many in the mountains that were unflinchingly loyal to Sertorius. On the Atlantic side of the Pyrenees, what is today (and was probably even then) the Basque country was allegedly loyal to the Roman government.[2] In reality this probably means that the local Vascones disliked their nearby rivals of the Arevaci who were among the most committed followers of Sertorius, and so picked the opposite side. Neither the Vascones nor their neighbours the Cantabrians were particularly impressed by Roman rule when it was actually applied to them, and the Cantabrians at least were still fighting the legions in the time of Augustus.

What all this shows is that while the central government in Rome saw Iberia as neatly divided into Hispania Citerior and Hispania Ulterior this cartographic abstraction in no way reflected the situation on the ground. With a fine disregard for provincial borders Pompey and Metellus moved as the military situation demanded. Few tribes in the north or central interior knew whether the Roman government considered them Citerians or Ulteriorans and it is unlikely that any of them lost sleep over the question.

Sertorius, like Vercingetorix in Gaul a generation later, was trying to create a common national identity from tribes who had never considered themselves as anything but enemies occupying the same peninsula. It is to his project that we now turn.

Firstly, we must acknowledge the injustice of the designations used heretofore in this chapter and before. For convenience, Pompey, Metellus and their armies are referred to as 'Roman', as if Sertorius, Perpenna and their armies described themselves as anything but. In reality, from principle and for practical reasons Sertorius insisted that he was as Roman – actually more Roman – than his opponents. His was not an Iberian uprising against Roman rule. Sertorius was a functionary of the last legitimate government in Rome who continued the fight against an armed faction which had deposed that government by force. His war was a civil war, and while he and the Sullani might have very different ideas about the Rome they were fighting for, at no time did Sertorius see himself as fighting for Hispania against Rome.

Therefore, Sertorius faced the challenge of creating a Roman province with a common identity that in no way diminished the necessary blood-lust of its warriors. This was a tricky challenge, for the one thing that kept many of the tribes fighting together was their mutual hatred of Rome. For example, among Sertorius' most dedicated followers were the Arevaci. These Celtiberian tribesmen had been the proud occupants of Numantia when Scipio Aemilianus had flattened it a generation before. This, and a string of other grievances (see ch3ff) made them less pro-Sertorian than deeply sincere supporters of anyone who would help them to kill Roman legionaries. In fact elements of the Arevaci were still trying to do this in AD 25, almost a century later.[3]

Yet Sertorius still dreamed of returning to Rome should a future Lepidus manage to bring about a change of government. To do this, he would have to show that his stewardship of Hispania had been that of a

Roman governor, and not that of an Iberian rebel. The problem was that many of those fighting for him were doing so precisely because they saw him more as an Iberian rebel than a Roman governor.

Somehow Sertorius had to square the circle, and his technique for doing so is not considered radical only because it was so successful that it thereafter became standard operating procedure for the Roman Republic and Empire, and also for the British Empire long after that. In summary, the Sertorius procedure was simple and logical. Romanize (or Anglicize) the local elite – the top merchants, aristocrats and administrators – and the rest of the population would follow. Yet Sertorius did it first. And it was not so obvious back then.

True, Rome had long been the most inclusive of empires. Had not the sixth king of Rome, Servius Tullius, first entered the city as a captive in a Roman triumph? Were not both Marcus Tullius Cicero (no relation) and Caius Marius both prime examples of Roman citizens though their forebears had bitterly fought the Romans from their ancestral home of Arpinum? By freely granting Roman citizenship to the conquered at a time when other states jealously guarded this privilege, Rome had grown great.

Now Sertorius planned to extend the policy from the Italiot peoples, who were in any case close to the Romans in culture, to those whom those same Italians would have regarded as wild and unconquered barbarians. Not to all of these 'barbarians', and not at once, but Sertorius made it plain that advancement in his Hispania would depend on how enthusiastically candidates embraced Roman culture. Heretofore the rule had been conquest first, Romanization afterwards, and technically Sertorius was following that rule. After all, he was a Roman promagistrate, and these men were obeying his commands. So therefore, *ipso facto* they were under Roman authority and Romanization could and should proceed. It was a daring experiment. As the great German historian Theodor Mommsen remarked of the provinces of the empire: 'It was the first attempt to accomplish their Romanization not by extirpating the old inhabitants and filling their places with Italian emigrants, but by Romanizing the provincials themselves'.[4]

It helped that the first aspect of Romanization had been an unqualified success. Roman military weapons, formations and signals had led to unprecedented military achievements by the Iberians. Admittedly the most glorious of these achievements had been against the Romans that

Sertorius was trying to get the leading Iberians to become, but as Sertorius explained, those Romans were Sullani, so it didn't matter.

The conversion to Roman-style weaponry was easily accomplished through a deft perversion of traditional Iberian warrior values. By these values, a great warrior had an expensively decorated helmet and a gloriously ornamented shield. His clothing was of the finest quality, for the perfect Iberian warrior did not just overcome his enemy on the battlefield with his martial ability, he overawed him first with the splendour of his person.

Sertorius was lavish with his gifts of silver-chased helmets, and swords, and tunics and cloaks to those who supported his programme, and to those who distinguished themselves on the battlefield. And naturally all those helmets, shields, swords and clothing were Roman-style material. Consequently, the Iberian elite not only gave up their old military clothing and hardware, they did so cheerfully and practically fell over themselves in their eagerness to obtain the Roman replacements. And as did those whom the common people considered their betters, so did the common people.

The next step in creating a unified culture and identity was to give the people a common capital. For practical reasons this had to be Osca, as this was the optimal point for thumping Roman reinforcements wearied by crossing the Pyrenees and from fighting the warlike tribes the mountain range contained. By arguing military necessity, Sertorius could sidestep the thorny political issue of which tribe should have the honour of hosting his headquarters.

Iberian menfolk Sertorius could keep in his retinue and teach Roman manners by example. But the mothers and children could not be part of this retinue, both because local custom dictated otherwise, and because that retinue was often engaged in high-speed hit-and-run operations against the Romans. So Sertorius set up a school for the offspring of tribal leaders at Osca. Membership of the school was a keenly-sought honour.

At Osca, a large city, he gathered those [children] of the highest birth. These he put under teachers who gave them a Greek and Roman education. Actually, under the guise of educating these princelings Sertorius had made hostages of them. But he promised the fathers that when the children were grown they would share his administration and power. So the fathers watched in delight as their sons decorously went to their lessons in purple-bordered togas. Sertorius paid for their education, held frequent examinations, and awarded prizes as appropriate.

(Plutarch, *Life of Sertorius*, 14)

Before we accuse those fathers of gullibility, it is worth noting that they had a lot to gain. However the on-going war turned out, Rome was not going to go away. Someone who could negotiate with the Romans on their own terms, knowing their jokes, laws and customs was far more likely to get a good deal for his people than someone whom the Romans regarded as a hairy barbarian, no matter how sophisticated his actual culture. And someone would have to administer Iberia for Rome, whichever side won Sertorius' civil war. Those people would need in positions of influence men who understood both the local people and the Roman way of doing things. The administrators of the Hispania of the future would need – or actually be – graduates of the Academie Sertorius.

Furthermore, every local tribal grouping of note was represented at the academy. These tribal leaders of the future would grow up knowing each other at a personal level. For Sertorius this was an important step in creating a single people from the Iberians, but to the more calculating type of Iberian chieftain there were advantages to the idea even if the whole scheme came smashing down. After all, a tribal leader was more likely to do deals with another tribal leader who had suffered the same Latin lessons in the same class. Someone whose trust had been earned in boyhood exploits was more likely to marry his daughter than a possibly imperfect stranger, and so be drawn into a tribal alliance.

In short, the academy offered the younger generation the opportunity to create the first old-boy network in Iberia, and no tribal leader wanted his offspring to miss out. The carrot of Roman citizenship was dangled before these leaders, with Sertorius offering his good offices to ensure this valuable reward once he was securely again in a position to influence the Roman senate. In the meantime he made clear what benefits such citizenship could bring by making it clear that though the chieftains were honoured allies, Hispania was to be a Roman province run by Romans.

But the generosity of spirit of Sertorius was demonstrated, firstly, in the title of 'Senate' to that group of senatorial exiles from Rome who had joined his cause. He appointed 'quaestors' and 'praetors' from among them, and had all these organized in the fashion of his native land.

(Plutarch, *Life of Sertorius*, 22)

(The historian Appian saw this differently saying 'He enrolled a council of 300 members from the friends who were with him, and called this the 'Roman Senate' in mockery of the real one'.[5] Despite this cynicism, the fact remained – to be in the inner circle of Sertorius, one had to be a Roman.)

Secondly he used the armies, cities and wealth of Iberians without ever pretending to the Iberians themselves that they had any share of his power. Instead he put Roman generals and officers to command them. This gave the impression that he was fighting for freedom [from the Sullani] for the Romans, and not taking the side of the Iberians against Rome.

(Plutarch, *Life of Sertorius*, 22)

This was an enormously complex feat of diplomacy. Sertorius had to persuade the Romans that he was in charge of a Roman province, while at the same time leading Iberian tribesmen against Roman armies – and beating them. He had to persuade those Iberian tribesmen to fight Romans while at the same time insisting on the primacy of Romans at every level of the civil and military administration. There was only one way to do this – and that was by suggesting to the leaders of the Iberian people that they (or their sons) would become Romans too one day.

Thus the Romanization of a provincial elite was pioneered by Sertorius not as a matter of enlightened government but as a desperate measure adopted because it was the only possible solution to the conundrum which Sertorius had to resolve. As it turned out, it was a very good solution, and if it seems obvious to us today, it should be remembered that one of the definitions of a very good idea is that it should be blindingly obvious – when seen with hindsight.

Sertorius' promise of citizenship to his Iberian supporters carried all the more weight because other generals in Hispania, including Metellus and Pompey had been well aware of the persuasive power of that same promise, and exercised it in the areas which they controlled.[6] Cicero at one point mentions in passing how Spanish poets praised Metellus in Latin while the latter was in Cordoba, and indeed, one of Cicero's closest business associates L. Cornelius Balbus was originally from Gades, and had been given Roman citizenship by Pompeius the late, unlamented father of Pompey.[7]

So the idea of attaining the citizenship for one's family was not a pipe-dream but a very real prospect, and one which Sertorius used to keep his Iberian allies in line. The sight of their children in Roman tunics was not merely the sight of Sertorius teaching the lads to emulate Romans, but the physical demonstration of the promise that these children could well become Romans themselves, and should be prepared for their new status.

For the present Sertorius presented one aspect of Roman power which was highly unusual for a Roman governor of that period anywhere in the empire – he did not abuse it. We have no idea whether this was due to Sertorius' natural moral reticence or because it would have been suicidal for him to do otherwise, but in either case, the Iberian people under the rule of Sertorius found themselves ably-governed and with a degree of justice and prosperity unusual in that war-wracked land. In part this prosperity was due to the fact that tribute was no longer rendered to Rome (the archaeology of this period has revealed that locally-produced silver denarii appeared in unprecedented numbers).

There are also indications that Sertorius, now he had a base of operations on the east coast, renewed contact with his former associates, the pirates with whom he had allied before his expedition to Mauritania (p.58). These he set up in a base at the 'promontory of Diana' between Valencia and a settlement whose Greek name of *Acra Leuca* (White Mountain) became modern Alicante.

These pirates had the same utility for Sertorius as they had for that inveterate enemy of Rome on the other side of the Mediterranean, Mithridates VI of Pontus. That is, the pirates served to interdict trade from and to Roman-held cities on the eastern seaboard of Hispania, and to intercept supplies to the armies of Pompey and Metellus (Pompey later complained bitterly about how few supplies reached him (p.150)). The produce of this maritime pillage was duly exchanged for the silver which Sertorius possessed in abundance, and thus linked the Sertorian portion of Iberia with the products of the rest of the Mediterranean world. At the same time the pirates acted as intermediaries between Sertorius and the rest of the world, bringing him packets of mail from his sympathizers in the senate (not all followers of Lepidus fell with their leader), and without doubt being the medium by which Sertorius established diplomatic contact with Mithridates (of which more anon).

For the leaders of the Iberian people, the fact that Sertorius offered the continuity of their power and influence even in a Roman world was reason enough to accept his leadership. For the average Iberian, the lead given by their traditional leaders was a considerable incentive in itself, but more important was the fact that even in trying circumstances, Sertorius contrived to establish the basics of good governance in each area – internal security, justice and a sound economy. Added to which, of course, Sertorius was up to this point a wildly successful war leader, and the sound economy of those tribes which followed him was partly based on plunder taken from those who had been slower to see the light.

His success in war led to thousands of warriors being literally devoted to him. In Iberia it was usual for a war leader to have warriors who tied their fortunes to his by swearing a vow that they would under no circumstances survive should their leader happen to fall. Given the fact that Iberian leaders were expected to lead by example in battle and suffered a disproportionate casualty rate, few men took the personal risk of so dedicating themselves to a leader, unless that leader was Sertorius.

> The barbarians call a 'consecration' that custom of the Iberians which demanded that the shield-bearers who surrounded their leader should die with him if he fell. Consequently other leaders had few such shield-bearers and companions. However Sertorius had a bodyguard of many thousands who had sworn themselves to live or die with him.
>
> (Plutarch, *Life of Sertorius*, 14)

Future events show that the enthusiasm which Plutarch says the Iberian people felt for their leader was rooted mainly in the success that Sertorius had enjoyed up to this point. Such loyalty was widespread, but the roots were shallow. There are also indications that the popularity of Sertorius was less widespread than his biographer wishes us to believe. One reason for this is that Plutarch has the literary aim of demonstrating – as he explicitly says in his preamble to Sertorius' biography – that 'fortune ever changes her course' and proved 'a more intractable opponent than those who were openly his enemies'.[8] Therefore having shown how low Sertorius had fallen earlier in his career, it must now be shown that fortune had led him to completely dominate the stage in Iberia, and any recalcitrant native tribes booing from the stalls must be drowned out with a fine literary flourish.

Yet the fact that Celtiberian campaigns consumed what little spare time Sertorius possessed tells us that the tribes in the hills north of the river Baetis looked not at the charisma of Sertorius but at the marching distance of the legions based around Italica for indications of where to place their allegiance. We have seen that the Vascones supported the Romans simply because their rivals supported Sertorius. It is almost certain that in every town and tribe there were factions which, to a greater or lesser extent, supported one side or another. Since both Sertorius and his opponents were explicitly fighting for a Roman Hispania, ideologies such as freedom, independence and nationalism were outside the debate. Therefore it was reasonable enough for those living in the province to opt for the side which offered them the best deal. Despite the thousands sworn to die alongside him, overall loyalty to Sertorius was shallow precisely because his cause had little to offer the Iberians that was worth their dying for.

Sertorius was shrewd enough to understand that the best way to keep his allies loyal was to keep defeating the people to whom those allies might otherwise be tempted to defect. Therefore, his objective in the year 75 BC was pretty much as it had been in previous years: to defeat the Romans in the peninsula, and hope for a change of government among the Romans in Italy. His contribution to a change of government in Rome would be to embarrass the present government by its inability to make progress in Hispania, while at the same time making the stalemate as expensive as possible.

It will be remembered that Spanish silver had in the past made wars in Iberia self-financing, and even profitable. But that was when the mines were producing their silver for the government in Rome, and the treasury was swelled by the loot from defeated Iberian tribes and cities. Under Sertorius Hispania kept its silver to itself, and loot was extremely hard to come by. Therefore, the government in Italy had to pay for the war and supply the troops (with Sertorius' pirate colleagues taking their cut) at a time when the empire was financially strained from the damage and expense of the recent civil war and the on-going issue of Mithridates in Asia Minor.

During the winter, Pompey may well have had to deal with reproachful messages from his allies in Rome. They had stuck out their necks to support his unconstitutional appointment to command in Hispania, and unless the wonder boy started to deliver on the promises they had made, Pompey's backers were vulnerable to their enemies in the senate.

Even without such urging Pompey had reason enough to want to start the year's campaigning with a victory. His men needed a boost in morale, and one should not discount the wounded pride of a young man who had previously considered winning to be almost his natural right.

For both Pompey and Metellus there were two first priorities for the campaign of 75. One was strategic – the Sertorians had to be cleared from the east coast and a clear line of communication established that ran without interruption from Emporion in the north to Carthago Nova in the south. This would allow the two commanders to link up when the military situation demanded it, and to move supplies and manpower as necessary between their two armies. Secondly – and in a wider perspective just as importantly – the two commanders had to do something to prove that they were doing something to justify the huge expense of money and manpower which the Iberian war was costing the central government.

The chronology of events becomes ever more confused as the war went on, and what follows is a reconstruction based on a reading of the fragmentary and confused sources. The reader must remember that other interpretations are possible.[9] However, and notwithstanding this caveat, there could be little doubt that the start of the campaigning season saw Metellus preparing to march north while Pompey marched south. The Sertorians on the east coast had the choice of abandoning their gains or being caught between the two armies.

Sertorius had invested a lot of effort and prestige in taking his bit of the east coast, and he had five legions of regular Roman infantry and a host of Iberian tribesmen with which he intended to keep it. Being on the defensive meant that for much of the time he would be able to choose his ground, and even on the relatively benign east coast, there was plenty of terrain that a good general could get to work in his favour. And friends and enemies alike were agreed that Sertorius was a good general. If Pompey and Metellus wanted to join their forces, they would have to fight for the territory which currently separated them.

Fortunately for Pompey, it would appear that over the winter the Sertorian commanders had switched their responsibilities. Perpenna faced Pompey while Sertorius and Hirtuleius took on Metellus. There were good reasons for this. Pompey had a weakened and demoralized army which might well fall apart if defeated in a regular battle. But even in its current state Pompey's army would be too much for Iberian tribesmen alone to handle in a stand-up fight. And if Pompey was not to be delayed and harassed but actually defeated and stopped on his march south, at some point a stand-up fight was inevitable.

The regular Roman infantry were now under the overall command of Sertorius, but it is clear that Perpenna remained their immediate commander in the field. Sertorius had no reason to believe that Perpenna was not a competent commander – after all he and Lepidus had extricated their army from defeat near Rome and brought it largely intact to Iberia.

Therefore, it probably seemed best to let Perpenna get on with beating Pompey while Sertorius and Hirtuleius took on the less glorious, but trickier job of making sure that Metellus did not interfere. Since Perpenna had the heavy infantry, Sertorius had no way of stopping Metellus in a direct confrontation. So it was back to delay and ambush, playing cat-and-mouse with Iberians against legionaries. This was a dangerous game, but one which Sertorius could play like no-one else, and this is probably why he was not present when the first clash of the year came against Pompey near Valentia. (Another possibility was that he was in the far north sorting out matters near Osca.)

The ease with which Sertorius had beaten Pompey the year before may have caused Perpenna to under-estimate Pompey as an opponent. The pride of the aristocratic Etruscan refused to allow that Sertorius was his better in anything but rank. So if a country yokel like Sertorius could run rings around Pompey – and Pompey was himself a country yokel from Picenum, after all – well, how hard could it be?

Much of what we know of the battle which followed comes from a single sentence from Plutarch's *Life of Pompey*.

Near Valentia he [Pompey] crushed the generals Herennius and Perpenna, men of military experience among the refugees with Sertorius, and slew more than ten thousand of their men.[10]

The Herennius referred to here is an obscure character, and since it appears he was among the slain in this battle, there is no opportunity to know him better. Perpenna was humiliated and had lost the Sertorians two irreplaceable legions of Roman infantry. He also lost the Sertorians the city of Valentia, a disaster that sent Sertorius hurrying to take charge of the northern front in person.

The dilemma which Sertorius faced is known to military strategists today as 'The Napoleon problem'. When a general enjoys the confidence of his men they are more assured of victory and also fight harder to impress their commander. Since the general earned that confidence by being a superior general in any case, his chances of success in any given situation were far greater than the chances of a subordinate in the same position. The problem which Napoleon faced was the same as that which Sertorius faced eighteen hundred years before him – one cannot be everywhere at once, and the enemy can take liberties with the marshals that they cannot with the master.

So, even as Sertorius set about retrieving the situation in the north, Hirtuleius made things worse in the south by getting himself drawn into a pitched battle with Metellus. For all that Plutarch relishes Sertorius' description of Metellus as an 'old woman', slow and over-fond of luxury, the fact is that even Sertorius himself had failed to land many telling blows on Metellus at a time when his generals were demolishing other Roman armies. The 'old woman' was a capable fighter who had the misfortune of being matched against a genius. Hirtuleius was good, but he was not in Sertorius' class, and Metellus was his equal. And if the generals were evenly matched, it came down to the soldiers, and as Sertorius had repeatedly pointed out, in a battle between Roman legionaries and Iberian *scutati*, the legions were going to win.

We have a few details of this battle. It is recorded in a brief mention in a summary of the historian Livy. (Livy, like Sallust produced a complete history of the Sertorian war. Frustratingly, nothing but a few fragments remain of Sallust, and a hugely abbreviated version of Livy called the *Epitome*. It is the *Epitome* which tells us 'The Proconsul Quintus Metellus defeated Lucius Hirtuleius, a quaestor of Sertorius, and his army.')[11] Our best description comes from two extracts from Frontinus.

When Metellus Pius was fighting in Hispania against Hirtuleius, his opponent mustered his army soon after dawn and marched on Metellus' encampment. Metellus kept his men behind their entrenchments until noon. The reason was that this time of year was extremely hot. Once the enemy began swooning in the heat, he easily defeated them as his legionaries were fresh and at their full strength.

(Frontinus, *Stratagems*, 2.1.2)

Since his enemy remained drawn up in front of his camp for hours, Metellus had plenty of time to examine the enemy's dispositions and make his own accordingly.

In Hispania when Metellus defeated Hirtuleius in battle, he had observed that Hirtuleius had posted his strongest units in the centre [of his battle-line]. Accordingly he held back the centre of his own army. Thus he avoided meeting that part of the enemy's forces in combat until he had won on the flanks and could completely envelop those remaining in the middle.

(Frontinus, *Stratagems*, 2.3.5)

This was the classic tactic used by Hannibal at Cannae almost a century and a half beforehand. It had worked then, and it worked now. The historian Orosius wrote much later, but probably used Livy for at least part of his account, which tells us that the battle, fought near Italica, was a bloody defeat costing the Sertorians 20,000 men. Chastened, Hirtuleius fled north.

The defeat of Hirtuleius temporarily dispersed the Sertorian threat to the Roman heartland south-east of the River Baetis. Even if he had not been on the move before, Metellus now had nothing stopping him from joining his army with Pompey's. Sertorius had to work fast to avoid being caught between two. This is because he had taken over command of the Roman regular infantry. With Iberian tribesmen the issue would not arise, because Iberian tribesmen were almost impossible to trap.

His men were accustomed to disperse ... and then to come together again, so that often Sertorius roamed unaccompanied, then took to the field again with an army of a hundred and fifty thousand men at his back, just as a winter stream suddenly swells into a torrent.

(Plutarch, *Life of Pompey*, 19)

However, if Roman legionaries could not vanish like smoke before an advancing enemy, they could certainly demonstrate their solidity in no uncertain fashion. Sertorius advanced rapidly northward with the intention of taking the young pretender out of play before this veteran colleague could enter the game.

An older, wiser commander than Pompey would have played for time and held back until Metellus could close off Sertorius' retreat and both armies could engage their elusive opponent simultaneously. But Roman commanders were never keen on sharing the glory of victory, and Pompey was flushed with his success against Perpenna and burning to avenge the humiliation he had suffered at Lauron. Consequently, far from playing for time, he rushed into battle with the express intention of having it all done and dusted by the time Metellus showed up.

With his opponent obligingly coming at him, Sertorius sent Perpenna to keep Metellus at bay until the issue with Pompey could be decided at a time and place of Sertorius' choosing. He chose late afternoon as the time, and the banks of the river Sucro, not far from the town of that name as the place. The late afternoon was chosen since it gave both sides time to complete the engagement. Thereafter, if Pompey was victorious, Sertorius would be able to pull his beaten army away under cover of night. If, on the other hand, Pompey was routed, his beaten army would be caught by the mobile Iberian infantry in the dark in unfamiliar terrain, and cut to pieces before it could reach safety. It was a good example of the attention to detail at which the conscientious Sertorius excelled.

The evening was an ominous one, lit by flashes from a thunderstorm over the horizon.[12] This the veteran troops on either side ignored, and each general took station on his army's right wing. This meant that Sertorius faced Afranius, Pompey's second-in-command, while Pompey faced an unknown subordinate of Sertorius.

Battles in antiquity were always a gamble. However well a commander prepared, and no matter how well-drilled and disciplined the troops, the slightest chance could turn the tide. When this happened, it was up to the general to decisively take events by the forelock and drag them in the appropriate direction. Both Sertorius and Pompey fought well in the battle, but the end result was another lesson in generalship for Pompey, and one that he was not soon to forget.

Like almost every Roman general, Pompey was not lacking in courage. He and a huge enemy infantryman soon engaged in a hand-to-hand fight, and though Pompey was on horseback, he and his opponent fought almost eye-to-eye. (An exaggeration, perhaps, but Roman horses were much smaller than their modern cavalry counterparts.) Pompey managed to lop off his opponent's hand, but was himself wounded in the thigh. Nevertheless, his wing pushed hard and the enemy in front began to fall back in disarray.

When Sertorius realized that his left was in danger of collapse, he turned over command of the fight against Afranius to his subordinates, and took over the left wing himself. The presence of Sertorius in their ranks inspired his men. 'Those of his men who were already in retreat he rallied, those who were still holding in their ranks he encouraged, then he launched a fresh attack on Pompey, who was following up hard.'[13]

Again the difference between the two generals became apparent. When the tide of battle began to turn in Pompey's favour, Sertorius had been quick to detect the change and had reacted promptly, decisively and so effectively that he not only rallied his wavering troops but shocked the attacking forces of Pompey with a counter-attack so vigorous that it put his opponents into disorder which quickly turned into a near-rout. On the other hand, Pompey misread the course of the battle to the point where the collapse of his advance took him by surprise, and he was totally ineffective at doing anything about it. Partly this was not his fault. The soldiers of Sertorius trusted him to get them out of a dangerous situation. Pompey's men had seen Sertorius spank their commander up and down the Iberian peninsula and were fully prepared to believe that it was about to happen again.

Pompey did his best to stem the tide of his men's retreat. His failure to do so meant that he left his own retreat until somewhat beyond the last possible moment. He was saved by his horse – not because it carried him to safety, but because it was captured by the enemy. Anyone who knew Pompey could have guessed that his steed would be an example of the finest horseflesh ever to set hoof in Hispania, and this equine apparition was further decorated with golden headgear and exquisite and valuable trappings.

It was all too much for the mercenary Lybian mercenaries who had been in the vanguard of Sertorius' army ever since his return from Africa.

Given the choice of capturing the horse or the general who abandoned it in his flight, the Lybians opted for the horse and fell to quarrelling about how to divide their booty. In the confusion, Pompey, despite his wounded thigh, quietly retreated to the safety of his own ranks to fight another day.

Pompey's men had not managed to fight off the Sertorian advance, but Sertorius was still grappling with the Napoleon problem. He was now forced to leave the promising situation on his left to return to the right wing. Here Afranius had overwhelmed the opposition and pushed it back into its camp. (This is another indication that we are looking at a battle fought between regular Roman legionary armies. Iberian irregulars would simply disperse after a defeat, but legionaries made a marching camp.) The camp had not held either, and Afranius' men, convinced the victory was theirs, busily set about pillaging the place. Consequently the appearance of a vengeful Sertorius and half his army came as a dreadful shock – and for a great many of the pillagers, it was the last shock of their lives. 'Returning from his victory on the other wing, Sertorius fell upon the straggling and confused soldiers of Afranius and slew great numbers of them'.[14]

Meanwhile, back at the rearguard, Perpenna encountered Metellus for the first time. The historian Appian tells us baldly 'Metellus defeated Perpenna and plundered his camp'.[15] This meant that Metellus was now able to continue his advance in time to make an appearance the next day just as Pompey and Sertorius, their armies battered but undaunted, were squaring up to go another round.

Orosius, with his usual bloodthirsty relish, gives the casualties in the fighting to date at 10,000 men on each side.[16] Even half this figure would have represented a disaster for Sertorius, for it meant that the force of Roman regular infantry which Perpenna had brought to Hispania had, in the course of three brisk battles been knocked down to about a single legion. True, Pompey had been mauled to an even greater degree, but (given resolve on the part of the central government in Rome) his troops could be replenished from Rome's huge reserves of Italian manpower. Perpenna's troops had been a one-off windfall for Sertorius which had now largely been spent.

With Perpenna's failure to delay Metellus, there was no chance for Sertorius to have another go at Pompey on equal terms. He had lost his chance to take Pompey out of the campaign, and he knew it. His bitter remark has been preserved by Plutarch 'If the old woman had not made an appearance, I'd have thrashed the boy and packed him off to Rome.'

But the old woman had indeed turned up. When he came to meet Pompey, the latter ordered his lictors to lower their fasces. The fasces were symbols of the rank of a Roman magistrate – or promagistrate – and by having his lowered Pompey acknowledged that he was in the presence of a superior rank. Metellus was aware that his young ally's morale was desperately fragile, so he insisted on treating Pompey as his equal. He was well aware that the army Pompey commanded obeyed its general rather than the senate in Rome, and the last thing Metellus wanted was for Pompey to get so discouraged that he picked up his toys and went home. A bit of flattery was in order.

Furthermore, Metellus had reason to be grateful. While Pompey had been serving as Sertorius' punching-bag, Metellus had been able to make considerable progress with the war. Pompey might have suffered, but his opponents had suffered also. In fact so rough a start to the campaigning season had the army of Sertorius endured that it was in no condition to deal with the combined forces of the battered Pompey and the seasoned and (so far that year) consistently victorious Metellan army. Sertorius had no choice but to abandon the coast and retreat towards Clunia in the highlands of Celtiberia – something he could now do more easily because he had far fewer Roman legionaries to shepherd through his retreat.

Like many a guerilla leader afterwards, Sertorius had discovered that the moment of greatest vulnerability comes at the moment when an attempt is made to stand one's ground against the soldiers of a regular army in head-on combat. Perpenna had provided the men to make such a stand, but he had not provided the generalship to go with it, and had lost the better part of the army he had brought. Nevertheless, Sertorius still had his Iberians, and they were on their home ground in the Celtiberian interior. Metellus would follow him there at his peril.

Chapter 8

The Turn of the Tide

S ertorius had fought hard for the east coast, and had matched his enemies blow-for-blow in battle. Nevertheless, by his retreat he had to publicly concede that he had suffered a large-scale setback. But as the poet Horace remarks 'Good fortune conceals the ability of a general, adversity reveals it.'[1]

The first concern of Sertorius was for the morale of his men. For this he required his white fawn. Since things had been proceeding unsatisfactorily for much of the year, there had been little occasion to produce the animal to announce glad tidings. So Sertorius let it be known that in fact his cervine advisor had wandered off, with the implicit explanation that the lack of this creature's divinely-inspired advice lay behind the ill fortune and misjudgements that had marked the year so far. (According to the grammarian Aulus Gellius, writing much later, the doe was safely secluded in a nearby swamp.[2]) Fortunately, as Sertorius now informed his lieutenants, the beast had now been retrieved, and he awaited only the right moment to make the fact public.

He concealed the doe and waited for several days. Then he went to the council with a joyful expression on his face. He informed the barbarian chieftains that in his dreams he had been told by a god that good fortune was on its way. Then he took his place and began to judge the cases of those who had appealed to him.

At this point those keeping the doe released her from somewhere close by. Seeing Sertorius the doe bounded joyfully towards his judgement seat, and stood to put her head in his lap, and, as was her habit before, licked his hand. Sertorius returned her affection, stroked her and even cried a bit. After being initially dumbfounded, all those watching were convinced that the amazing Sertorius was the beloved of the gods. They escorted him home with shouts and applause, and were high-spirited and full of confidence.

(Plutarch, Life of Sertorius, 20)

Of course, having his doe back, Sertorius had to deliver on the idea that military success was now going to follow, or a second, yet more devastating collapse in morale might ensue. Fortunately, Metellus had taken the bait, and followed Sertorius into the Celtiberian uplands. This allowed Sertorius, the veteran guerrilla leader, to return to his area of core competence. Roman armies on the march were wonders of logistics, and not a few Roman victories came about simply because Roman legionaries could remain fed and active in the field long after the enemy had been forced to disperse through lack of supplies.[3] Sertorius was having none of that. With his superior cavalry and local intelligence network as his tools, he launched unrelenting attacks on the Roman supply trains.

Even as things went well, Sertorius contrived a further divine prodigy to boost the morale of his men. The shield faces of the cavalrymen and the breasts of their horses were miraculously splattered with blood, though none knew from where the blood came. Sertorius explained that this was the gods announcing a further victory, as the blood had fallen on those parts which a fallen foe usually sprayed on a cavalryman.[4]

As a further sign of changes for the better, without supplies reaching his legions, Metellus was forced to do exactly what Sertorius wanted him to do – leave his camp and attempt to forage his supplies off the land. Sertorius was doing what he could to ensure that the land had as little as possible left for the Romans to forage, and we can safely assume that he wanted the enemy to spread out as much as possible before launching one of his patent ambushes. In the event, this is not what happened. It turned out that the Romans intended to pillage not merely another stretch of farmland, but the substantial Celtiberian town of Segontia.

It may be surmised that Sertorius had done all too good a job of raising the morale of his men. Seeing the Romans coming out to pillage, the Iberians correctly surmised that their general had got Metellus exactly where he wanted him. Therefore they had no intention of waiting until one of their settlements was destroyed. Instead they promptly fell on the foragers with great ferocity and absolutely no subtlety.

This we can read from Plutarch, who remarks that Sertorius was 'forced' to give battle when the enemy came out to forage. Sertorius had done a good job of interdicting the Metellan supply lines without the need to fight, and there was nothing Metellus in his current situation could do to force Sertorius to battle. Therefore the obvious conclusion is that Sertorius' own warriors forced him into the battle by engaging in a large-scale action without consulting him first.

As incentive Perpenna's men would have known that their performance had been unsatisfactory so far, and be keen to make amends. But the attack was probably launched by Iberians, as there was kudos to be won by taking down a Roman army where Perpenna's legions had failed.[5] Furthermore, some of those Celtiberians in the army were locals unimpressed by the idea of letting Roman pillagers loose on their native city. So battle it was: a confused extempore affair into which combatants on both sides became involved in increasing numbers until it became plain that a full-scale confrontation was under way.

The fight is described by Plutarch as being on 'the plain of Saguntum', a description which has puzzled historians aware that the city of Saguntum is on the east coast of Hispania and both Sertorius and Metellus had left the coast behind some time ago. A modern study has convincingly shown that the 'Saguntum' in question was one of the several towns in Celtiberia called Segontia.[6] Modern Langa de Duero (Segontia Lanca) is the best candidate, as Sallust informs us that the battle was fought on the banks of the river Duoro, some two hundred miles inland.[7] If this is the site, one can imagine that Metellus advanced on Segovia up the valley of the Duoro, while Sertorius lurked in the hills alongside. Seeing themselves on the flank of the Roman army, some of the more enterprising among the Iberian warriors decided to seize the moment, and the flank attack became a general melee as both sides fed troops into the conflict until finally an unplanned battle commended.

The battle lasted from noon till night, with all combatants giving of their best.[8] So ferocious was the conflict that one of the early casualties was Pompey's brother-in-law Caius Memmius. Memmius was a veteran of the Spanish wars who had served under Metellus in previous years. He was currently with Pompey in the capacity of quaestor, and Plutarch calls him 'the most capable of Pompey's lieutenants'.[9] It was his misfortune to be in the thick of the fight when Sertorius launched one of the personally-led surges of the type which had almost disposed of Pompey on the banks of the Sucro a few months previously.

From descriptions of the battle it seems that Sertorius intended to make the clash of generals as personal as possible. At Gaugamela in 331 BC, in a battle Sertorius had surely studied, Alexander the Great smashed the Persian army by taking a wedge of select troops and driving it straight at Darius, the Persian king. When his royal bodyguard was destroyed, Darius saved himself by fleeing, and taking his army in flight along with him.[10] The Alexander-style onslaught on Pompey had come within an ace of capturing or killing him, so now Sertorius intended to put Metellus under identical pressure. Would the luxury-loving 'old woman' break and flee, as Sertorius was gambling he would?

Sertorius was gambling, because in focusing his attention on Metellus, he had to leave the rest of the battle in the hands of his subordinate, the hapless Perpenna. As with all the battles fought by Sertorius, the information available is scanty and often contradictory, so what follows is only one reconstruction which takes into account all the available evidence.

It appears that Hirtuleius (probably accompanied by Perpenna), stung by recent setbacks, was the first to engage Metellus while Sertorius set about his customary task of beating up Pompey. Metellus' army not only effectively pushed back its opponents, but also killed Hirtuleius in the course of the fighting.[11]

As Plutarch remarks 'though Sertorius suffered a number of defeats, he and those who fought under him were victorious. The crushing defeats came where others were in command'.[12] Sertorius was exasperated by yet another setback, and one which had cost him his most loyal subordinate. He reacted swiftly and ruthlessly to keep the news from demoralizing the men who were currently pushing back Pompey. 'Quintus Sertorius was engaged in battle, so he stabbed his dagger into the barbarian who reported to him that Hirtuleius had fallen. His fear was that the messenger would inform others of this news and that as a result the spirit of his own troops would be broken.'[13]

As he was fighting on horseback at this point, and able to move swiftly across the battlefield, Sertorius now decided to switch places with Perpenna to deal with Metellus once and for all. Therefore, he took over the troops of Hirtuleius and launched the *ad hominem* attack on Metellus described above. It was a failure.

Metellus stood his ground with vigour unexpected in a man of his age. However, in the course of his splendid fight he was struck by a spear.

(Plutarch, *Life of Sertorius*, 21)

Up to this point things were going well for Sertorius. Pompey's army had once again been mauled. Metellus' men were falling back, and their commander was wounded (though not seriously, as it transpired). However, that spear which brought Metellus down changed the course of the battle. After his victories earlier in the year, the soldiers now rather liked Metellus.

All the Romans who saw or heard of this [Metellus being wounded] were filled with shame at the idea of deserting their commander. The same event filled them with fury against the enemy. So, they covered Metellus with their shields and carried him out of danger. Then they fell energetically on the Iberians and pushed them back. The victory changed sides.

(Plutarch, *Life of Sertorius*, 21)

This was the last pitched battle that Sertorius was to fight, and probably one which he had not wanted in the first place. The result further convinced him of what he already knew. Taking on the legionaries in a direct confrontation was a recipe for disaster. Besides, after yet another hard-fought losing draw, he had nothing left to fight with. Appian gives the butcher's bill.

Sertorius vanquished Pompey, killing nearly 6000 of his men but himself losing about half that number. At the same time Metellus wiped out some 5000 of Perpenna's men.

(Appian, *Civil Wars*, 1.110)

The writer Valerius Maximus tells the moving story of a soldier who was looking through the corpses of the Sertorians slain in battle. One of the bodies he discovered was that of his brother, against whom he had unknowingly been fighting.[14] This is a reminder both that the Sertorian war was basically a Roman civil war, and that the Sertorian legionaries suffered greatly in this year's campaign.

Attrition earlier in the year's campaigning had already whittled Perpenna's army down to a single legion before the battle at Segontia. Five thousand more casualties at this point meant that Sertorius had lost his legionaries altogether. Add to this the horrendous death toll that the *scutati* of Hirtuleius had suffered both here and near Italica before that, and it can be seen that this single year's campaign had not only cost Sertorius more men than all his previous battles put together, but had virtually wiped out all his heavy infantry. There would be nothing for it but a further retreat.

Made complacent by victory, Metellus situated his camp casually. So on the evening of the day after the battle Sertorius showed that he was ready, willing and able to resume guerrilla warfare as usual. He launched an unexpected attack on the camp, and attempted to exploit its vulnerable position by cutting it off with a trench. However, by then Pompey had mustered his army and he advanced to Metellus' rescue, forcing Sertorius to withdraw.

Such inter-general co-operation was far from the rule among Roman commanders. It is probable that the two generals worked so closely together because both were uneasily aware that though Sertorius was outnumbered by better-equipped and better-trained troops, he was still quite capable of beating either general separately. As his later record shows, Pompey was a reluctant collaborator when military glory was a possibility. He collaborated with Metellus despite his natural inclination, because he knew that if he did otherwise military embarrassment and disgrace was almost certain. It is not just that Sertorius had convinced Pompey that he alone could not win a battle against him; it is highly likely that Sertorius had convinced Pompey that he could not win battles at all.

It is often noted that Segontia was the last major battle fought by Sertorius. Less noted is that this is the penultimate major battle ever fought by Pompey. As he had so often promised to do, Sertorius did indeed give the 'schoolboy' a lesson he never forgot. For Pompey, repeated defeats hammered home one lesson time and again, and that lesson was that he was lousy at fighting battles. Fortunately there is much more to being a great general than fighting battles, and for the rest of his brilliant career, in all his strategic victories, Pompey took care to win without having to fight another major action.

For all that Sertorius had come close to terminally embarrassing him with that opportunistic attack on his poorly-sited camp, Metellus might well have believed that he finally had Sertorius on the run. The enemy's heavy infantry was gone, the morale of his own men was sky-high, and he had convincingly demonstrated to the cities of Iberia that Sertorius could not defeat him in the field. This was something worth celebrating; and after three years with precious little to cheer about, Metellus was not about to let the chance slip by.

> Having won a victory over Sertorius, Metellus was ecstatic. He was as delighted with his own success as were the soldiers who saluted him as 'Imperator' [i.e. conquering general] and the cities which celebrated his visits to them with sacrifices on [specially dedicated] altars.
>
> He accepted wreaths that were set upon his head and invitations to formal dinners at which he drank his wine while sporting a triumphal robe. Mechanical statues of the goddess of Victory were made to descend and give out golden victory tokens and celebratory wreaths, while choirs of boys and women lauded him with hymns. He called Sertorius Sulla's runaway slave, and a relic of Carbo's doomed faction.
>
> Naturally he became a laughing stock, being so puffed up with pride and joy when all he had achieved was to get enough of an advantage over Sertorius that the latter had been forced to retire.
>
> (Plutarch, *Life of Sertorius*, 22)

Here, in defence of his hero, Plutarch goes well over the top. Since a triumphator's robe might only be worn once the senate had decreed a triumph, and then properly only for that triumph and accompanying celebrations, it is highly unlikely that the punctilious Metellus would have jumped the gun by wearing such a garment before he was officially permitted to do so. Secondly, Metellus knew the importance of propaganda, and by celebrating his success as a significant victory he made it plain that others should consider it so. By his ostentatious celebration Metellus was broadcasting the news across Hispania that Sertorius had suffered a major setback.

Finally, Plutarch understates the importance of the battle at Segontia far more than Metellus overstated it. The heavy infantry that allowed Sertorius to contest the field against the legions were gone, wiped out in battle. Sertorius could no longer threaten the east coast or Turdetania, and while Sertorius would make it as uncomfortable for them as he could, Roman legions could march to anywhere in Iberia they pleased. The destruction of his heavy infantry meant that Sertorius could no longer win his war – it was Rome's to lose. But so long as the senate kept its nerve and found the resources to keep the legions in Iberia paid and supplied, a military victory might be slow in coming, but come it inevitably would.

In fact, victory might come almost at once, were Metellus only able to pin down Sertorius himself and finish the war by cutting the enemy off at the head. Sertorius had made the war personal by his direct attacks on his opposite numbers in battle. In turn Metellus was beginning to realize that Sertorius was not just the leader of the Iberians, he was the heart and soul of their resistance. If Metellus could put an end to Sertorius, he would put an end to the war.

Even now Sertorius was as frustratingly elusive as ever. He extricated his army from the defeat on the battlefield near Segontia by the simple expedient of disbanding it.

> When defeated in battle by Quintus Metellus, Sertorius was convinced that even an organized retreat was too risky. So he ordered his army to break up and the soldiers to withdraw [individually]. They were to reassemble later at a place he now designated.
>
> (Frontinus, *Stratagems*, 2.13.3)

As Frontinus himself points out immediately afterwards, this tactic was not unprecedented. Viriathus, the great Lusitania guerilla leader, had been forced to the same expedient, and indeed so had the Romans over a century before. When fighting Hannibal in southern Italy the generals were informed of the incursion of a further Carthaginian army into northern Italy. The only way to get the legions to meet the new threat in time was to disband the army and instruct each man to make his way north as swiftly as possible. The legions dissolved, reformed in north Italy in time to win a victory at the Metarus River, and were back facing Hannibal before Hannibal even knew that they had gone.

The problem with pulling off this trick with a defeated army, as Sertorius well knew, was that it exposed beaten men to an acute temptation to abandon their military careers altogether and quietly make their way home. Retreat by disbandment required a great deal of mutual faith between commander and soldiers – the commander had to believe that the soldiers would eventually turn up again, and the soldiers had to believe that their commander would make it worthwhile for them to do so.

Livy tells us that, while the rest of his army escaped to safety, Sertorius led his pursuers towards that secure stronghold to which he had been retreating before the unfortunate clash at Segontia – the fortress town of Clunia.[15] Sertorius had prepared this mountain town to resist a siege, repairing the walls and strengthening the gates. His intention was not, as his enemies surely hoped, to set the scene of a glorious last stand. Rather Sertorius wanted Pompey and Metellus to focus on him while the rest of his army withdrew.

Even as he fortified the ramparts of Clunia, Sertorius dispatched messengers to those tribes and cities under his control, ordering them to raise new levies. Once the levies had been raised, Sertorius ordered that he was to be informed. He actually had no intention of remaining at Clunia any longer than it took for his old army to get away and for a new one to be raised.

Of course, until then there remained the matter of holding off two vengeful Roman armies skilled at siege warfare, and afterwards escaping when the time was right. However, if there was one thing that Sertorius possessed in abundance it was confidence based on a sound assessment of his own abilities. It is probable that in the following account Frontinus has preserved for us a fragment of the siege that followed.

Quintus Sertorius was completely outmatched by the cavalry of the enemy. [Since he was defending a city, Sertorius would have had little use for his own cavalry and had sent it away with the rest of the army.] The enemy cavalry were so cocksure that they habitually advanced right up to his fortifications. Observing this, Sertorius [secretly] constructed trenches during the night and drew up his line of battle in front of these. As had happened on previous occasions, the cavalry closed in on him, and Sertorius pulled back his men. The enemy, pressing hard behind, fell into the trenches and in this manner they were defeated.

(Frontinus, Stratagems, 2.12.2)

The *Epitome of Livy* gives us an overview as general as the above fragment is detailed. 'Sertorius was besieged at Clunia, but by repeated sallies he was able to inflict as much damage on the besiegers as he received.'[16] After several weeks of stalemate, the end of the siege came when Sertorius was informed that his reconstructed army was ready and waiting. Plutarch relates 'After the cities sent their messengers, Sertorius cut his way through the enemy without difficulty and joined up with his new troops.'[17] In terms of cocking a snoot at Pompey and Metellus, Sertorius could hardly have managed better. He had managed to extricate his army from a tricky position, had tied up the Romans for several more profitless weeks of the campaigning season, and had effortlessly escaped their efforts to bottle him up in Clunia. He was ready to resume the war.

Fortunately for Clunia after the departure of Sertorius the Romans departed hot-foot after their opponent. If they stayed to take out their frustration on the city, Clunia would have paid a terrible price for its gallant defence. As it was the reckoning was delayed.[18]

Sertorius had an army once more, and no intention of losing it. It was pointless to throw the new recruits into battle against the Romans. He had tried that with veterans backed by legionaries, and had lost both. Even if he won a victory, previous experience indicated that the death toll among his recruits would be terrible, and for that Sertorius would pay the cost in support from the Iberians.

In another way, the Iberians were already paying the price for supporting Sertorius. This was through the tactics to which Sertorius had returned. As the Romans advanced, Sertorius retreated, and as he went he destroyed or carried away anything animal or vegetable which might support the armies marching against him. And should the Romans come across land not already stripped by Sertorius, their desperation for supplies caused them to strip it themselves, and then destroy anything that might be of use to the enemy before they moved on.

For the peasants concerned, it mattered little whether their lands and livelihoods were destroyed by friends, Romans or countrymen – as the duelling armies circled one another they spread a swathe of desolation and misery in their wake. It was a futile, inglorious war, and the question was whether the Roman government in Italy or the people of Iberia would tire of it first.

Inglorious it may have been, but in the short term it was undoubtedly effective for Sertorius. We have no reports of any further military actions for the rest of the campaigning season. The time was spent by hungry Romans doggedly pursuing an Iberian army as it withdrew through an ever-more resentful countryside which it stripped of supplies as it went. This burned-earth policy combined with the Celtiberian cavalry's interdiction of Roman supply chains made it difficult for the Roman generals to keep their men provisioned, and impossible to accumulate sufficient reserves to feed both armies through the winter. As the autumn drew in, Metellus was forced to an inescapable conclusion. If his army were to fight in Hispania the following year, he would have to leave the peninsular at the end of the current one.

This was not as bad as it seems at first blush. After all, the Iberian warriors of Sertorius also needed the winter off – someone had to replace the grain devastated in the fields during the current year. Therefore, the manpower for any campaigning Sertorius could do in the winter would be severely limited, and certainly he lacked the means to take any of the cities which were the main bastions of Roman support. Away from the east coast and Turdetania, Roman armies anyway held little more than the ground they were currently camped on, so they were not surrendering much territory. Therefore wintering outside Iberia was not a military problem. In fact the men would welcome a change to the friendly atmosphere and plentiful supplies of Transalpine Gaul, and would return to Iberia rested and recuperated.

The damage was political. Sertorius could justifiably claim to have driven Metellus from Iberia, further proof to the senate in Rome that the war in Hispania was going nowhere. Pompey did remain in Iberia, stubbornly camped among the Vaccaei in central Iberia, where he had a miserable time of it. His men suffered badly from a lack of supplies, and without much reaching them from the coast Pompey had to make good some of the deficiencies by buying what supplies he could locally from his own pocket. Yet Pompey held on because he had little choice.

The young general was well aware that his ambition and unconventional rise to prominence had made him disliked and feared by many senators who considered him a dictator in the making. Anything less than an unambiguous victory in Hispania would weaken a reputation built upon effective generalship and leave Pompey vulnerable to a charge of *maiestas* when he returned to Italy.[19] So Pompey could not return until the war was won, and the retreat of Metellus into Gaul made it seem as though that victory was further away than ever. The fact that Pompey was stuck in Hispania until he could convincingly beat Sertorius led to the joke that Sertorius would be back in Rome before Pompey.[20]

Sertorius was more than ready to negotiate such a return. After all, he was not fighting for freedom for the Iberians or to set up his own private empire. He was a Roman who happened to be in Hispania under particularly trying circumstances, and he had never abandoned the idea that he might one day contrive a return to his native Italy. Consequently, 'even after his victories he would send messages to Metellus and Pompey. In these he said that in exchange for the privilege of returning home, he was prepared to end his war. He said that, so long as he was home, he would prefer to be the least of Rome's citizens, rather than to be considered master of the rest of the world, but an exile'.[21]

It was a futile hope, and Sertorius knew it. The senate would never make terms with Sertorius after he had just beaten the Romans, as this would make it appear that they had been forced to make peace from weakness. And the senate would not make peace with Sertorius after he had been beaten, because there was no need. So Pompey and Metellus rejected the envoys of Sertorius out of hand. Each of the pair was keen on the glory that victory would bring, but the unconventional circumstances in which he had entered the war meant that Pompey needed to safeguard his political position as well. Any negotiated settlement would be a political disaster for him.

Furthermore, unless Sertorius wanted to totally undermine the morale of his officers, there was no way that he could have sought amnesty for himself alone. His entire 'senate' of Roman exiles would need to be forgiven and readmitted to the Roman civic body. This would re-introduce a substantial bloc of known dissidents into a still-delicate political situation, and raise the sort of factional strife that had been buried with Lepidus.

Even more to the point, many of the exiles, such as Perpenna, had been men of wealth and property – wealth and property which the current senators had incorporated into their estates. So Sertorius was effectively asking the senate to bring back ideological foes and rivals into the already frantic senatorial competition for electoral office, and for the senators to do so at considerable financial cost to themselves. It was never going to happen.

Well, if the senate was not going to negotiate, there was another offer on the table. Lacking a navy of his own, Sertorius continued to support and encourage the pirates who infested the Mediterranean, urging them as far as possible to focus their efforts on Roman supply ships bound for Valentia and Carthago Nova. However, the resources and encouragement that Sertorius could offer paled in comparison to the resources available to the true sponsor of the pirates – Mithridates of Pontus.

Good relations between Mithridates and Sertorius had existed for some time, inspired by a mutual antipathy toward the Sullan government in Rome. Both Sertorius and Mithridates had fought against Sulla, and neither had particularly enjoyed the experience. However, Mithridates had by far the worst of it, for the expert generalship of his opponent had destroyed two large Pontic armies in Greece, and forced Mithridates to retreat from a land he had almost entirely brought under his control. In the end Sulla had been forced to make peace with Mithridates because he had the more pressing business of a civil war waiting for him in Italy (in the course of which he met Sertorius). Nevertheless, both Romans and Mithridates were well aware that the day of reckoning had only been postponed.

The Romans tried again in the late 80s BC when a subordinate of Sulla's named Murena had launched an (allegedly unauthorized) invasion of Pontus, and his army had been thoroughly beaten for its pains. Since then Roman prestige in Asia Minor had waned, and while allegedly at peace, Rome and Pontus did all they could to sabotage each other. Rome encouraged economic warfare and minor provocations by King Nicomedes IV, ruler of Bithynia, the client kingdom on the western border of Pontus, and Mithridates encouraged the pirates to wreak havoc on Roman shipping. When Mithridates – a man with an excellent intelligence network – heard of a rebel general discomfiting the Roman authorities on the other side of the known world, he naturally offered to help in any way he could.

This offer of help was something of a poisoned chalice. Mithridates was perhaps the most notorious enemy of Rome since Hannibal. When he conquered the whole of Asia Minor in 88 BC, Mithridates had ordered the execution of some 80,000 Romans and Italians who had been trapped there by his sudden onslaught. Most of these were civilian traders and their families, and the relatives of the deceased had neither forgiven nor forgotten. Sertorius could accept help from Pontus only by publicly allying himself with the man who publicly yearned for Rome to be destroyed. Unless he handled matters with extreme delicacy, any negotiations with Mithridates would extinguish the last faint hopes of negotiating a safe return to Italy with the Senate.

Cicero was later to make exactly this point the other way around, by pointing out the danger of Mithridates allying with Roman generals such as Sertorius.

> But Mithridates did not forget the previous war, but prepared for a new one. After he had built and equipped enormous fleets, and mustered mighty armies from every nation he could. He sent ambassadors and letters as far as Spain to those commandeers with whom we were at war at the time. The plan was that in this way as it were, he would wage war against you [i.e. the Roman people] in two remote parts of the world most separate from one another.
>
> Then you, with two separate enemies united in a single strategy and fighting on two fronts, might find that you were fighting for the empire itself. The danger from Sertorius and Spain, had by far the most solid foundation and the most formidable strength ...
>
> (Cicero, *On the Manlian Law*, 4.6)

Interestingly, Cicero mentions later in the same speech that Mithridates also sent an envoy to sound out Pompey and the depth of Pompey's allegiance to the republic. It was a ploy worth trying. Pompey was in military difficulty in Hispania and consequently in political peril at home. Since many senators considered Pompey a danger, it was worth checking if that danger was at all real. After all, Pompey had an army that was loyal to him rather than to the senate in Rome, and Sertorius too had a private army. Between them, the pair could crush Metellus and present a credible threat to Italy, especially if Mithridates launched his huge and meticulously prepared army from the east at the same time.[22] So just how did Pompey feel about being king (or dictator, or whatever) of Rome, with Sertorius as his second-in-command?

Pompey was not interested. With all the optimism of youth, he reckoned that the war in Hispania could be turned around, and soon. Sertorius had lost an army, was losing popular support, and Metellus would be over the Pyrenees in spring. With a bit of luck the whole thing could be over by autumn. The same thoughts had occurred to Sertorius. Consequently he took the Mithridatic offer a lot more seriously, and after some diplomatic to-and-fro terms were hammered out. From a hint in later sources, this diplomatic effort may have involved Perpenna. It was a welcome bonus for Sertorius to find something that both kept his prickly subordinate out of his hair, and was sufficiently important and prestigious that Perpenna could not complain about it.

Soon after the start of his first war with Rome, Mithridates had captured the only Roman province in Asia Minor, the former kingdom of Pergamon, which the Romans called Asia. Sulla had forced Mithridates to withdraw, but now the Pontic king saw a chance to regain his lost conquest. Furthermore, Mithridates wanted to have a go at reconquering the non-Roman territories of Cappadocia and Bithynia. To date the Romans had obstinately refused to allow Mithridates to occupy either – now in exchange for Pontic ships and money, Mithridates wanted the Romans to stand aside whilst he expanded his empire.

As was usual for a Roman faced with a tough decision, Sertorius called a *concilium* to discuss it. His council was more formal than most, being made up of those senior exiles whom he dignified with the title of 'senate'. The senate was all for the proposal.

> They accepted the terms with delight, and wanted to accept the offer immediately. All that was asked for was the meaningless right to occupy places which they could not stop him from taking in any case. In return they would receive those things which they most badly needed.
>
> (Plutarch, *Life of Sertorius*, 23)

Ships Sertorius could certainly use, though he might have trouble keeping them safe from the Roman navy. But it is interesting that Plutarch says that Sertorius needed money at this point. A fragment from Sallust states 'Sertorius spent the empty [i.e. non-campaigning] time building up his resources'.[23] He had after all, lost most of two armies at Segontia and

Italica and reconstituting these might well have strained his resources to the utmost. Mithridates did not offer men, because his Pontics were not noticeably better than Sertorius' Iberians, and getting them from one side of the known world to the other was problematic enough without the hostile Roman fleet in the way. Sertorius too was in favour of accepting the Mithridatic proposal, with one significant exception.

> He was prepared to let King Mithridates exercise his royal power and authority over Bithynia and Cappadocia. These countries did not belong to Rome and were customarily ruled by kings. But there was no way that he could agree to allow Mithridates to take or hold a Roman province. This one [Asia] was Roman in fact and law. Mithridates had taken it from Rome, and then had lost it in war ... and abandoned his claim in his treaty with Sulla.
>
> He [Sertorius] regarded it as his duty to increase Rome's territory by force of arms, not to shrink that territory in order to increase his own power. For a man with true nobility of spirit will happily accept victory with honour, but if the terms are dishonourable, he will not accept them even to save his own life.
>
> (Plutarch, *Life of Sertorius*, 23)

Nothing is said here about the other two significant kingdoms in Asia Minor – Galatia and Paphlagonia – but we can safely assume that Mithridates wanted them as well. The reference to Bithynia is useful, because it gives us a secure *terminus ante quem* for the negotiations. We know that Nicomedes IV, king of Bithynia died early 74 BC, and like the king of Pergamon he left his kingdom to the Romans. Therefore after 74 BC Bithynia, like Asia, was Roman by right of inheritance, and Sertorius would have refused to cede it by the same argument that he had refused to cede Asia. Given that it took ambassadors at least three months to make the trip to Iberia (the winter made sea travel a dubious proposition), we can assume that the negotiations were drawn out over the winter of 75.

Mithridates was not best pleased with the idea that the province of Asia was to remain Roman. 'So this Sertorius, who had been pushed with his back to the Atlantic Ocean nevertheless sets limits to my rule in the east, and threatens war if I attempt to recover Asia? So what will he have us do if he ever returns to the Palatine in Rome?'[24] Despite this, the king was prepared to yield the point and the province, mainly because he was aware of earlier deficiencies in his army's performance against the legions. Sertorius had offered to send officers to train the Pontic army in Roman warfare, and it was this training that Mithridates was prepared to pay for. We know from Appian that Mithridates not only wanted to train his men to fight the legionaries, he wanted at least some units armed and equipped Roman-fashion as ersatz legionaries themselves. Who better to command such units than men accustomed to commanding the real thing?

And pay Mithridates did with three thousand talents. A talent was about 30kg (67lbs) of gold worth about six thousand denarii at a time when keeping an Iberian warrior in the field probably cost Sertorius around 200 denarii a year. In other words Mithridates had just subsidized an army of 90,000 men for a year. The ships were to await the sending by Sertorius of the legionary training officers that Mithridates had paid for. Once they arrived a handy little fleet of some 40 warships was dispatched to Spain, where they made themselves at home in the same base which sheltered Sertorius' pirate allies. Although under the command of Sertorius, it is plain from its later conduct that this fleet retained its Pontic officers, just as Perpenna had remained in command of his legionaries.

The little naval force was in a precarious position, given that Sertorius had few links with the east coast. In the next year's campaigning a fragment of Sallust tells us that when 'the Roman army went into the territory of the Vascones to gather food, Sertorius also moved his position. It was vital for him to keep open his links with Gaul and Asia'. This scrap of information tells us that the 'link with Asia' was then open, and this link must have been the fleet. So though Sertorius was operating inland he took care to prevent any Roman armies getting between him and his outpost on the east coast.

So with his war chest replenished, his army rebuilt, and with a small fleet operating under his command for the first time, Sertorius prepared to take his war into its sixth year. There was still no sign that the coming year held more than a continuation of the prevailing stalemate. If the previous year had shown that for Sertorius fortune was a fickle mistress, the coming year was to test the Roman Senate's resolve to the limit.

Chapter 9

The End Game

E arly in 74 BC Nicomedes IV of Bithynia died. The Bithynian king had been an inveterate enemy of Mithridates and a close friend of the Romans (so close was his relationship with the young Julius Caesar that a homosexual relationship was suspected, and Caesar's enemies called him 'the Queen of Bithynia'). The kingdom of Bithynia had acted as a buffer state between the predatory kingdom of Pontus and the even more predatory Romans in their province of Asia. So with malice aforethought, Nicomedes stripped away that buffer by leaving his kingdom to the Romans.[1]

Having the Romans right on his border and only a few days' march from his capital represented an intolerable threat to Mithridates. He was well aware that it was only a matter of time before the Romans did indeed cross that border and march on his capital, so he decided to get his retaliation in first.

The senate in Rome, deliberating policy for the coming year, received in quick succession the news that they were heirs to the former kingdom of Bithynia, and that they would have to fight Mithridates for it. Mithridates had crossed the border with a huge army and taken Bithynia almost in passing on his way to the province of Asia. Once in Asia Mithridates stuck scrupulously to the letter of the law of his agreement with Sertorius. Marcus Marius (no relation of Gaius Marius, Sertorius' former commander) was one of the training officers despatched to Mithridates by Sertorius. He was now promoted to the rank of governor of the province of Asia, and officially it was he who conquered cities there in the name of the Marian cause.

He was 'assisted' by Mithridates in the capture of these cities, and when he entered them with <u>fasces</u> and axes [the symbols of a Roman governor], Mithridates would follow him in person, choosing to

assume the inferior rank of a client king. Marius gave some of the cities
their freedom, and wrote to others announcing that, by command of
Sertorius they were exempt from taxation.

(Plutarch, *Life of Sertorius*, 24)

These tax breaks were shrewd propaganda, for nowhere did the ugly face
of Roman imperialism get any uglier than in Asia Minor, where Roman
tax-gatherers colluded with corrupt governors to bankrupt entire cities
with such exorbitant demands that men had to sell themselves and their
daughters into slavery to meet the bill. The fact that Sertorius had been
mild in his exactions when he took over Hispania may have persuaded
many cities to hope for similar treatment in a Sertorian province of Asia.
Likewise the suffering of Asia under the Roman senate was a fate which
Sertorius doubtless prophesied for Iberia should the Sullans ever get to
rule the peninsula once more.

For Sertorius it was excellent news that Rome had a major war on its
hands in Asia Minor. Then came news of a rebellion within Italy itself –
the gladiator uprising of Spartacus. All this meant less money and fewer
supplies were going to be available for the Roman armies in Hispania.
And these were already feeling the pinch – one army so badly that it
was currently making its way back from Gaul. Sertorius could hope that
perhaps the senate was feeling the same war-weariness that afflicted the
Iberian peninsula, and would make peace with its Roman enemy in order
to deal with the even more severe threat from the foreign foe. In fact Rome
was facing a military crisis of massive proportions.

There were wars and wars. The Sertorian war still raged in Hispania,
and the Mithridatic war had erupted in the east. The war against the
pirates was fought right across the entire sea, and another war broke
out in Crete against the Cretans themselves [partly due to Cretan
support for pirate bases on the island]. Besides all this, there was the
gladiatorial war in Italy itself which started suddenly and quickly
became very serious.

(Appian, *Civil Wars*, 1.111)

After years of misgovernment, Rome's chickens were coming home to
roost as a single threatening flock. Both Sertorius and Mithridates enjoyed

popular support because they were more honest and less greedy than their Roman counterparts. The pirates had become a major threat because the Romans had been too busy fighting each other to police the seas, and yet they had jealously refused to allow anyone else to develop the naval power to do so. Rome's political squabbles had left thousands homeless as their lands were devastated as collateral damage by warring armies. Abroad many of the dispossessed had joined the pirates. Now in Italy they flocked in such numbers to the banner of the renegade gladiator Spartacus that he had to turn some recruits away.

So 74 BC started with Rome fighting on the east and west, across the Mediterranean Sea but particularly in Crete, and getting regularly thumped in Italy itself by Spartacus as he devastated his way across the countryside.

Yet Rome had not forgotten the war in the Hispania, and like the legions it commanded, the senate was stubborn and terribly persevering. Despite the threats pressing in on all sides, the senate still somehow dug up the resources to send another two legions to join Metellus as he returned from his winter sojourn in Gaul.[2] There was to be no relenting of the effort to beat Sertorius.

As Metellus crossed the Ebro, and Pompey moved to join him, Sertorius and Perpenna advanced from Lusitania to meet them. Iberia wearily braced itself for another season of warfare, and for the first time its people showed signs of large-scale dissent. After all, they had opted for Sertorius because he offered them a better future than the Sullan senate. Yet, as the contemporary Roman proverb had it 'Even a bad peace is better than a just war', and all that Sertorius seemed able to offer was war without end. The question of whether to keep supporting Sertorius or side with the Roman armies split tribes and families. A fragment of Sallust tells the story of one unknown city –

Whenever the men went to war or out on raids, the womenfolk had reminded them of their forebears' achievements in war, and celebrated the heroic feats of their ancestors. Yet when it was discovered that Pompey was marching on them with his army, the elders persuaded the men to peace and obedience.

The women were unable to dissuade them, so they left their husbands and took over the very secure Meorigan stronghold. They announced that the men had given up their country, their freedom and the mothers of their children. So the wives were giving up breast-feeding, childbirth and their other obligations too. Their husbands could take over these roles. The young men were stung by this insult and so ignored the decrees of the elders.

(Sallust, *Histories*, 2.75)

We do not know where this city was, nor the outcome of the warlike women's strike, but it is certain that this sort of division afflicted communities across Iberia. As Romans and Sertorians again began their fruitless warfare, both devastating the lands that their armies crossed, it became increasingly clear that the Iberian dedication to the Sertorian cause was waning fast.

At this point some of the soldiers of Sertorius abandoned him and went over to Metellus. It is uncertain whether these were the remnants of the legions of Perpenna or the first of an increasing stream of defectors from the Iberian army. In any case, Sertorius took the desertions badly, and took out his ill-temper on those of the defectors' unit who remained. This hurt morale: 'The men considered it most unjust that they, who had remained with the standards were punished because others had deserted.'[3]

Details of the war, always scanty and confused become yet more so in this year, as there were none of the major set-piece battles which the historians of antiquity loved to relate. Unable to pin down Sertorius and force the issue with him, Metellus set about the same strategy that he worked with his father in Africa during the war against Jugurtha. That is, he methodically began to secure the cities and tribes of Iberia one at a time. At Langobriga (p.84) Sertorius had frustrated the first attempt at this policy, but Metellus had learned a lot since. He kept his soldiers on a tighter rein, for a start.

When Quintus Metellus was in Hispania he wanted to keep his troops in order. Therefore when about to break camp he announced that he had intelligence of an enemy ambush. He ordered that no-one should break ranks and leave the standards. He did this only to keep his troops disciplined, yet happened to meet with an actual ambush. His soldiers dealt with it calmly, since they were expecting it.

(Frontinus, *Stratagems*, 4.7.42)[4]

Pompey had less luck in central north Celtiberia, where, following the Metellan strategy, the young general attempted to take the city of Palentia (modern Palencia). He was in the process of laying logs against the walls as a base for his siege towers, when Sertorius turned up. Pompey, chastened by his earlier experiences, did not even attempt to remain to dispute mastery of the city with his rival. He set fire to the logs around the wall to discourage an enemy sally, and pulled his army back.

Thereafter, he and Metellus operated more closely together, each remaining close enough to fall back on the other's support should the need arise. With each army protecting the other, the Celtiberian cities became harder to defend. Bilbilis and Segobriga were among the many towns that fell to the advancing Romans. 'The forces of Metellus overran many of his [Sertorius'] towns and subjugated those living in them', Appian reports laconically. [5]

However, if the Roman armies were together in central Iberia, this meant that the rest of the peninsula was lightly defended. Sertorius and Perpenna split up. There was good reason to divide the command anyway, because relations between the pair were getting somewhat rocky.

Not just the Iberians, but also the Romans of the Sertorian senate were becoming disaffected. The Iberians were discouraged by the two extra legions of Metellus and his subsequent progress in Celtiberia. The Roman faction, on the other hand, was greatly encouraged by the problems Rome was facing in the wider world. With Rome's general position deteriorating across the Mediterranean, there was a real chance that the senate would so badly need the twelve or so legions operating in Hispania that it would try to patch together a peace that would allow the legions to be deployed elsewhere. It is improbable that Perpenna believed that the republic would ever forgive what it saw as his treason, but if Perpenna could never return to Rome, he had hopes of at least leading the Romans in exile to making peace.

The senators and men of rank began to feel confident that they were a match for their enemies. Once they had shed their fear they instead began to feel envy and foolishly jealous of their general. Perpenna, whose high birth allowed him to believe that he should be the man in overall command, encouraged these sentiments.

In secret conferences with his associates he would maliciously enquire 'Tell me, what evil genius is rushing our destiny from bad to worse? We were not prepared to remain at home under the command of Sulla when he ruled all the world. No, we came to this war-torn land to live as free men. And instead we are slaves in the retinue of Sertorius the exile.'

(Plutarch, Life of Sertorius, 25)

Sertorius was not unaware of the mutterings, and his response was to draw closer to the Celtiberians who still supported his cause. Because the legions of Perpenna had been spent, along with the money which Perpenna had brought, Sertorius had less reason to consider Perpenna's very real reservations about the way that the war was being fought. So his public reaction to perceived disaffection among the Romans was to replace his Roman bodyguard with one of Celtiberian cavalry.

This caused further problems; since seeing that the Romans were under suspicion, the Celtiberians took this as licence to insult the foreign exiles. The exiles in turn took out their frustration my making exorbitant demands of money and supplies from the native tribes and harshly punishing those who failed to deliver. Since they did this in Sertorius' name, this led to a number of cities deserting to the Romans. This further exasperated Sertorius, who feeling that he was threatened with disloyalty by both natives and his fellow Romans, began to slip into a state approaching paranoia. For their mutual health it was definitely time for Perpenna and Sertorius to separate.

Perpenna went around the Romans operating in the interior to the west coast. He found that the city of Cale was lightly defended enough to be vulnerable, so he promptly captured it.[6] (In Roman Hispania, Cale (pronounced 'Cah-lay') became Portus Cale, which gave its name to modern Portugal.) While Perpenna went west, Sertorius stayed to rebuild the walls of Palentia before going east to the valley of the Ebro. Here, the Romans had been intermittently trying to take the fortress town of Calgurris since 76 BC. The besiegers had no warning that Sertorius was even on his way. 'Because of the rapidity with which he could move the Celtiberians nicknamed him [Sertorius] Hannibal' remarks Appian, and the great Carthaginian commander himself might have admired the dispatch with which Sertorius fell on the Romans at Calgurris, killing some 3000 of them.

Sertorius had another reason for being in the east. He wanted to keep in touch with his fleet, which the Romans were making a serious effort to destroy. A chunk of the fragmentary *History* of Sallust gives us a taste of this campaign. The Roman side of the naval campaign was led by an admiral called Antonius, of the Antonine clan (which currently included a ten-year-old lad whom later history was to know as Mark Antony, the triumvir and lover of Cleopatra).

Antonius had trouble even getting to Hispania, as he ran into trouble with the Ligurian tribes, who were supported by 'hostile ships', a phrase which could refer to either Sertorius' fleet or pirates acting on his behalf. The weather was calm, and the enemy ships parked themselves on the Roman flank, a move which paralyzed the fleet, since the far less experienced Roman rowers would be unable to compete if it came to a battle in open water. 'For if any one ventured to put out against them [the pirates], he would usually be defeated and die; but even if he was victorious, he would be unable to capture any of the enemy because their ships were so fast' observed the historian Cassius Dio.[7]

It was only after an otherwise unknown tribe called the Terentuni were persuaded to help push the Ligurians inland that Antonius was able to continue to Hispania. There he set about patching up his fleet 'in the territory of the Aresinarii' who were apparently a Catalonian tribe.

Antonius' first task was to rescue Emporion. Sertorian forces, operating by land and sea, appear to have taken this city out of the conflict, not by capture (as the sources would have informed us of such a significant event) but by a close siege which deprived the Romans of the use of their trusty base by the Ebro. The operations of Antonius took place both on an unknown river (possibly a tributary of the Ebro) and on an island just off the coast from the city.

A fragment of Sallust is worth quoting in full as it gives a flavour of the combined forces of ships, infantry and cavalry used by both sides:

being separated from the enemy by the Dilunus, the depth of which river meant that even a handful of men could deny him a crossing. So he [lured away the enemy] with pretended crossings not far away, and having recalled the fleet, ferried his men across with this, and some jerry-built transports. He then instructed the cavalry and some warships to go on ahead under the command of Manius and get to the island [near Emporion?]. He thought that, being unexpected, this would cause a panic and so free the town which was very conveniently situated for receiving supplies from Italy.

But the enemy had confidence in their position and remained firm in their intent. They had fortified the small hill with a double wall which could only be approached by a narrow sandy frontage and sloped steeply on the seaward side.

(Sallust, *History*, 3.6–7)

The 'double walls' were possibly siege walls, one facing the besieged and the other facing outwards to repel relief troops. Caesar was later to build such a 'double wall' when beseiging the Gauls at Alesia in his Gallic war.

The overall effect of the Roman fleet was weakened by the fact that Antonius was not a very competent commander. He made so little progress that apart from Sallust no other histories of the war mention his contribution at all. In the end it appears that the senate decided that if the fleet was doing little against the Sertorians, it should be sent elsewhere. At this time, largely due to pirate predations, Rome was desperately short of grain. A young quaestor called Marcus Tullius Cicero had made extraordinary efforts to ease the shortage by getting supplies sent from Sicily, and was very disappointed to find how little his efforts were appreciated at home.[8]

This shortage of supplies crippled the war in Iberia. If Emporion was blocked by siege, then Roman supplies had to be brought up the coast from Valentia, with all the hazards that this entailed. And even to get to Valentia, merchantmen had to escape interdiction by both pirates and the Sertorian fleet. At the same time, Metellus and Pompey had learned the hard way that allowing their men to scatter and forage for what scanty supplies remained in territory already devastated by Sertorius was a recipe for disaster. So the legions were crippled by a lack of food and other supplies, which severely hampered their movement.

In later life, Pompey became known as a master of logistics. It was his ability to move men and supplies around the enemy that allowed him to eventually tame the pirate threat, conquer much of the Middle East, and bring even Julius Caesar to the point where his men were forced to try baking cakes out of grass. To a very large extent his mastery of logistics was learned in Iberia. A man who could keep his army fed and supplied when Quintus Sertorius was doing his best to prevent it was a man who could keep his army fed and supplied under almost any other circumstances. The student had taken some hard lessons from the master, but he was an able student, and he learned his lessons well.

Nevertheless, if Sertorius appeared to be getting the better of his opponents, it was only in that his men were marginally less hungry and battered than the enemy. The war in Iberia was grinding down both sides and hammering the infrastructure and economy of a land which now struggled to support the armies struggling for mastery of it.

Very little was achieved in the remainder of the year. At the end of the campaigning season the opposing armies reeled apart like punch-drunk boxers. This time it was Pompey's turn to take his army into Gaul. The governor, Fronteius, had laid on stores for Pompey to collect while his men enjoyed some much-needed rest and recuperation. The stores were the best that the Roman authorities had been able to scratch up under very difficult circumstances. The 'best', however, was apparently pathetically inadequate, for Pompey wrote bitterly to the senate. The letter (purportedly in Pompey's own words) is worth repeating in full.

From my early youth I have endured peril and privation whilst the armies under my command put to flight the most criminal of your enemies and made you safe. Yet, Fathers of the Senate, now that I am absent, you could do no more against me than you are now doing if I had spent my time fighting you, my fatherland and my father's gods.

For now, despite my youth, you have left me exposed in the cruellest of wars. You have, to the best of your ability, condemned both me and a faithful army to that most wretched of deaths, that by starvation. Is this what the Roman people expected when they sent their sons to war? And after being wounded, and so often shedding their blood for their country, is this how they are rewarded?

When I got tired of fruitlessly writing letters and sending envoys, I used up my personal resources, and even my credit, while in three years you have barely supplied me with enough to keep going for one. By the Immortal Gods! What do you think I am – the treasury, or someone capable of running an army with neither food nor pay?

I'll admit that I started into this war with more zeal than discretion. Forty days after you gave me the empty title of general I had raised an army. The enemy [i.e. Perpenna] were already at the throat of Italy, and I drove them from the Alps into Hispania, in the process opening for you a route far superior to Hannibal's.

... Outnumbered and with inexperienced troops I held off the first onslaught of the conquering Sertorius. Thereafter I spent the winter not in making myself popular or in the towns but in camp among the most savage of enemies. Do I really have to recount the battles and campaigns, the towns destroyed or captured? The matter speaks for itself; the taking of the enemy's camp at Sucro, the fight on the River Turia, Gaius Herennius, the enemy commander, wiped out along with his army; Valentia; you know all this well enough. So, grateful fathers, in return for all this – we get want and hunger.

They are in the same condition, the enemy army and mine. Neither has any pay, and both can march into Italy to get it. Take note of this and please give my warning your full attention – you do not want me to take into my own hands the job of providing myself with what I need. Those parts of Hispania Citerior not held by the enemy are actually a costly burden for us because apart from the coastal towns both we and Sertorius have devastated it into total destitution. Gaul supplied cash and crops to Metellus last year – this year crop failure means the province can barely support itself.

So I'm out of options, money and credit. It is up to you. Either you save the situation or my army will come to Italy and bring the war with it. It's not what I want, but you have been warned.

(Sallust, *Histories*, 2.82)

It says much for the exasperation of Pompey that he did not bother with veiled threats, but simply uttered them outright. The senate, struggling to contain Spartacus, thought what another hostile army could add to the prevailing chaos, and dug deep into its reserves. In fact Pompey's threat so galvanized Rome's aristocrats that many contributed towards the army's supplies from their private fortunes. The general Lucullus, though no friend of Pompey's, was the leader in the fund-raising because he wanted Pompey out of the way while he prepared to take the war to Mithridates in the east. By spring Pompey's army was adequately prepared. The young general's tantrum had not gained him many new friends in the Senate, but it had got his army the resources it needed. Those resources could not be matched by the army of Sertorius, which had finished the previous season's campaigning in at least as desperate a state as the Romans they were fighting.

So as both sides braced themselves for another year of war, it became plain that the advantage lay with the Romans. They could draw on the resources of their empire, beleaguered as it was. Corn could be brought from Sicily and Africa, Gaul could supply recruits, and the mineral resources of Macedonia could pay the legions thus raised. Sertorius had only Iberia, and only those parts of Iberia he still controlled. These were in the north and west, where crops and infrastructure had both been comprehensively wrecked by unending warfare. Nor was it easy to raise the manpower to continue a war which many considered already lost.

Many chieftains used the break in the campaigning season to make clandestine diplomatic approaches to Metellus. Once assured it was safe for them to change sides, these men started the new season's campaign fighting against Sertorius. Sertorius was cornered and desperate, with his army falling to pieces around him. He responded to the desertions with the same savagery that he had shown in his very first years in Hispania. 'He laid aside his former mercifulness and mildness', remarks Plutarch sorrowfully, 'and perpetrated injustices'.[9]

Among those who felt the brutal force of those injustices were those children at the 'school' in Osca. These were now exposed as what they had been all along – hostages for the good behaviour of their families. It was rare for the Romans to actually act against hostages in their power, but Sertorius had no such scruples. Depending on the extent he felt he had been betrayed, or acting on a personal whim, he had some of the boys killed and sold others into slavery. The careful campaign to win hearts and minds was now in tatters. Sertorius held no power as a popular governor, but through an ever more erratic despotism that created enemies and made friends uneasy.

Sertorius may well have been acting through despair. He was a capable general who, though stubborn, was far from blind. He could see that his long war against the Sullan senate was coming to an end, and that for him it was going to end badly. With their armies resupplied and restored Metellus and Pompey started the new season confidently and with hard-earned competence. The easy victories which the Iberians had won over the Romans in the past were no longer possible.

These victories had been gained by exploiting the mistakes of the enemy, but Metellus seldom made mistakes any more, and Pompey was learning fast. Also, exhausted and depleted by continual warfare, the army of Sertorius was a shadow of its former self.

To some extent, Sertorius gave up. 'He fell into luxurious living, abandoning himself to wine women, and song. Since he no longer concentrated on his business, he was regularly defeated. He suspected this was from treachery, and became evil-tempered and cruel in punishment.'[10] Metellus had seen the change in style of the rebel government and had long ago decided that removing Sertorius was the key to ending the war. Accordingly he made his pitch directly to the Romans still with Sertorius. 'Should any Roman kill Sertorius he would be given a hundred talents of silver and twenty thousand acres of land. If he was an exile, he would be free to return to Rome'.[11] It was a powerful incentive, and one designed to increase Sertorius' feelings of suspicion and isolation. 'He changed into a savage and dissolute man' says Livy – one of the few character assessments in his abbreviated *Epitome*.

By all accounts, it worked. Sertorius had unjustly suspected his Roman retinue of plotting his betrayal – now those same suspicions made real the very conspiracy which Sertorius had feared. A group of Romans began to actively plot his downfall. To no-one's surprise Perpenna was foremost among them. Perhaps more surprisingly, Perpenna remained one of the few Romans whom Sertorius still trusted to some degree, perhaps because Perpenna was as committed to the war as was Sertorius himself. Sertorius may well have believed that the senate considered Perpenna as much a threat as himself, and Metellus may well have excepted the rebel leaders from his bounty offer. Without hope of mercy, both Perpenna and Sertorius were committed to fighting to the bitter end.

An early conspiracy was betrayed, but Perpenna had distanced himself from the plot. Those whom Sertorius discovered either died or fled to safety with Pompey or Metellus. It is quite possible that there were some whom Sertorius executed just to be on the safe side, for the historian Appian remarks that those who formed a second conspiracy did so in self-defence. Perpenna joined this second group of plotters, not necessarily out of jealousy of Sertorius, or even because he felt he could do a better job of waging the war, but because Sertorius' paranoia had made him feel that he had to get Sertorius before Sertorius got him.

Every plotter fears betrayal, and it was the threat of betrayal which finally drove the conspirators to act.

Manlius was one of those in high command. He was infatuated with a beautiful boy, and to show how much he loved him, he revealed the conspiracy. Since he, Manlius, would be a very important person once the conspiracy had succeeded, he urged the boy that now was the time to abandon his other lovers and focus his attentions on himself.

The boy promptly ran to another whom he loved even more, one Aufidius, and told him the entire story. Aufidius was appalled. He was himself one of the conspirators, but had no idea that Manlius was also. And here was this boy now also implicating Perpenna, Gracinus and a number of others whom Aufidius knew for himself were in the plot.

Aufidius pretended to laugh it all off, saying that the boy should despise Manlius for his false boasting. Then he hurried to tell Perpenna that they were all in peril [since security had been compromised]. Matters were at a crisis, and if the deed was to be done, it must be done soon.

(Plutarch, *Life of Sertorius*, 26)

Soon after that Sertorius received a dinner invitation from Perpenna. The banquet was a necessary ruse, for in those days Sertorius spent most of his time behind the hedge of spears carried by his bodyguard. The problem of persuading their moody commander to come to the meal was overcome when the conspirators faked dispatches from a commander in the field. These claimed a totally imaginary victory and a great slaughter of the enemy. Since news of the war had previously been uniformly grim, Sertorius was delighted. Even then it took the entreaties of all present before Sertorius was persuaded to drop his guard for as long as it took to attend the celebratory dinner.

At the dinner the wine flowed freely. It flowed particularly freely in the direction of the bodyguards who surrounded the banqueting hall. It was only when Perpenna received word that these men had been soused comatose that the plot moved to the next stage. Meals with Sertorius were not the culinary orgies of the type in which many of his contemporaries indulged. Both the food and the conversation were limited, both by Sertorius' natural inclination and because riotous parties would not go down well with the starving people of a land ruined by war. 'He allowed only merriment that was both decorous and restrained' says Plutarch.

Because of this Sertorius must have felt increasingly uneasy as the banquet drew to a close. Those present became drunk, and acted even more drunk than they were. They used vulgar language and ignored Sertorius when he commanded the guests to behave themselves. The intention was to get Sertorius off the relative security of his banqueting couch and into a crowd where a knife could be shoved through his ribs without difficulty. However, Sertorius refused to get up and physically intervene to stop the increasingly indecent behaviour on display. This presented something of a problem, for though in late middle age Sertorius had a well-deserved reputation as a fighter.

But in fact the fight had been knocked out of him. A life of battling the headwinds of inclement fortune had brought Sertorius here – to a room full of potential assassins in a foreign land that was turning against him and where the commanders of two substantial armies actively sought his death. It must have dawned on Sertorius, that he might be one of the greatest generals of his day, but that at that moment he had not a friend in the world, and an awful lot of enemies. He'd had enough. 'Either to show his exasperation at their conduct, or because he had become aware of their intent from the violence of their talk and their unexpected contempt for his wishes, he changed his position by throwing himself back on his couch as though he did not want to see or hear them any more.'[12]

Perpenna seized the moment. The plan was that he would clatter his wine cup loudly against something as he raised it to drink, and this would be the signal for Antonius, the man reclining on the couch beside Sertorius, to use the hidden sword which he had smuggled into his hand. At first it seemed as though even now Sertorius was not so weary of fighting that he would go quietly. He turned at the blow from the sword, and tried to rise and engage his opponent. But Antonius rose faster, and fell on Sertorius, pinning the wounded man down with his weight, and holding him by the wrists. With their victim pinioned and helpless, the conspirators rushed in and repeatedly stabbed Sertorius until he was dead.

It was an end that Sertorius had known was coming. The war was lost, and had been from the moment when Pompey's threats had procured the supplies his army needed. It had been a close-run thing, but in the end the senate's determination to continue the war had outlasted that of the Iberians. To some extent Sertorius had involuntarily contributed to his own downfall, for he had little choice but to fight the Romans by starving their armies, even if it meant that his own people starved as well. Ever since the battle of Segontia his had been a war of attrition, and had Rome the will, the empire always had the resources to outlast Iberia.

In fact at this point Sertorius' army had so few resources that it was being handily rolled back by Pompey acting alone. Metellus was elsewhere in the peninsula, pacifying restless tribes, and bringing others under his control by the very effective propaganda point that one army alone was now more than enough to defeat Sertorius, leaving Metellus and his army free to give their full attention to anyone else who objected to the restoration of the *pax Romana*.

The only question that had remained for Sertorius to contemplate was whether the Romans would get him or whether, as turned out to be the case, his own side turned on him first. The basic fact was that his was a personal war, a war waged by the last Marian commander against the Sullan senate. All Sertorius had to offer the Iberians who followed him was the prospect that they would be better off in a Hispania governed by himself than a Hispania governed by the senate. This had proven not to be the case. Despite losing army after army and spending a fortune in what must at times have appeared a war without end, the senate persevered. They may have grudged their generals resources desperately needed elsewhere, but in the end they never gave up on Metellus and Pompey. And because the war continued, Sertorius was unable to deliver the better government that he had promised, and eventually the Iberians gave up on Sertorius.

Once Sertorius was losing control of his Iberian allies, the exiled Romans had no further need of him. By terminally retiring their commander they could make a pitch to his men that the army would do better under new management. The assassins could not say what they planned to do differently, but it was plain that the previous strategy of Sertorius had failed. A fresh start might bring new hope, and if a revitalized army managed to deliver the unwary Pompey an unexpected setback, then perhaps the exiles would have breathing space in which to consider their next move.

There was a gaping hole in this argument, and the Iberians were quick to notice it. If Sertorius, an undoubtedly brilliant general, had been unable to hold the line against the Romans, how did a lesser man such as Perpenna propose to do so? Even when he had command of five legions Perpenna had contrived to lose battle after battle. Where the genius of Sertorius had failed to keep a desperate situation under control, the sub-mediocrity of Perpenna was unlikely to change things for the better. The Iberians were already discouraged. Once news got out that Sertorius was dead and Perpenna was in charge, morale promptly nosedived further.

Now that he was dead, the virtues of Sertorius were remembered, and his recent atrocities forgotten.

> People are generally less angry with those who have died, and when they no longer see him right in front of them they tend to dwell tenderly on his virtues. So it was with Sertorius. Anger against him suddenly turned to affection and the soldiers clamorously rose up in protest against Perpenna.
>
> (Appian, *Civil Wars*, 1.114)

No-one seems to have challenged Perpenna's claim to be the new leader of the rebel cause. The question was if he would have anyone left to lead. With their leader dead, his followers were leaving the fight in droves. Deserting Romans sought sanctuary with Pompey or Metellus, and Iberian tribesmen simply went home. This was particularly true of the Lusitanians who had originally invited Sertorius to return to Iberia. They had followed Sertorius through personal attachment to their charismatic battle leader, and had very little interest in his cause or in fighting for Perpenna.

Matters were not helped when the will of Sertorius was opened and it was revealed that the chief beneficiary from Sertorius' estate was Perpenna, his assassin. Few bequests could have been as unwelcome. Perpenna, already disgraced as the murderer of his commanding officer and the man who had given him sanctuary in Hispania, was now also revealed as having slain his friend and benefactor.

If Perpenna intended to lead he needed to show leadership at once. So parlous was his situation and so low his stock that it would not take much to convert his grumbling and protesting men into a lynch mob. So sticks and carrots were used freely. Sertorius' legacy might be unwelcome, but whatever hard cash was now available was used to convert those who put their faith in solid silver. Promises of high rank or future benefit swayed others, and the release of the surviving Sertorian hostages brought some goodwill from the Iberians. The judicious execution of the loudest protesters quickly silenced the rest, and the three nobles (including Perpenna's own nephew) who had appeared to want to replace Perpenna with themselves were executed to discourage the ambition of others.

In this way, though not without making even more enemies than he already had, Perpenna strengthened his tenuous grip on power. With Sertorius' friends now under his control, there remained the far from minor matter of Sertorius' enemies, starting with Pompey. As soon as he had heard of the assassination, Pompey had marched directly for Osca. He sent scouts and skirmishers ahead to test the morale of the enemy, and Perpenna responded in kind. For different reasons, both generals were eager for a decisive battle. Perpenna needed a victory to cement his position. Nothing succeeds like success, and if Perpenna could show that he was capable of defeating Pompey when Sertorius had not recently been able to do so, this might win the Iberians back to his side.

Pompey just wanted to get the war over with. He and Sertorius had respected each other as opponents, and until now Pompey's advance had been justifiably cautious. Perpenna, on the other hand, Pompey knew as a man who had lost every action he had ever fought. 'Pompey despised him as a general' remarks Appian bluntly.[13] It was clear that Perpenna had taken over with no clear idea of what to do next, and having no fixed idea of campaign, sought instead to wrap things up quickly. So just ten days after he had disposed of Sertorius, Perpenna took to the field to do the same to Pompey and Pompey readily answered the challenge.

It was time for the student Pompey to show what he had learned from his years of fighting Sertorius, and Pompey did not disappoint. He fought a textbook engagement – literally. Over a century later when Frontinus was preparing to govern Britain, he compiled for himself a textbook of various military manoeuvres and tactics with which to inform his own campaigning. Pompey's defeat of Perpenna was lesson 32, section five of Book 2 'On ambushes'.

> Pompey put troops here and there, in places where they could attack from ambush. Then, pretending fear, he pulled back drawing the enemy after him. Then, when he had the enemy exposed to the ambuscade, he wheeled his army about. He attacked, slaughtering the enemy to his front and on both flanks.
>
> (Frontinus, *Stratagems*, 2.5.32)

From other sources, mainly Plutarch and Appian we get a few more details. The force that Pompey sent out to lure Perpenna's army consisted of ten cohorts. This was about 5,000 men – enough to make a tempting target without being so many as to be intimidating. Perpenna took the bait and rushed to attack.

A feigned retreat and ambush was a military cliché even in the days of the late Republic. It is highly unlikely that Sertorius, the master ambusher, would have done more than sneer at so transparent a ruse. But Perpenna was so desperate for a victory that he seems to have seen only what he wanted to see – the enemy falling back in confusion before his advancing army. Pompey's successful ambush proved Plutarch's disparaging comment 'Perpenna was as bad at command as he was at following orders'. His army collapsed right down the line, and in a morning the Marian cause that Sertorius had sustained through a decade of war was forever wiped out on the battlefield.

Perpenna receives further discredit in our sources for not even having the decency to emulate the majority of his officers and die fighting. In fact, immediately after the debacle he was more concerned about the vengeance of the men he had led to disaster than the legions which had beaten him in battle. With Pompey, there was at least the chance of striking a deal. The only thing his own disaffected men wanted to strike was his head off his shoulders.

Accordingly, Perpenna lay low until Pompey's men had chased the last of his army from the field. The Roman cavalry found him hiding in a thicket and brought him to Pompey's camp. There, with his fellow prisoners of war howling execrations at him, Perpenna shouted that he had to be brought before Pompey. As successor to Sertorius' command,

Perpenna had come into possession of a number of letters. These were from Sertorian sympathizers in Rome, some of them men of the highest rank. Dissatisfied with the Sullan senate, but afraid to voice their feelings, these men had urged Sertorius to come to Italy. With Sertorius as their figurehead they would stir up a revolution and forcibly change Sulla's constitution. Some of these correspondents had been rash enough to affix their names to the letters, thus compromising themselves beyond doubt.

Who these would-be revolutionaries were, and whether they existed at all, has been a matter of some speculation since Pompey, we are told, did the statesmanlike thing. Executioners were sent to silence Perpenna, and once the letters were found, Pompey burned them unread. The reason for so doing was that if their treason was made public these men would have nothing to lose. Made desperate, they might well plunge Italy into the civil war they had wanted Sertorius to bring down on their behalf. And with Spartacus' rebellion still convulsing Italy, a further civil war might have unpredictable consequences for Rome and her empire.

Those who have followed Pompey's subsequent career can only applaud his actions at this point. The execution of Perpenna was not an extra-judicial killing such as others which blight the 'teenage butcher's record. Perpenna was already condemned to death, and as with Sertorius, his sentence had only been pending on Rome attaining the ability to carry it out.

It was certainly a wise decision not to make the letters public. However, the cynical historian cannot but wonder whether Pompey did not consider burning, for example, the previous month's army requisition dockets while he kept the original letters close to his chest. After all, public exposure could be disastrous to the state, but private blackmail could be very advantageous to Pompey. Certainly, Pompey had been in considerable political danger just a year before. Soon after the battle he was close to being a favourite son of Rome, with a triumph and a consulship awaiting only his return. Skilful propaganda built on the victory over Perpenna, or skilful propaganda combined with skilful leverage applied to the right quarters? We will never know.

Chapter 10

Aftermath

The Sertorian war basically ended with the death of Sertorius. 'If he had lived, I do not think the war would have ended so soon or so easily' says Appian by way of his personal conclusion.[1] But even after the destruction of Perpenna's army and the capture and execution of its leader a certain amount of tidying up remained to be done. The Celtiberians were famously bad losers, and even without a chance of relief, towns such as Clunia and Calgurris held on grimly.

Even though the last embers of the Sertorian war ceased to flicker, Rome could hardly claim to have conquered Iberia. Many of the tribal chiefs who had deserted Sertorius did so assuming, not that they had submitted to Rome, but that they opted out of the war altogether. With Sertorius gone these chiefs expected to go back to the largely autonomous condition that many tribes had lived in before Sertorius had briefly united the peninsula.

In the short term, this expectation was largely met. Rome had problems enough without embarking on a war of conquest in Hispania. Though 72 BC was the year that Rome turned the corner in coping with the numerous challenges facing the state, the finish line was still distant. In Asia Minor Mithridates and his huge army were bottled up by Lucullus, who had trapped the Pontic king as he besieged the city of Cyzicus. However, at this point the outcome of the siege was uncertain, let alone the outcome of the war as a whole – and in fact the Mithridatic war was to rumble on for a further decade.

In Italy, Spartacus had shown that he and his misfit army were equal to the best Rome had to offer when they defeated the veteran legions brought against them by the proconsular governor of Gaul, Cassius Longinus. However, this victory inspired the senate to finally take the gladiator threat seriously. The veteran Sullan commander Marcus Crassus took the field against Spartacus with ten legions and Crassus soon had his opponent penned in the toe of the Italian peninsula.

In Hispania, Metellus and Pompey worked quickly to tie up the loose ends. Not only Calgurris and Clunia remained faithful to Sertorius. Cities such as Uxama (modern Soria) in north central Iberia held on grimly. After Pompey took Uxama, the prosecution of such sieges was left to subordinates while the proconsuls concentrated on restoring what they could of their devastated provinces. Defiant Calgurris came to a particularly grim end.

They obstinately kept their word, even to the ashes of the murdered Sertorius. They continued to frustrate Pompey's siege even when there was no other living thing [for them to eat] in the town. So they turned on their own wives and children, feeding their flesh with those of their flesh and even salted down the remnants for later. ... This was savagery beyond comparison with any wild animal or reptile. Those to whom they pledged their lives, and who should have meant more than life itself instead became lunch and dinner.

(Valerius Maximus, 2.7.6)

All for naught. The town fell to Pompey's subordinate. 'Afranius destroyed Calgurris with fire and massacre'.[2]

Metellus, in one of his last acts as governor raised taxes to help to pay for the restoration of ravaged infrastructure. Hispania Citerior particularly needed all the help it could get. The countryside had been ravaged, and only a few Roman-held cities such as Carthago Nova had escaped damage by the warring armies.

Prostrated by eight years of war, Iberia briefly became a peaceful province. In 71 BC both Pompey and Metellus were recalled to Rome. Pompey left a memento in the form of a massive victory monument intended as the first thing a visitor to Hispania saw as he entered the Pyrenees. This depicted Pompey himself and the '846 towns' to which he had restored Roman rule.

At the end of the year the proconsuls were to celebrate a joint triumph in Rome: Pompey for his victory over Perpenna and Metellus for his win at Segontia. Though, in truth, the triumph was awarded by the senate not so much for a particular victory in battle but as a grateful 'thank you' for the pair's dogged effort in often unrewarding circumstances.

With Rome recovering well from a bad few years, the legions of Metellus were needed less than the money it took to keep his men in the field. Therefore, Metellus disbanded his army as soon as he left Iberia. Pompey, as might be expected, held onto his men and was already looking for other ways in which they could be employed. Since he wanted to be in Italy for his triumph, the obvious candidate for this attention was the army of Spartacus. Spartacus was desperately trying to escape the trap that Crassus had forced him into. Should Spartacus succeed in breaking out, Pompey wanted his legions there to meet him.

As it turned out, Pompey's legions were also surplus to requirements. Spartacus and his army did indeed break out of confinement in south Italy, but Crassus was quick to respond. He brought the slave army to battle as it struggled to reach Brundisium, and in that battle the rebels were defeated and destroyed as a fighting force. All that was left for Pompey's returning army was to mop up the remnants of the defeated army as the survivors fled north. Pompey's letter to the senate that 'Crassus had won a victory, but it was he who had torn the rebellion up by the roots' was regarded in Rome as the somewhat pathetic attempt at self-aggrandizement it was.

With nothing left for it to do, Pompey's army became something of a political liability. He kept it with the excuse that the men were entitled to join him in celebrating his Iberian triumph, but thereafter his legions were finally stood down. Among those now seeing home again were probably such Roman legionaries as had survived on the Sertorian side. We know that while Pompey executed the proscribed leaders of the Sertorians, he had little interest in the others. He was certainly not vindictive towards the common soldiers, whom he happily welcomed into the ranks of his semi-private army.

The Iberians captured in the last battle of the Sertorian war may have been settled by the Romans somewhere near Transalpine Gaul. As related further below, some of these forcibly retired warriors were later enthusiastic combatants against Rome in Julius Caesar's Gallic war.

Julius Caesar himself had some experience of Iberians by then, as he went out to Hispania Ulterior as a junior official in 69. At this time the province was relatively peaceful. The Iberians had no intention of provoking the Romans, and the Romans for all that they claimed to rule most of the peninsula, were careful not to push those claims too hard. There was sporadic fighting, for this was Iberia, after all. The successors of Pompey and Metellus both appear to have claimed triumphs for obscure confrontations, but by and large the province was peaceful enough to escape the attention of historians. When Iberia returned to the record it was because Caesar had returned to Ulterior as governor.

Like many of his gubernatorial predecessors, Caesar came to Iberia needing a war, not for reasons of state but for personal advancement. Caesar was bankrupt. In fact he had only been allowed by his creditors to come to Hispania because Crassus had stood surety for his debts. As a footnote, some of these debts had been incurred in Caesar's campaign for election to Pontifex Maximus.[3] This was one of the top priestly offices in Rome and the vacancy had been created by the death of its previous holder. This was Sertorius' old opponent Metellus Pius, one of the few eminent Romans of the early first century who could honestly have called himself a decent and honourable man.

The same description even Caesar's friends hesitated to apply to him. He was 830 talents in debt – an amount sufficient to keep a medium-sized city running for several years. Therefore the currently peaceful *status quo* in Hispania was unacceptable. Given the prevailing poverty and the desperation of some in the province, it was inevitable that they would return to the time-honoured Iberian tradition of banditry. This was Caesar's *causus belli*. He began by increasing the army by a third, from twenty cohorts to thirty. Then he selected his target.

The historian Cassius Dio describes the events of the next year.

Though he might have remained at peace, he proceeded to the Herminian Mountains and ordered the inhabitants to move into the plain. He claimed that this was so that the people could not use their mountain fortresses as bandit bases, but really this was to give himself an excuse for war, because he well knew that the people would never accede to his demand. And this is exactly what happened.

Those in neighbouring areas feared that he would march against them too. So they sent their children, wives and most valuable possessions to safety across the river across the Duoro. Caesar first occupied their cities then went to battle with the men themselves.

(Cassius Dio, *History*, 37.52)

The tribes whose towns Caesar plundered for public order and private profit were the Callaeci and their neighbours the Lusitanians. Caesar summoned the fleet from Gades, and took his conquests as far north as Brigantium (A Coruña).

Having cleared his debts and established a military reputation, Caesar then set about governing his thoroughly cowed province, and did it rather well. 'After successfully finishing his war, he just as happily set about tackling the problems of peace. He established harmony among the cities, particularly by resolving the strife between debtors and creditors.'[4] Caesar also successfully petitioned the senate for the abolition of the extra taxes imposed by Metellus.[5]

The historical spotlight of these years is firmly on Caesar, so what we get to know of events in Hispania is often because these events are reflected from Caesar's adventures elsewhere. It is evident that the people of Ulterior did not forget their militarily-minded governor, and when the chance came for some payback, they took it enthusiastically.

As mentioned above, when Caesar was conquering Gaul, a southern tribe sent for help to Iberia. Among those responding were some who had fought under Sertorius. Caesar noted that these veterans showed disconcerting proficiency at fighting Romans.

> Summoned by ambassadors from Hispania Ulterior, they waged war with great confidence. Those who had been with Sertorius throughout were appointed leaders, as it was assumed they would be most skilful in military matters. In a Roman-like manner these proceeded to pick prime spots to fortify their camps. They made raids and attacked the passes, yet left enough men in their garrisons. They began to cut our men off from their provisions, so that corn and supplies were no longer readily available to them.
>
> (Caesar, *The Gallic War*, 3.23)

Metellus Pius did not care much for Caesar while he lived, but he would have well understood and sympathized with what the Romans were now enduring.

Though Caesar's legions eventually overcame the spirited resistance of the Sertorian veterans, Caesar and Iberia were not yet done with each other. Caesar returned to the peninsula in 49 BC at the time when he was fighting a civil war with the Roman senate. The senatorial forces were led by none other than Sertorius' former opponent Pompey.

A special law (the Lex Trebonica) had made Pompey governor of Hispania from 55 to 50. By then Pompey had indeed become 'great' – and fantastically rich – thanks to successful campaigns against Mithridates and the pirates. He had no desire to leave the cockpit of Roman politics to return to a province of which he had some less-than-fond memories, so he sent a legate to do the actual governing. Nevertheless, patronage and favours were distributed in his name, so Pompey could hope that he had cultivated loyal followers in the peninsula.

But in the event, the legacy of Sertorius determined the politics of the war in Iberia. The tribes living around the old Sertorian capital of Osca immediately favoured Caesar for no other reason that he was an enemy of Pompey. The people of Calgurris jumped at the chance of revenge, and the Celtiberians happily supplied Caesar with the cavalry he needed to encircle and outflank the senatorial armies in true Sertorian style.

The Celtiberians put a bit of extra effort into their war because one of the generals on the senatorial side was Afranius, Pompey's second-in-command in the Sertorian war, and the man who had masterminded the Roman sieges which had caused such hardship at Calgurris and Clunia. Afranius concentrated his efforts on interdicting Caesar's supply trains, evidently something which he had learned to do from Sertorius. In fact, Caesar remarked that Afranius' men tended to fight Sertorian-style altogether.

> Afranius's soldiers fought in this way, they would advance rapidly against the enemy, and boldly take over a position. They were not particularly bothered about holding formation, and did not consider it necessary to fight in compact ranks. If hard-pushed they found no disgrace in abandoning their position and retreating, and in this they followed the custom of the Lusitanians. ... This novel manner of fighting was unexpected, and it confused our men. When they saw the enemy advance in broken formation they were afraid of being surrounded ... the first ranks became disordered, and as the legion on that wing started to give ground it retreated to a nearby hill.
>
> (Caesar, *Civil Wars*, 1.44)

To Celtiberian delight, Caesar relentlessly pushed Afranius towards the Ebro, forcing Pompey's commander to make his last stand among the very hills into which Pompey had forced Sertorius. Finally at the town of Ilerda (Leida in modern Catalonia), not so very far from Osca, Afranius was brought to bay and forced to surrender after a siege that ended when Afranius was betrayed by his own men. Those Sertorian veterans now serving as auxiliaries in Caesar's army must have found the irony delicious.

After this victory, Caesar proceeded to take over Hispania Ulterior. It was not exactly hard work. The Lusitanians were longing for the opportunity to do to the local Romans what the Celtiberians had done to Afranius in Citerior, but they did not get the chance. Varro, the governor, was a lukewarm Pompeian in command of a thoroughly pro-Caesar army. Varro was also a personal friend of Caesar. Thus, with people, army and commander all aligned in favour of the attacker, Hispania Ulterior fell with hardly a fight. The peninsula secured, Caesar left for Rome where he made himself dictator.

However, Iberia had not heard the last of either Caesar or Pompey. In 46 BC there was yet again a Pompey campaigning in Hispania. This was Sextus Pompey, one of the sons of Pompey. Pompey had been defeated by Caesar at Pharsalus in northern Greece, and had fled to Egypt where he was murdered. Now Pompey's sons had come to Hispania to raise their father's former allies into an army to sustain the Pompeian cause.

Yet again the conquerors of Sertorius were doomed to repeat his story. The remnants of a former regime, driven from Rome by a general-turned-dictator had come from Africa to make Iberia their last bastion.

> He gathered a considerable force, partly by entreaty and partly by force. With this he began to devastate the province. Under these circumstances some states voluntarily sent him supplies, others shut the gates of their towns against him.
>
> (Caesar, *The Spanish War*, 1)

These words, written a generation after the death of Sertorius, could have described him as easily as they described the son of Sertorius' former opponent. Like Sertorius, Pompey the younger was neither gentle nor particularly fastidious about how he raised funds.

> If any of these [Caesarian cities] happened to fall to his assault, even if a citizen living there deserved well of Cn. Pompey [the elder], if

he was wealthy enough, some excuse was found to condemn him to death so that his fortune might become the reward of the soldiers.

(Caesar, *The Spanish War*, 1)

So Caesar returned to Iberia, bringing with him a sickly young relative called Octavian. Octavian was later to campaign in Iberia in his own name, which was by then Augustus, Emperor of Rome. Like his predecessors Caesar noted the problems Iberia presented to an invader. His comments might as easily have been uttered by Metellus a generation before, or one of Napoleon's marshals eighteen hundred years later.

The war was protracted because the country is full of mountains and extremely well adapted to marching camps. Almost the whole of Ulterior has extremely fertile soil, and plentiful springs, yet, nevertheless, it is very difficult to get access to much of it. Here too, thanks to frequent unrest, anywhere any distance from the main towns is fortified with towers and castles ... located in places commanding an extensive view of the country on all sides. Actually, even the towns of this province are built on mountains, and other naturally defensible places all of which are extremely difficult to approach. Sieges are rare and hazardous in Hispania, and it is altogether difficult to subdue a town by force.

(Caesar, *Spanish War*, 8)

Though the Pompeys were overcome at the battle of Munda even now the entire peninsula was not under the control of Rome. As Livy remarked, Iberia was among the first places outside Italy into which Rome's empire had expanded, and one of the last places to be subdued by those arms.

When Augustus returned to Iberia in 29 BC some tribes were still fighting. In fact both the Cantabrians and Astures were to wage a vicious guerrilla war for another decade, and when beaten many chose suicide rather than surrender. Some of those who were captured nevertheless refused to submit to their Roman conquerors and sang defiant war-songs even as they were crucified.[6]

Yet the tribes of the far north-west were by now the exception. By this time, the Romanization of the rest of Hispania was fast progressing. In fact the operations by Augustus against the Cantabrians gave merely the final touches to a process of conquest and assimilation that had lasted over a quarter of a millennium.

And far from being a war of independence, the Sertorian war probably increased the pace of this Romanization.[7] The war not only served to draw Iberia further into Rome's orbit, but because it was essentially a civil war between two Roman factions, those fighting tended to identify with Rome, even if with differing versions of it. Likewise, both Sullans and Sertorius tended to promote and favour Romans, and used Roman citizenship as a bribe for the co-operation of high-ranking Iberians.

Caesar further speeded up the process by establishing several citizen colonies in Iberia, for example at Urso in Turdetania. Yet even in his time Varro commanded a Vernacular Legion (that is, a legion of Spanish-speaking Roman citizens) and Caesar mentions that some 300 Roman knights on the Pompeian side died at the battle of Munda, and many of these must have been Iberians.

Once the citizenship had been liberally distributed among the upper classes of the peninsula and colonies of full-fledged Roman citizens were founded (a process that involved the wholesale conversion of former Spaniards), many of the more influential inhabitants of the peninsula started to think of their homeland as an integral part of the Roman empire. It helped also that, for the next generation, from Metellus Pius through Pompey to Caesar, the leaders in Rome had first-hand knowledge of Iberia and were linked to the province by personal friendships and clients.

A good example of the latter is Lucius Cornelius Balbus, a naturalized Roman born in Gades in the 90s BC. As a young man, Balbus served against Sertorius in the armies of both Metellus Pius and later Pompey. Balbus accompanied Pompey to Rome in 71 as a personal friend, and when Pompey briefly allied himself with Caesar, Balbus became a friend to both, and later widened his circle to include Cicero and the young Octavian. In 40 BC the Iberian-born Balbus was consul of Rome. In later years the colony of Italica in the Baetis valley was to produce two of Rome's better emperors, Trajan and his successor Hadrian.

In the interim, a poet who never thought of himself as anything but Roman – Marcus Valerius Martial, was born in the Hispanian colony of Augusta Bilbilis in AD 40. Yet Martial makes no secret of his ancestry, proudly saying he is 'sprung from the Celtiberians, of the country of the river Tagus' and contrasting his bristly Iberian hair with the oily locks of effeminate Greeks. Martial saw no contradiction in being both a Roman and an Iberian. There is no irony to the verse in which he rebukes a German shoving his way to a drinking fountain: 'this belongs to the conquerors, yet you keep a lad from getting his drink. It's for citizens, not captives'.[8]

By the imperial period a genuinely Romano–Hispanic culture existed in Iberia. After centuries of wrenching warfare the peninsula enjoyed a matching period of peace. In few parts of the empire did the *Pax Romana* become as firmly entrenched, and there were no major military events there until the arrival of the Vandals in the fifth century AD. Even then the Vandals and the Visigoths who followed did not displace the Romano–Hispanic culture of the peninsula. Rather they preserved and further entrenched it, and it is this culture (despite a number of quite radical alterations) which is essentially the culture which survives in Iberia today.

Notes and References

Chapter 1

1. Plutarch, *Life of Sertorius*, 2. We do not know exactly when Sertorius was born, but best estimates are in the range of 127–118 BC.
2. And he tells us that he served twelve years. Plutarch, *Life of Gaius Gracchus*, 2. Exactly when young aristocrats joined the army appears to have been flexible – several of Sertorius' near-contemporaries only served when in their late teens or early twenties.
3. The history of Orosius, 5.15-16.
4. Even though the passes of Piedmont lay open, which meant that the Cimbri would have had a much easier route than Hannibal's crossing of a century before.
5. Plutarch's description of the Cimbri in his *Life of Marius*, 11.
6. Plutarch, *Life of Sertorius*, 3. Where Sertorius was, if not with the barbarians has been discussed by several academics, with alternative theories suggesting he was with the army, or unsuccessfully trying to re-start his political career in Rome.
7. A king whom Marius had almost certainly met in Spain, as the young Jugurtha fought as a Roman ally of Scipio Aemilianus.
8. The necessary time between consulships had not elapsed, and Marius was still in Africa and the law required him to campaign in person.
9. Plutarch, *Life of Marius*, 27.
10. Plutarch gives a figure of 60,000 prisoners. *Life of Marius*, 27.

Chapter 2

1. It would be a decade before constitutional reform made holding the quaestorship an automatic qualification for the Roman senate. But even before then a quaestorship was a big step in the right direction.
2. Apparently Marius was so 'greatly upset' about this that Sulla specifically mentioned it in his memoirs (which have not survived but were used by later Roman historians).
3. It is uncertain whom this governor was, but a credible case has been made for C. Coelius Caldus, the consul of 94 BC.
4. Sallust, *Histories*, frag 1.88. The Marsi were one of the leading tribes in the war against Rome, so some contemporary historians named the war after them.
5. A fact which has attracted the attention of academics – cf for example W. Moeller in *Historia*, 1975, 'Once More the One-Eyed Man against Rome.'
6. Says Appian, *Civil Wars*, 1.65.
7. Marius' son joining Cinna – as argued by H. Bennett, *Cinna and His Times* (Menasha: Wisconsin, 1923).
8. Plutarch, *Life of Sertorius*, 5.

9. From an influential article of that name: E. Badian's 'Waiting for Sulla', Journal of Roman Studies, vol 52 (1962), pp 47–61.

Chapter 3

1. Not all of Gaul, as bits of Cisalpine Gaul remained unconquered; Transalpine Gaul had been Roman for almost a century but, on the other hand, Caesar also conquered most of what would later become Belgium and bits of Germany and the Netherlands.
2. Scipio Africanus got the name 'Africanus' because he finally won for Rome in Africa. Scipio Calvus got his name because he lost his hair. Calvus means 'bald' in Latin.
3. Hannibal only got to see a part of his brother. The rest of him was defeated at the Metaurus in northern Italy along with his army. The Romans took Hasdrubal's head to Hannibal's camp in southern Italy and triumphantly flung it over the ramparts.
4. Those sniggering at the back are correct. This is linked with the word 'turd' – the region was rich in small brown thrushes, which in Latin are 'turdes'. It is uncertain whether the thrush gets its name from the proto-Germanic *torde*, or vice-versa.
5. In 13 BC the emperor Augustus was to rearrange Spain into three provinces – Baetica, Lusitania and Tarraconensis. Very approximately and somewhat inaccurately, this was done by splitting Ulterior into its Turdetanian and Lusitanian bits and renaming Citerior as Tarraconensis.
6. Polybius (34.9) says that in his time (the mid-second century) Roman mines in Hispania produced 2,500 drachmae a day for the Roman people.
7. For example – even in the 170s – Livy (41.15), says both Publius Crassus and Scipio Maluginenses were appointed to Hispania, and both ducked out of the job.
8. In the words of Appian, *Iberia*, 51.1.
9. These were recovered later by the surviving part of the Roman army.
10. A useful account of the founding of these and later cities is to be found in T. Fear's *Rome and Baetica Urbanization in Southern Spain 50 BC–AD 150* (Oxford, 1996).
11. It has been estimated that sinking and shipwreck caused more casualties in the first Punic War than the Carthaginians did. In one incident in 255 BC alone they lost 284 ships, and at least 40,000 men. (Polybius, 1.37).
12. J.S. Richardson, *Hispaniae* (Cambridge, 1986), p.175.

Chapter 4

1. This was Crassus the future Triumvir with Caesar and Pompey.
2. Strabo, *Geography*, 4.6.7.
3. Appian, *Civil Wars*, 108.
4. Postulated by, among others, the great Italian historian Gabba in his *Social War*.
5. Plutarch, *Life of Sertorius*, 7.
6. Oddly enough there is an Islamic tradition that Adam too was 60 cubits tall when god created him. (In the narrative of Abu Huraira.)
7. In legend, Aeneas was ordered by the gods to abandon his new-found love Dido, queen of Carthage, and get on with starting the Roman race in Italy. Dido did not take this development well.
8. C. Konrad, 'Some Friends of Sertorius', *American Journal of Philology*, Autumn, 1987, pp. 519–27.

9. Later this became the prosperous town of Baelo Claudia and did well out of shipping fish sauce to Rome.

10. Whether Fufidius was actually the governor has been disputed. Spann, P. 'C., L. or M. Cotta and the "Unspeakable" Fufidius: A Note on Sulla's Res PublicaRestituta', *The Classical Journal*, Vol. 82, No. 4 (Apr. – May, 1987), pp. 306–309. However, in the absence of a clear rebuttal, the unambiguous opinion of Plutarch should stand.

11. We know not which Cotta. There were a number of them about at this period, and we have neither praenomen nor gentilictum for further identification.

Chapter 5

1. Plutarch, *Life of Sertorius*, 22.
2. Valerius Maximus, 7.3.2.
3. Vegetius, *De re Militari*, Book 1.
4. More precisely, 480 men with a first cohort of double that strength. In fact, as the legions were always chronically short staffed, a cohort could be anywhere from 300 to 500 effectives, with the norm at the lower end of that figure.
5. The modern town of Murcia today still offers horse-riding for tourists, features horse racing and has horse-drawn carriages in the streets.
6. Strabo, *Iberia*, 15.
7. Florus, *Ep.* 2.10.
8. Livy, fr 91.
9. C. Konrad, *Plutarch's Sertorius: A historical commentary* (Chapel Hill, 1994).
10. Cicero, *De Finibus*, 2.20.
11. Which in fact only arrived the following year.
12. Plutarch, *Life of Pompey* 18.
13. Florus, *Ep.* 2.10.
14. Sallust, *Histories*, 1.113.
15. The chronology of this period is highly uncertain. It is probable that the events described here happened at this time, but the siege could have occurred as late as 76 BC.
16. Plutarch – presumably because his readers would understand the designation better – actually uses the anachronistic imperial name of the area as Gallia Narbonensis.
17. Plutarch's *Sayings of the Romans*, 2.2 in the *Moralia*. (The same quote is given by Valerius Maximus) Leonard A. Curchin, *The Romanization of Central Spain: Complexity, Diversity and Change in a Provincial Hinterland* (Routledge, London & New York, 2004).

Chapter 6

1. Cf. Cassius Dio, 44.28: 'After that Lepidus, ostensibly with the purpose of punishing these men, got together a faction of his own'.
2. Appian, *Civil Wars*, 1.68, is pretty clear on this. However, some modern historians believe this is simply too neat, and suggest that instead Pompeius died of the plague.
3. Veiento is given as 'Vento' by Plutarch, almost certainly in error.
4. Appian, *Civil Wars*, 1.109.
5. Plutarch *Life of Sertorius*, 16. It is after this episode that Plutarch (who is rather suspect in his timing of such incidents) gives the anecdote of the horses' tails – a story which seems to fit better in the first year of training, where I have placed it.

6. Something Sertorius may well have picked up from his reading of earlier campaigns. Frontinus tells us this tactic was also employed with success in the first Punic war of two centuries before.
7. Velleius Paterculus, 2.29.
8. Orosius, 5.23, calls this river the Palantia, which would help, if we knew where the River Palantia was.
9. Appian, *Civil Wars*, 1.109.
10. This is probably the best way of squaring Orosius, 5.23 with other accounts.
11. Appian, *Civil Wars*, 1.109.
12. Letter of Pompey to the senate: Sallust, *Histories*, 2.82.

Chapter 7

1. In fact Pompey's move might have been aimed at driving the Sertorians away from Contrebia Belaisca. If so his gamble failed, and his winter camp was less comfortable than he might have hoped.
2. Basque country? If we accept that the archaeological remains show a definite continuity of culture and that the ancient name of Vascones has mutated to the modern Basqu(ones).
3. Cf. Tacitus Annals 4.45.
4. Theodor Mommsen's *History of Rome*, 'The Establishment of the Military Monarchy', p.7.
5. Appian, *Civil Wars*, 1.108.
6. Cf. S. L. Dyson, 'The distribution of Roman republican family names in the Iberian peninsula', *Ancient Society*, 11/12 (1980/1).
7. Cicero, *pro Balbo*, 3.6.
8. Plutarch, *Life of Sertorius*, 1.
9. For example, Konrad's *Plutarch's Sertorius* (North Carolina Press, 1994) places many of the events described below at the tail end of the campaign of 77 BC.
10. Plutarch, *Life of Pompey*, 18.
11. Livy, *Ep.*, 91.4. From the placement in the epitome, it is even possible that this battle was fought at the end of 77 BC, though the unfolding of events makes early 75 a better choice.
12. Appian, *Civil Wars*, 1.110. The editor of the Loeb translation, H. White, places this battle in 75 BC, which again shows the problems with chronology in this war, since either he or the summarizer of Livy (see note above) has to be wrong by at least a year.
13. Plutarch, *Life of Sertorius*, 19.
14. Plutarch, *Life of Sertorius*, 19.
15. Appian, *Civil Wars*, 1.110. This appears to be the only way to make sense of Appian's account of the battle, which otherwise would have Metellus both present and turning up later.
16. Orosius, *History against the Pagans*, 5.23.11.

Chapter 8

1. Horace, *Satires*, 2.7. Horace had a brief military career himself, being on the losing side in the civil wars of Octavian.
2. Aulus Gellius, *Attic Nights*, 15.22.
3. One such victory was the landing in Britain in AD 44. Delays in getting the legions embarked meant that there were no Britons left to contest the landing when it happened.

4. The incident, documented in Frontinus, 1.12.4, is undated, but this seems the most likely point into which this prodigy can be fitted into the chronology.

5. Appian, *Civil Wars*, 1.110.

6. Spann, 'Saguntum vs Segontia', *Historia*, 33 (1984).

7. 'proelium apud flumen Durium', Sallust, *History*, 2.98.

8. A better-documented case of an army attacking on its own initiative is provided by the supposedly well-disciplined troops of Caesar at Thapsus in 46 BC.

9. Plutarch, *Life of Sertorius*, 21.

10. Or at least that is what the Roman tradition says, and being a Roman, that's the theory Sertorius was working on.

11. Putting Hirtuleius into the combat at this point is the only possible way of reconciling reports by historians such as Florus that Hirtuleius fled north after his defeat at Italica and yet – according to Livy – was killed by the army of Metellus in battle. Some historians have attempted an alternative explanation that Hirtuleius was in fact a pair of brothers with one killed at each battle, but the description of events given in this text seems less of a stretch.

12. Plutarch, *Life of Sertorius*, 19.

13. Frontinus, *Stratagems*, 2.7.5.

14. Valerius Maximus, 5.5.4.

15. Livy, *Epitome*, 92.

16. Livy, *Epitome*, 92.

17. Plutarch, *Life of Sertorius*, 22.

18. Florian, 2.10.9, shows that Clunia remained in Sertorian hands until the end of the war.

19. *Maiestas minuta populi Romani* was a crime against the people introduced in 103 BC and refined in 81 by Sulla as an instrument against his enemies. Any Roman who was considered derelict in his duties or rebellious in his conduct could be charged and exiled. Pompey returning to Rome without a satisfactory victory in Spain could be considered guilty on both counts.

20. It is highly unlikely that – as some have read into this claim – anyone seriously considered that Sertorius might march his Iberians Hannibal-style through the Alps. And in any case, in such an event, Pompey would be ordered hot-foot back to Rome. The joke was about the political situation, not the military.

21. A realistic hope, when one considers the famous double-cross that Octavian pulled on the Senate a generation later when he abandoned their cause to join his army to that of Antony and Lepidus and become master of Rome.

22. Sallust, *History*, 2.34.

23. Plutarch, *Life of Sertorius*, 24.

24. Sallust, *History*, 2.7.

Chapter 9

1. Naturally this was not the only reason. Death by assassination was practically death by natural causes for a Hellenic monarch, and letting it be known that he was leaving his kingdom to Rome, Nicomedes made it in no-one's interest to kill him.

2. At least we know the Senate sent two legions. Pompey complained later of getting no reinforcements, so unless he was exaggerating, he did not get them. And Metellus in Gaul was more handily situated to receive the men than Pompey in the wild interior.

3. Appian, *Civil Wars*, 1.112.
4. Frontinus does not give either full names or dates, so from the placement of the event, we cannot even be certain that our Metellus or the Sertorian war are meant.
5. Appian, *Civil Wars*, 1.112.
6. Says the ancient writer Servius: 'A town of this name [Cale] is in Callaecia, which Sallust commemorates as captured by Perpenna.' Since we have a reasonable idea of where Perpenna was in preceding years, this incident is best placed here.
7. Cassius Dio, 36.20.
8. Cicero, *Pro Plancio*, 64–66.
9. Plutarch, *Life of Sertorius*, 25.
10. Appian, *Civil Wars*, 1.113.
11. Plutarch, *Life of Sertorius*, 22.
12. Romans dined reclining three to a couch with the food placed between the couches.
13. Appian, *Civil Wars*, 1.115.

Chapter 10
1. Appian, *Civil Wars*, 115.
2. Orosius, 5.11.
3. Plutarch, *Life of Caesar*, 7.
4. Plutarch, *Life of Caesar*, 12.
5. Caesar, *Spanish War*, 42.
6. Strabo, *Geography*, 3.4.18.
7. As argued by Richardson, p.125, *The Romans in Spain*, (London, 1998).
8. Martial, *Epigrams*, 11.96.

Bibliography

Astin, A.E., Walbank, F.W., Frederiksen M.W., and Ogilvie R.M., *The Cambridge Ancient History*, revised Feb 1990

Badian E., 'Waiting for Sulla', *Journal of Roman Studies*, vol 52, 1962

Bennett, H., *Cinna and His Times. A Critical and Interpretative Study of Roman History During the Period 87–84 B.C.*, Menasha: Wisconsin, 1923

Collins, R., *Spain: An Oxford Archaeological Guide*, Oxford Paperbacks, 2003

Curchin, L.A., *The Romanization of Central Spain: Complexity, Diversity and Change in a Provincial Hinterland*, Routledge, London & New York, 2004

Dyson, S., 'The distribution of Roman republican family names in the Iberian peninsula', *Ancient Society*, 11/12 1980/1

Fear, T., *Rome and Baetica Urbanization in Southern Spain 50 BC–AD 150*, Oxford, 1996.

Keay, S.J., *Roman Spain*, Berkeley: University of California Press, 1988

Konrad C.F., *Plutarch's Sertorius: A Historical Commentary*, University of North Carolina Press, 1994

'Metellus and the Head of Sertorius', *AHB*, 1988

'Some Friends of Sertorius', *American Journal of Philology*, Autumn, 1987

Lovano, A., *The Age of Cinna: Crucible of Late Republican Rome*, Franz Steiner Verlag Wiesbaden GmbH, 2002

Moeller, W., 'Once More the One-Eyed Man against Rome.' *Historia*, 1975

Richardson, J.S., *Hispaniae Spain and the Development of Roman Imperialism, 218-82 BC*, Cambridge, 1986

Spann, P., 'C., L. or M. Cotta and the "Unspeakable" Fufidius: A Note on Sulla's *Res Publica Restituta*', *The Classical Journal*, Vol. 82, No. 4 Apr.–May, 1987

Quintus Sertorius and the Legacy of Sulla, University of Arkansas Press, 1987

'Saguntum vs Segontia', *Historia*, 33, 1984

'M. Perpenna and Pompey's Spanish Expedition, *HAnt*', 7 1977

Syme, R., *Sallust*, University of California Press, 2002

"The conquest of northwest Spain", in *Roman papers*, ed. Ernst Badian Oxford: Clarendon Press, 1979

Celtic Tribes of the Iberian Peninsula: Tribes of Gallaecia, Tribes of Lusitania, Lusitanians, Celtiberians, Astures, Vettones, Coelerni, LLC Books, 2010

Ancient Texts

Appian	*Iberian Wars*
	Civil Wars
Frontinus	*Stratagems*
Orosius	*History against the Pagans*
Plutarch	*Life of Sertorius*
	Life of Pompey
Strabo	*Geography*
Sallust	*Histories*

Index